BEST COACHES
BEST PRACTICES

by

ANDY HIGGINS

Foreword by Ken Dryden

**HIGGINS
HOUSE**

Jacket design and interior artwork: Finucci Graphic Communications
Book design: Joan McDonald

Printed by Webcom Ltd.
Printed in Canada

Dedicated
To

GEORGE AND MARIE HIGGINS

Who gave me the gifts of being grateful for what I have,
a positive attitude, and strong values that included
using what I have to make a difference in the world. They then
gave me the opportunity to get the education required
To do this in the only way I could.

AND

To all parents everywhere who love their children enough to be
Best Coaches for them.

CONTENTS

ACKNOWLEDGEMENTS

I am indebted to generations of men and women who cared enough, had the courage to act and the persistence to stay with the struggle to make a difference in the world. I cannot begin to name all those who wrote stories that have inspired and informed my life nor can I thank every one of the wonderful men and women who directly gave of their time and experience to change my life.

I do, however, want to thank my editor of this project Larry Hoffman for his attention to detail, his patience, and his constant reminders that what I was doing was significant. As I have said on many occasions, every coach needs a coach. Larry has been a great coach to me in making this book a reality. Vic Finucci brought his special creativity to the cover and interior of the book along with an enthusiastic attitude. Joan McDonald brought the attitude of an Olympian because she is one, her incisive mind, and her incredible computer skills to making the book ready for the printer. I am grateful for the Best Practices of all three of you.

One last Thank You to all the Best Coaches who took the time to tell me, or write for me their coaching stories that fill this book and make it richer and more interesting for you the reader.

Andy Higgins,
Toronto, Ontario
October 3, 2003

A NOTE TO THE READER

I chose the Inukshuk and the Medicine Wheel as symbols to represent Best Coaches and their Best Practices because I have such respect for the spiritual teachings of the First Nations people. I believe each symbol is perfectly appropriate.

INUKSHUK

The word itself looks like a person and these carefully arranged rocks serve many purposes for arctic travelers. Some were directional markers for those who follow. Another indicated the presence of a food cache intended to sustain a traveler on the next leg of a journey. Always, the Inukshuk was a sign that another human being had been there and survived. The Inukshuk is a timeless sign of the mortal, a part of the human continuum. It represents our interdependence and our human bonds of friendship. The Inukshuk is a symbol of trust and reassurance for travelers in the arctic vastness.

For more on the Inukshuk and Arctic Nunuvut see: www.ndcorp.nu.ca

I believe the Inukshuk represents Best Coaches because they are directional markers on the path of personal excellence. They recognize and teach our human interdependence and global bonds of friendship. They are symbols of trust and reassurance for all who travel the vastness of life on the little marked path of becoming who they truly are. And, they definitely "sustain a traveler" on every leg of expressing their own special gifts.

MEDICINE WHEEL

Greg Henhawk, the son of Sidney and Doris and brother to Cheryl and Dan, is a Mohawk of the bear clan from the Six Nations of the Grand River. Greg has lived all of his 41 years on Six Nations. He is the Head of Physical Education at Hagersville Secondary School for the last 18 years. I asked Greg to share his understanding of the Medicine Wheel."

"The medicine wheel represents a view of life that is whole and shows the interdependence of all facets of life. Everything is important since all things are connected. The teachings of the wheel are all expressed in sets of four. All human beings have four aspects to their nature - mental, physical, cultural and spiritual. Each of these aspects must be equally developed in a healthy well-balanced individual.

The wheel also represents the ongoing cyclic nature of change and transformation that is fundamental to all things. The power of the wheel is its' fundamental principle of harmony and balance in all four directions; the goal of all learning and change. It connects an individual to the earth, all the children of the earth, and all living things.

The circle (wheel) teaches that the journey (path) never ends. It continues from generation to generation and all learning and change must take into consideration the fact that all we do affects generations to come, not just the now."

To keep from repeating "Best Coaches" continually throughout the book the word coach, unless it appears in Quotation marks will always mean Best Coach.

FORWARD

Several years ago, I spent a year in a high school in a Toronto suburb and wrote a book about the experience, called *In School*. I sat in a classroom just as students sat, getting to know them and their teachers, trying to figure out who was learning and who wasn't, and why; who was a good teacher and who wasn't, and why. Later, when I spoke to groups about schools, to get them off the politics of education and into the classroom where the discussion really mattered, I asked them to think of a favourite teacher in their life. It might be a parent, an in-school teacher, a coach, but now being old enough to know who had been important in their lives, someone they knew had made a real difference to them. I could see tiny smiles come onto their faces as they began to remember. I could see their heads nod. Everyone had a favourite teacher.

I bet there are lots of kids, now adults, whose favourite teacher was Andy Higgins. In everything he does, Andy is a real teacher. He loves to see kids do better than they did yesterday. He loves to see kids see themselves do better even more. He loves the little miracles that can happen in a life. Everything going a certain way, irresistibly, inevitably it seems, then something happens. Someone decides to do something, interrupts destiny with understanding, time and caring, and a life changes. It changes for 50 years. It changes for a lifetime. It changes for entire families, for friends, for children later born, and their children. And their children too. One little interruption that no one had to make, but did. The flap of the butterfly's wings that affects generations.

This is a book of stories. Andy gets people to tell us about themselves, what their lives were like, about the teachers and coaches who changed all that, what they did, how they did it, and why it worked. The stories tell us that good teachers don't teach subjects or game strategies, they teach people. The stories remind us that no matter how much a teacher knows, if teachers can't help the other person know, they haven't done their job. And Andy knows, as a writer, that if his reader doesn't understand, he has also failed. So the stories he tells us are personal, emotional and clear.

We know we are all learners. This book reminds us that we, all of us, are teachers as well. To Andy Higgins, there is no higher calling.

Ken Dryden,
Toronto,
September 2003.

INTRODUCTION
Let me tell you a story...

Best Coaches are wonderful and wise story tellers.
With their stories, they share the experiences of all who have
gone before and create a sense of possibility in others.

"Coaches change kids' lives..."
~ *Jerry Osborne, former Principal, Central Technical H.S., Toronto, Ontario*

Years ago I was guest speaker at the athletics awards dinner for Central Technical School, the largest high school in Toronto. I was seated at a table with the principal, seven other teachers and coaches and the head coach of track and field, who was an English teacher. The room was a large hall filled with tables of ten young, vibrant student-athletes and teacher-coaches. The room was alive with youthful, athletic energy. It was an evening of celebration, a recognition of achievements with awards for many.

I was familiar with the programs and knew their success was due largely to the support of the principal. When I leaned across the noisy table and said, "Jerry, I really admire the support you give coaches at your school," his reply defined the value of coaching as succinctly and clearly as I've ever heard. "Andy, coaches change kids' lives. We don't do that in geography class."

A lifetime of working with other people's children has validated the importance of the coach and, especially, the parent, the first coach. Parents make all the difference. After a very few minutes in a social situation with a youngster I can tell you a good deal about the parents. I cannot recall where I first heard this, but it is a truth – parents who are fortunate to have terrific kids, usually have kids who are fortunate to have terrific parents. Maybe more than anyone else this book speaks to parents.

Coaches change lives by creating environments that are physically and emotionally safe to make learning easier. All things done by the coach are based on positive values, values that are critical to long-term success and that honour the best within each individual. Coaches share an expectation of significant positive change. They are aware of the unbounded possibilities that reside within each of us. Their high energy creates an equally high measure of vitality and vibrancy in the people with whom they work. They develop leaders who are passionate about learning, growth, and achievement.

STORIES THAT TEACH

"Stories are beings. You invite them to live with you. They'll teach you what they know in return for being a good host. When they are ready to move on they will let you know. Then you pass them on to someone else." A Cree Storyteller.

A powerful method of learning and teaching that supports the growth and development of both coach and learner is story telling. From long before the time of Homer, stories were told and re-told to inspire and teach. Stories are a common factor in successful coaching and coaching environments.

Rob Pitter is a former National level high jumper. He is now an associate professor at Acadia University in Wolfeville, Nova Scotia. Rob relates his experience with stories.

I learned about stories during my adolescence, about how captivating they can be and how they can educate, inspire and bond athletes together. I learned this as I sat silent, crammed into the back seats of cars with my club mates during road trips to track and field meets around Southern Ontario, Western Quebec, and the Northern United States. I heard stories around tables in restaurants during these two to three day trips. For a long time I felt left out because I didn't have any interesting or exciting stories of my own to tell. Mine never seemed as captivating as the stories being told by the other older, more experienced athletes and coaches. Any lesson, I discovered, could be conveyed via a story. Every story, whether profound, inspiring, humourous, sad, or even a little boring contained a lesson. It might be a lesson about relationships, about commitment, about the perils of taking life too seriously, or about what is possible.

A story I will always remember is about the young Lynn Davies, who later became Olympic long jump gold medallist in Tokyo. He and his coach had spent months trying to master the last two strides before the take-off of the world record-holder Igor Ter Ovanesyan. Lynn was a great admirer of Ter Ovanesyan and was thrilled when he got a chance to speak with his idol face-to-face. He eagerly asked Ter Ovanesyan what he needed to do to master this technique. He was stunned by the response. "Master it? My coach and I have been trying to change this for years." Appearances can be deceiving. To simply copy anything can be a problem.

Several years later, I found myself in the front seat telling stories and sharing the lessons I had learned from them. After that I become a coach still telling stories, not only to novices, but to experienced and accomplished athletes who still had lessons to learn. I no longer coach people for track and field. Now, as an academic, I work with young people interested in careers in what is called kinesiology; we used to call it physical education. I try to help them understand how our social world works and how they can impact upon it. I use stories to illustrate how they, as leaders will be telling their own stories and how through these stories they are shaping the lives of each person they work with - and shaping the stories that will be told in the future.

My life has been informed and transformed by coaches and their stories. The best coaches are incurable storytellers. They know the power of stories and they carefully choose the stories they tell. Every story has a clear purpose. Combined, over time, these stories change lives.

Reflecting on the experience of my lifetime, with my family, in education, and in sport, I felt a great need to share the stories of my experiences and what I have learned from many excellent coaches. Lately our society has been discarding experience and dismissing wisdom. The "elders" who for millennia have carried the stories that inspire and inform the next generation are no longer heard and are less and less present. They are shipped off to retirement communities, given "packages" and retired early from the world of education and work. In amateur sport they are "burned out" and discarded. I believe we are a society suffering from an immense wisdom waste. We need to hear the stories these elders can tell.

As a youngster I was excited and inspired by stories of great sporting achievements. Many of these stories were about coaching, coaching strategies and tactics. Many were remarkable tales of perfect planning, clever execution and wise interventions made at the right time in the right situation. I will always remember reading of the legendary Brutus Hamilton, coach of many American track and field greats describing, in his inimitable way, what was needed to achieve success. An experienced and competent high jumper expressed some doubt at a critical height in a major competition and Mr. Hamilton advised, "Son, first throw your heart over the bar, the rest of your body will follow." Later, I came to understand that even stories of individual athletic heroics were supported and shaped by coaches, for there was a dedicated coach behind every great athlete. Coaches are the essential factor in all great achievement.

Coaches know that the activity about which they care and teach is only the medium in which they work with people. It is the person they coach. When successful, the person they coach can become who they were meant to be and do all they are capable of doing. Coaches bring to bear all the resources they can access to accomplish this. At the heart of the process, running through it as a unifying thread, are the coach's stories. Coaches use stories with intention and wisdom, to inspire, clarify priorities, evoke passion, support progress, put performance in perspective and always with one goal: To actualize the potential of the person.

GETTING TO THE CORE
BELIEFS, ATTITUDES AND AWARENESS

More than forty years working in education, and sport at every level has taught me that coaching embodies management, teaching, and leadership. Management creates and sustains the learning and working context. Teaching creates opportunities to learn skills, and leadership inspires others to move toward a clear and compelling vision on a challenging learning and performance path.

Coaching incorporates all these aspects and is distinguished by its focus on the person. Coaches work with individuals. Managing and teaching are important but in the final life test do not make the difference. Nor does inspirational leadership. The difference lives in the head, heart and soul of the performer. Skill, preparation and motivation are essential but, to some extent, everyone has skill, is prepared, and wants the prize! Those who claim the prize have that critical difference which Antoine de Saint-Exupery in *The Little Prince* said: "…is invisible to the eyes."

The coach understands that it is the person, a human being with all the amazing strengths and possibilities, all the frailties and limitations that make us human, who must perform, whatever the task may be. The coach knows that the greatest limitations in learning and performing are neither genetic nor environmental. Our greatest limitations are how we feel about ourselves, our feelings of inadequacy, and our lack of self worth that fuel beliefs, and attitudes that do not serve us well. These incapacitating feelings, and beliefs that are "invisible to the eyes" are acquired very young.

Peter Warren is a retired Physical Educator and Coach. He tells the story of his son Bill:

Our son Bill was quite young when he expressed an interest in playing hockey. From the onset we encouraged him to do his best and try to improve each time out. We stressed fair play and playing for enjoyment. Learning to be a good loser as well as a good winner was part of the teaching over the years. In his peewee year Bill played on a team that had a lot of fun, but only won 3 or 4 games.

One day near the end of the season we were driving home from a game, another loss, when Bill said to us; "I think I have learned how to lose this year, do you think I could get on a team next year where I could learn how to win?"
P.S. Bill was invited to play on a team the next year that won the championship.

Beliefs and attitudes drive our behaviour, most of which is habitual. These beliefs and attitudes are operating at the unconscious level. Coaches know that changing behaviour is a challenging process and that when the pressure is on we often revert to old habits. Real change must take place at the level of beliefs and feelings. Coaches help us see that our behaviour, expressed beliefs and feelings, is an indicator of our self-perception and self-esteem. They support change by inviting us to see ourselves more positively, to speak more positively, and to act from that more positive base. Over time we can all experience significant change. Where the best coaches work significant change happens all the time. And coaches know that among us are some whose limiting beliefs are deeply rooted in a complex ground of emotional damage and they are not equipped to deal with that. As with everything else coaches know when and where to get help.

Coaches make the differences they do by creating self-awareness. Coaches point out that the real challenges are within our selves. They assure us we can meet and overcome all challenges and we will be given both the skill and the support to do so. They know that the simplest and quickest way to bring beliefs and feelings to a conscious level is by becoming aware of our self-talk. We talk to ourselves constantly and much of it is negative and limiting in nature. When we become aware of what we say when we talk to ourselves and how we feel when we are saying the words, we begin to "know thyself." This was important enough to the Greeks to carve it in stone above the entrance to the temple to the oracle at Delphi. Knowing one's self is key to learning, performing and all that makes up a happy and successful life.

Frank Dick, coach of numerous world class athletes including Daley Thompson, two time Olympic gold medallist and world record holder in the decathlon, is an internationally recognized expert in training theory. Frank tells a story about the importance of creating a useful focus.

She was nine years of age and wanted to sprint 100m. "Bang", off she sprinted, finishing eighth out of eight in 18.0 seconds.
She ran back to me, "Mr. Dick, I was last!"

"No you weren't, you were 18.0 seconds.
"What do you mean?"
"Well I had you down for 18.0 seconds, that's a great performance, well done,
I'm proud of you!"
"Really?"
"Yes, in fact you are a first!"
"What do you mean?"
"You are the first athlete I've coached, who has run 18.0 seconds for 100m!"

In a week's time she has another race. What does she think winning is now?
Breaking the 18.0 seconds barrier of course!

I try to sum this up with my two daughters Erin and Cara when they stumble, just as you and I stumble. When this happens we have 'one to ones' which always finish with the same lines: "You are the best in the world at being who you are. Don't ever try to be someone else; just be better at being you, and you will always win."

So here is my definition of winning: "Be better today than yesterday, every day, in something".

Coaches support changes in people's lives by creating an environment that models and teaches the development of character, courage, commitment and confidence. It follows that this is a safe environment in which to grow. In this safe context coaches make clear the significance of personal awareness, self-reflection, and intellectual and emotional honesty with oneself. They inspire the person to follow a path of ever increasing self-discovery.

A LIFE TIME OF LEARNING

Coaching takes place in a multitude of situations. Possibly you are coaching a great deal and are not aware of it. Awareness allows you to coach more effectively. The best parents coach, the best teachers coach, the best managers coach, and the best people who work with people in any endeavour are coaching. The problem is that the coaching process is seldom taught, even in sport where the title "coach" is most commonly applied, and many with the title are not really coaching. That does not mean they are not being effective. Many "coaches" are effective because they manage the environment well, they teach well, and they bring their passion to the situation, which inspires others to learn. However, ultimate success demands the support of a best coach in order to move beyond limiting beliefs and attitudes.

Coaches are avid learners, open to new challenges and new ideas and this never seems to change over the years. Not knowing a good deal about something is never a reason not to begin it. Coaches believe, and rightly so, that they can learn whatever is needed as they engage in the activity and the learning process never ends.

Pat Shipton, is a retired educator and coach who still runs for pleasure. He coached at Monarch Park Secondary School and Lawrence Park Collegiate for many years.

In the late fifties and early sixties when I was at University, I was a distance runner, and was invited to turn out for the cross-country team. I did and became a competitive university athlete. I became addicted to the pleasures of running. Twenty years later I was a teacher and had transferred to a new school. One of the students saw me running and asked if I would coach the school's cross-country team. He explained that there were four keen runners, 'coached' once a week by a grade thirteen student from another school. They were allowed to compete in the weekly meets if a teacher would show up. The particular teacher was not a runner and was not interested in coaching, but probably to please the school's Principal he showed up at the weekly meets. They wanted a teacher who was a runner to be a 'real coach'. My first growth area was learning the progressions for improving teenage runners. What they needed to improve was very different from my routines of running for pleasure. I learned about fartlek, tempo running, LSD, intensity workouts, hill reps and all the repertory of training. However the biggest growth areas were in other skills, life skills.

PARENTS: THE FIRST BEST COACH

Parents are the first major influence to shape our sense of self and the lucky among us have parents who are "Best Coaches." Parents know that skills and competencies are essential to our life success, but the best know that a strong sense of self-esteem, self-worth, self-confidence is more important than anything else and must come first. They are aware enough to understand that each child is a special individual, neither an extension of themselves, nor someone to live out the unfulfilled dreams of their parents. Best parents support the best in the child. Here is a story of a mother as a coach who shaped a positive success attitude.

Paul J. Meyer is the founder of Success Motivation Institute a world-wide leader in personal achievement.

We lived two miles from the high school in Campbell, California, and I rode my bicycle to school. I went to a public school, but at the same time I feel as though I were in today's nomenclature, "home schooled." My mother made a special project of affirming and reaffirming the positives in life by frequently asking me the questions, "Did they tell you about anything in school today that you couldn't do, or that couldn't be done?" Sometimes I would report a teacher saying something like, "You have to be in a certain place to do this or that," or "You have to have a certain education to do this or that." To these limiting comments my mother would say, "Just remember that if there is anything you want to do, the only limitations there will ever be are the one's you place in your own mind. Where you are and what you are will always be because of the dominating thoughts that occupy your mind."

My mother's objective in spending time with her children was to listen to us and, at the same time, teach us principles and values. I like the way she did it. For example, when she visited people in our neighbourhood who were sick, she took me with her. That was her way of teaching me to be concerned with other people. After retuning home we would talk about our experience, how we felt about it, how it encouraged others, and what else we might do to help certain people.

One topic that my mother talked about often that I thought was particularly interesting had to do with attitudes, my attitude toward my teachers and my attitude toward other students, including their behaviour and their attitude toward me. She asked me probing questions to explore my instincts. I guess she was checking to determine what I was thinking and how my attitudes were developing. She wanted to determine where I was in my development and to teach me how to relate constructively to all different types of personalities.

My mother taught me that the space I occupy in life is determined by my mental attitude – no more and no less.

Mr. Meyer's mother was a best parent, living best coaching practices every day. She invested a good deal of time over an extended period, she was concerned with, and engaged her son in issues of personal development, especially attitude. She modeled values and held out a vision of unlimited possibilities, making it clear that Paul was responsible for what he became and achieved in life as an opportunity and a right, not as a burden.

Coaching is about "quality time," and I know for certain that quality time only occurs in "quantity time." Coaching cannot be accomplished in five minutes a day.

TEACHERS – THE NEXT BEST COACH

David Carmichael is a parent and educator who is passionately committed to promoting the values of physical education, recreation and sport for all. David tells the story of a teacher seeing beyond both his subject area and his after school activity. He sees beyond the troubled and troublesome boy to the person within who is unable to deal with his life issues. He sees the best in the youngster, which is there in all of us, and uses sport to first engage his attention. Later he uses sport, and other activities to build self-esteem and hold his attention while teaching him there is much more to life than sport. Education is more important, and great satisfactions can be gained by making a difference in one's community.

My teacher's name was Mr. Holland. He was an industrial arts teacher at R.J. Lang Junior High School in Toronto and the assistant wrestling coach. I don't know what he saw in me but he must have seen some good.

In September 1970, as a grade seven student I was getting into a lot of trouble. I was smoking, using marijuana and alcohol, and picking fights outside of the school property. By November I was in juvenile court.

Fortunately my first experience in court was my last. Mr. Holland assured that when he persuaded me to try wrestling. The last class of the day was shop and after the class finished, Mr. Holland walked me to the change room, waited for me outside, escorted me to the cafeteria, helped me set up mats, and became my first wrestling partner.

I enjoyed wrestling and I was good at it. At my first tournament I was second because I was injured out of the final. In a scramble, as we both moved quickly, my opponent's elbow hit me in the nose. We couldn't stop the bleeding so the match was over.

After wrestling season ended I was encouraged to run track and in grade eight I wrestled again. I came to believe I could be a great wrestler. Mr. Holland thought I could be more than just a great wrestler. At the beginning of my grade eight year he helped me prepare a slide presentation about vandalism. We shot pictures of all the damaged areas in the school. In November I offered my first slide presentation to the entire student body. I was nervous, but not as nervous as Mr. Holland was for me. It was a wonderful success and I received compliments from students and teachers, even the Principal.

What Mr. Holland didn't know at the time was just how significant his coming into my life and supporting those positive experiences would be. I continued wrestling in high school and university and made the Canadian Under-21 team in my first year of university. After I finished competing I began to coach wrestling. I completed a graduate degree in coaching, and have been committed to promoting the benefits of sport and physical activity ever since. In fact, I've made hundreds of presentations about the importance of building self-esteem through sport and have appeared on numerous radio and television shows talking about the benefits of sport and physical activity for all children and youth. My passion and my career are directly related to the positive experiences that Mr. Holland created in grades seven and eight.

Who knows where I would be today if Mr. Holland didn't see the possibility for good in me and supported that. I am simply grateful that he saw in me what I couldn't see in myself at that stage.

Coaches know that in every situation and at every age, people who feel good about themselves, who have high self-esteem and are generally happy will always perform well and generate quality results. They know the opposite is equally true. People with low self-esteem who are unhappy cannot produce good quality, not in their own lives, the lives of people around them, nor in their activity or work. Coaches see beyond the unhappiness, the lack of quality in the activity to the inner struggles of the individual and support the self-awareness, self-responsibility process and enhance self-esteem. Coaches change lives.

At about the same time as youngsters meet that second best coach, the exceptional teacher who sees who that young person is in her class, they also come in contact with a number of other potential coaches. The best coaches are those who give of their time in sports, arts, music and crafts. Exceptional men and women are coaching others in many situations.

COACHING IS MESSY

Managing is logical, detailed, and organized. Teaching is linear, following a logical progression: A must be learned so that B can be built upon it, and so on. Coaching operates with a plan, one that is responsive with the intention to intervene whenever appropriate. In coaching the process is more important than the plan. Teaching works well when the learner is not personally challenged. Coaching interventions move learners beyond their inner obstacles, which only appear when the learner is engaged in an activity that is challenging. We are all the same. We only come up against the limits of our confidence when we are thrust into new and different situations. Coaches know this and are there to support us to a new level of understanding our amazing potential and becoming more confident in our ability to express it. Their goal is always to create greater independence and self-reliance.

Coaches always remember that everything is relative, that we all come from different backgrounds and bring with us different experiences. We all have our limits. Who among us cannot walk across a three metre long, sturdy plank, fifteen centimetres wide, placed on the floor? Yet it begins to change for some when the plank is raised to only one metre, spanning the same distance and there are few among us who would even consider walking across that same sturdy plank, spanning the same distance three stories above the ground! In less dramatic ways this happens to every single one of us in many different areas of our lives and in different activities. We have limiting beliefs about our abilities that often make no sense at all.

In high school and university I was one of the best athletes among my peers. I had exceptional balance, was well coordinated and moved in games and sports with grace and fluid movements. Despite this, I believed I couldn't dance! So I couldn't. Years later I knew a young woman from among our married friends who was the best dancer in the entire group. She was musically gifted and moved with exceptional rhythm. When we organized an evening of fun badminton at a local gym she insisted she could not play games or sports and with that belief she was stiff and awkward on the court. In both of these instances the limiting factors were not innate ability or lack of opportunity or quality teaching. The block to doing, and thus learning was an old belief that needed to be changed. Coaching can undo the blocks.

Barbara Desjardins lives in Winnipeg, is a former National Team Handball player, and now assistant coach for that team. She is sensitive to the special interests, needs, and abilities of the young people with whom she works.

The first time I met James, I perceived a young man who, in my junior high days, would be described as a "nerd". He had a small frame, glasses, and he wore a shirt with a pocket protector for his pens. Whenever I saw him he would just have come out of either computer club or the chess club to come to practice. He taught me how to see past mere appearance to the heart of an athlete! He never missed a practice and was interested in playing the left wing.

I brought in videos to help show the athletes technique and how the games where played at elite levels. James watched one day as a winger on the video attacked and dove into the crease (scoring area) vertically and scored. He later approached me and asked if I would show him how to do it. We worked for 20 minutes after each practice going over the approach, technique, how to read the defence, how to jump and land correctly, how and where to shoot and the timing.

Finally we were invited to a tournament. James was very excited and had convinced his dad to buy him kneepads (for landing) and new shoes. In our first game, James sat on the bench taking in everything. Finally it was his turn to go on. He turned to me and asked if he could do the wing shot. I told him that if the correct situation presented itself as we had practiced, he could do it! I smiled at him and told him to have fun. A few offences later, James got the ball and tried to attack but was cut off. I called to tell him that he was to come off on the next offence. He signalled he wanted one more try. I nodded yes. This time he was ready. James received the ball on the move, faked past the defender, drove to the net, jumped, went PERFECTLY vertical and scored into the far corner of the net.

His first words as he came off were, "was that okay?" I laughed, hugged him and said that he was amazing. That was the only goal he scored. He never again shot throughout the tournament. When I asked him later why he didn't, he said it was the rest of the team's turn. He had accomplished his own goal and wanted the rest of the team to reach theirs. The next year James went on to high school, but was too involved with his other clubs to play. What did he teach me? Never judge people by what they do or look like, only by their actions and what they are made of inside!

Barbara Desjardins saw the boy's enthusiasm and chose to take the extra time from her busy life to work with him. She created an opportunity, especially for James to learn and grow, to experience a real sense of accomplishment. In the process the coach gained a wonderful lesson for herself! Coaches are open to taking advantage of every opportunity to engage with a person and make a difference, when that person is ready. We do not know when that readiness will occur.

In all my years of working with people, a classic "messy" coaching situation has repeated itself countless times at home, in the classroom, or the athletic arena. An example is a typical high jump training session and it could just as easily have been high school beginners or Olympians. It usually unfolds like this: I am well prepared for the session, all the necessary equipment is set up and I have a clear plan for what is to be achieved that day. Everything has gone well from warm-up through the preliminary drills and improved strength and power from all the training is evident.

The first few jumps look good and then on the first attempt at a challenging height, the approach is not smooth, the take-off hesitant and the bar is knocked down! This I have seen clearly and I also saw the facial expression and read the all-too-easy-to-read lips! "So, (and the name could be one of hundreds) what happened there?"

Initially, with every youngster the reply was always a variation of the same theme, "I jumped awful, knocked the bar down, it was terrible, I dunno!" At this point teaching would begin to do a review of what needs to be done to execute this jump. The leader in us wants to do an inspirational pep-talk, "you can do this!" But the youngster is neither stupid nor suffering from instant memory loss! And a pep-talk is a Band-Aid.

This is where coaching can do what teaching cannot. The coach has an opportunity to support the athlete in greater self-awareness, self-reflection, self-discovery and ultimately greater self-responsibility and confidence.

"Yes," I say, "I saw the bar come down. But what happened? What did you feel in the approach run? At take-off? That is what matters here today and in the biggest competition you will ever have. Be aware of every step, feel every movement because that is all you ever need to do to jump well." This was not a planned intervention. It came about as a result of what happened in the moment. It was about becoming aware of every subtle nuance of feeling and motion so that anything not exactly as it should be could be experienced. By so doing it leads to the key question: "What happened?" It is essential that the athlete learn to identify the thought or feeling that interfered so that it can be dealt with in the learning process. The problem looked like a technical one but in reality it was a belief or feeling one. This was not about being physically incapable of executing a run-up and take-off. This was about being fully present, fully focused and completely aware of what was happening in the moment. It was being aware enough to know when one is not focused, then stopping and re-focusing!

ATTAINING AWARENESS

Becoming aware and being able to respond more effectively is important in every test and exam a student ever faces, in job interviews, important meetings, and every life situation in which we feel the pressure of a challenge. Time with a coach prepares us well for life.

The path to personal excellence is a challenging path, and while the physical and mental work can be demanding, the real challenges on the path are the inner personal ones. Coaches are the guides on this journey. They are constantly there to remind us of the way and, when we have doubts, support us in getting beyond them. Most often the tool they use is a story, a story to illustrate that many before us have faced this same problem and overcame it, a story to inspire, to reinforce a value, to create perspective, to accomplish whatever is needed at the moment.

It is my wish that this book serves such a purpose for you. The ideas about coaching are not mine. They have been gleaned from the minds, hearts, and souls of some of the wisest men and women I have met, read about, heard speak, or whose books I have read. The many stories throughout give you access to the experiences of dozens of other coaches from all walks of life. They have all given generously and freely to you. The stories are now yours. Be "a good host" and when one is ready you will move it on. In the process you will create stories of your own.

My desire in creating this book is to stimulate your thinking about more effectively working with all the people in your life. You are already a coach, and we share our experience in the hope that you may become an ever better coach. Please take what is here that is useful to you and use it. When you are ready, and you will know, please share your wisdom with others.

Best Practice 1

A SAFE ENVIRONMENT

Best Coaches create an emotionally and physically
safe environment in which people can learn and grow.

"To aid life, leaving it free, however, that is the basic task of the educator."
~ *Maria Montessori*

Coaches create a safe place in which people can grow. An emotionally safe environment is characterized by clear boundaries. The boundaries are the "rules" that define the nature of the family, the team or the business. The rules are clear. They are the same for all and are consistently enforced. The intent of every rule must always be fair and equal treatment. A family in which one parent is strict and the other lenient creates manipulative children. Problems can occur when rules are not adhered to or enforced consistently by any person in a position of responsibility. Similarly, games are defined by rules that limit what is acceptable and not acceptable. So it is with every healthy "team." Inconsistency in anything from parenting to refereeing creates a negative experience. People must what to expect.

The safest emotional environment is always one in which actions are separated from the person. The child is loved and valued while actions may be acceptable or not. There is a world of difference between, "what a thoughtless kid you are!" and, "that was a thoughtless thing you just did." Both are strong statements of disapproval. The first is very damaging to the youngster. The other is not. Extrapolating from this principle, coaches never denigrate the person no matter how disapproving they may be of an action. A wise leader once said, "Praise in public, criticize in private." He could have added that neither should be directed at the person, only at what the person did. Sport psychologists spend hours helping athletes become clear on the reality that they are not their performance. Who they are is separate from what they do. They are valued as people whatever their level of performance.

The successful performance coach, Brian O'Reilly relates his experience coaching a group of word class skiers. His challenge was to help them move to a higher level of performance. He knew this task had little to do with skiing.

When I was working in Calgary I was invited to come to Banff to coach four world-class free style skiers. There was a lot of money in the group, which was a concern because money often determines who has power and the combination can cause serious personal problems and erode trust. These issues were threatening the group but it changed because of one small event.

I was in the dining room with three of the group when 'Jimmy' walked in pouting. He'd had a really bad day, in fact a bad week. He had not been getting along with his friends, but they put up with him because he had lots of money and paid for a lot of things. Tolerance for Jimmy was very high even in the wake of damaged relationships.

When one of the fellows asked, "What's wrong?" his terse response was "nothing."

Quietly, I interjected, "For someone who has nothing bothering him, you look pretty angry, Jimmy."

"Coach, I've had it. These guys are too much. They are always touching my stuff behind my back. They've no right to do that. They never ask me. They just take what they want. I'm fed up with it!"

I asked, "What's the straw that broke the camel's back, Jimmy?" He looked at the other three, and blurted, "Who touched my new Sony Walkman?"

One of the three responded with, "I did. I just wanted to relax with some music. It was lying there and I used it and put it back when I was done."

Jimmy pouted angrily, "You shouldn't have, you have no right to do that." I asked, "How important is that Sony Walkman to you?"

He mumbled something and I went on. "Jimmy, are you your Sony Walkman?" This got a response! "What are you talking about?"

I remembered I had my Walkman in my pouch and took it out and asked, "Jimmy is this my Sony Walkman?" Once he replied it was, I threw it hard against the wall. As it smashed into pieces on the floor, I had four pairs of eyes staring at me.

"What did you do that for?" asked Jimmy. "You must be crazy!"

"Maybe. But I do know this for certain – I am not my Sony Walkman. And I am here to do what I came here to do, coach all of you to be more effective.

The smashed Walkman got their attention and my comments were heard, maybe for the first time. The ensuing group conversation cleared up some unhealthy relationships. The next week of the camp was productive and Jimmy trained well. At the end of the camp, he came to say thank you and after a pause said, "Coach, I'm really stuck." My response, "Well, you are only as stuck as you want to be," led to a discussion about being at the mercy of factors he couldn't control and his allowing all kinds of things to get in the way of his performing well. After a time, Jimmy said, "Yeah, I guess I know what you mean, coach," and I replied, "Yes, maybe you do; maybe you are starting to see that." This immediately sent him back into his pouting attitude.

"There you go again coach – always maybe, never anything definite. How come you always ask us to evaluate our own work? You aren't really coaching us."

"Jimmy", I said, "aren't you tired of evaluating yourself by everyone else's standards?" When he 'guessed' he was, I suggested that if the bar was to be raised, he should be the one to do it.

He immediately said, "So you aren't going to coach." I asked if he felt like I had been coaching over the past three weeks and he agreed, yes, I had coached him on a whole lot of things. Then he said, "But this is different. You are coaching me on everything"

"That's not my intention. My intention is to care about you. I believe that care coaches. When you don't care about the others, and you don't care about what they think – well, are you getting along with them?" He admitted he wasn't and when I asked if he cared about his Walkman, and did that improve his relationship with it, he looked at me as if I was very strange and said one couldn't have a relationship with a Walkman! – " it's a thing."

I asked him how important things were in his life and at first he seemed puzzled and then admitted they were pretty important. When I asked, "Do you possess your possessions or do they possess you?" he became reflective and said, "I never thought about it that way." I pointed out that coaches do that, help you see new ways to think about things, understand the way you think about things and where that thinking is taking you.

I pushed a bit because I saw he was getting it and when he finally asked, "Do you ever let up?" I smiled and replied, "Nope! I'm a coach."

Brian O'Reilly knows the path and it is the inner path that renders the journey along the outer path of success possible. In this story Brian illustrates two essential concepts with which coaches work: The need to do whatever it takes to "get their attention" and the patience to wait for the right emotional moment to do that. In the grand scheme of what the skiers wanted, a Walkman was a small price to pay to get their attention, and the timing was perfect.

Another teaching tool that Brian uses well is asking questions that continue to turn people into their own inner wisdom. In the right situation, the right questions will always bring up our own answers that, for us, are the right answers.

Coaches use positive language even when dealing with clearly negative behaviour or extremely sub-standard performances. Sarcasm, belittling, or any abusive language is never used; it is against what we most desire to achieve – healthy, self-confident people who can perform at their best when it is important.

Tom Bourne, who lives in South Florida with his family and coaches youth baseball tells how he made a situation emotionally safer for one youngster in particular and the entire group in general.

I once had a player, Terry, who was introverted. He possessed great potential as a pitcher with a natural release and fluid motion that many never achieve through years of committed practice. He also had an autistic brother who was confined to a wheel chair and could only utter indiscernible exclamations. Now to an eleven year old this was embarrassing at best and it showed with Terry. For the others on the team it ranged from embarrassed laughter to complete avoidance. Eleven year olds do not have much compassion or understanding.

Terry's brother lived to go to the games and watch his brother play baseball. In years past it was noted that this situation was somewhat disturbing to both players and parents. Plain downright uncomfortable for some! Well this year was going to be different. The players on Terry's team learned about his brother and what Terry had to deal with in his life. More importantly, they learned what Terry's brother had to deal with.

As callous as it seemed I chose to use Terry's brother as a segue into talking about the privilege of health and physical well being that we often take for granted. Every time the players thought life wasn't fair when they struck out or couldn't play the position they sought, they were urged to reflect on Terry's brother. After all, he couldn't play at all but was always there to participate and cheer.

Once the players got over the initial strangeness of closer contact they became more comfortable with the situation and accepted it. They no longer were afraid and more importantly, when it was a non issue for others, Terry came out of his shell and developed the confidence he needed to excel at pitching. The team soon came to see Terry's brother as another individual like themselves, but with a difference and they committed to winning the season for him, which is exactly what they did.

A physically safe environment is based on respect for the individual and concern for his or her safety. It is planned and managed so that no undue harm can occur. Bumps and bruises to the body and psyche are a reality of life. Coaches make certain that these immediate hurts do not become long-term harm. Still these hurts are inevitable and coaches use them to create greater awareness and turn these into lessons in courage, confidence and whatever else can be extracted. The social environment is also assessed in terms of safety. Bullying in any form is not tolerated.

Unfortunately, some people have had experiences with bullying coaches. It is impossible to say how many people's potential has been ruined in this way. The fortunate ones find subsequent experiences to make repairs. Debbie Van Kiekebelt was Canada's female athlete of the year in 1971, as well as Track and Field's athlete of the year in 1971. She tells the following story of how bad coaching, with the best of intentions but an underlying negative attitude, wasted her greatest opportunity and almost destroyed her psychologically.

My coach, who had been only a short time in Canada had an Eastern European background and believed in berating, belittling, and badgering, which he felt would only make a competitive person work harder. In my case this method of coaching slowly destroyed my confidence and killed my passion for competing.

At the 1972 Olympics in Munich I was injured and pretty miserable after spending three months alone in Yugoslavia with him training for the games. When we reached Munich it was cold and I got sick. I had been over training and had a complete physical and emotional breakdown. Needless to say, I performed terribly. My coach made it clear that he was extremely disappointed. He did not even talk to me during my competition and left the games without speaking to me. I came back from the Olympics totally disheartened and disillusioned. On the verge of quitting track and field I was contacted by Lloyd Percival, a long time Canadian coach who was then running the Fitness Institute. He asked if I wanted to work with him. I did and for the next several months I trained alone with his guidance. He gave me workout plans, but he also gave me so much more.

Slowly and surely he began to restore my confidence. We would have long sessions just talking about my goals, my dreams, my fears, failure, success, and the future. He became my emotional and psychological guide to feeling good about myself again. He didn't really help me with my training but he did make me want to compete again. In March 1973 there was the first Canada/Russia dual meet in Canada at the Forum in Montreal. He told me to go to the track early, sit up in the stands and picture what I wanted to see happen that night, feel how I wanted to feel during and after the event. He told me to sit there and get excited about competing, not scared, not nervous, but exhilarated. Now you must remember these were the days before sports psychologists but I sat and looked out on the empty track and felt empowered. I was going there to be a contender. I won the event beating the Russian women and setting personal bests in two races. To me it spoke volumes about the importance of preparing an athlete for a big event not just physically but emotionally. A great coach must harness and then develop an athlete's physical potential but more importantly teach the athlete that their emotional and psychological confidence must be developed as well.

Truthfully, I do not believe I ever regained my self-confidence completely. Too much damage had been done and my career cut short because of that. This only reinforces the importance of the role a coach plays in a young athlete's life. A great coach must realize that it's vital to teach the right fundamentals of sport but it is also important to teach the fundamentals of life. These are the lessons athletes will take with them long after sport is no longer the focus of their lives.

Another strand that forms part of the boundary and strengthens it considerably is a clear agreement about the nature of the relationship between the learner and the coach. An important part of this makes clear that the real challenges are in the person, and what, exactly, is the role of each relative to those challenges. Responsibility and accountability are required of both parties and clear and honest evaluation replaces judging and blame. Openness, clarity, and respect are hallmarks of safe environments.

Sometimes that feeling of safety can occur when the sport is reduced to its original intention – FUN! Mark Lee, an announcer and producer of sport programmes with CBC Television tells a refreshing hockey story of boys and girls playing the game for the sheer delight of it.

It was a typical minor hockey practice, in the St. James Arena in Winnipeg, Manitoba. Stops and starts, the usual drills.

But a closer look revealed a team unlike any other I had ever seen. These were the Southside Dragons or 'The Outlaw Team', as they were known in Winnipeg hockey circles. Kids, ranging in age from ten to fourteen, many of whom had dropped out of competitive hockey. They all came from a system that pushed them away.

The team kept no statistics. There was no playoff race. No pressure. These kids did not have to face the devastation of being cut from the team or sitting on the bench while better players were on the ice.

"Is it true there was a coach who told you not to touch the puck?" I asked a twelve year old boy named Matthew Couture, one day when I met with the team.

"He told me not to touch the puck because I was not good enough", he said matter of factly.

"How did that make you feel?", I replied.

"At the time, I was really disappointed and sad. I did not like that at all", he replied.

Matthew's grandfather had formed the Outlaw Team. When I had coffee with him in the kitchen of his Winnipeg bungalow, Rollie Couture was 76 years old. He was a mild-manner man with thirty years of distinguished service as a coach and manager in minor hockey.

"What's different about this atmosphere?" I asked

Rishi Ramberran, a gangly forward said, "Well, the parents. If you make a bad play, they don't yell at you and stuff and if the coach wants to talk to you about something, he'll talk to you privately instead of yelling at you."

Bingo! Parents, for whom hockey was not a status symbol, had found a safe haven from the world of competitive hockey for their children.

"We were involved in a situation where the club seemed very geared to the elite or premier level hockey," said Bruce Hunt. "When it came to a player who was involved below that level they didn't seem to have much interest."

Even as these parents and their children left the orbit of organized hockey they could not escape the criticism. "The usual response is you're bucking the system, Outlaw Team, depriving your boy," recounted Randy Kouk. "I can't seem to figure that all out. The bottom line is they're all just kids and they're playing hockey," he said. "That's all that counts, and as parents, I've never enjoyed hockey so much in all my life."

On a brutally cold Friday night they loaded their gear and drove north to Selkirk, Manitoba. A Selkirk hockey official was waiting for them when they arrived.

One of the Dragons was dressed and ready to play for more than an hour before the game started. The anticipation was palpable.

The coach, Bernie Bowie, stood in the locker room to deliver his first pre-game speech of the year. "Make it special for yourself and the person next you", he said in the charged atmosphere of this hockey dressing room. "We've got three games and who knows what can happen!" The words could have come from any NHL head coach, but this was a volunteer with no vested interest except in the well being of the children on his team.

By the third period, the Dragons trailed 6-0. On the bench Rollie Couture was asked about the mood on the team. "I don't seem to see any indication of them giving up," he said, "but I think we're a little out-numbered."

The horn sounded. The final score: Selkirk 6, Dragons 0. "Take your gloves off and shake hands boys," Rollie shouted. This practice has long since been abandoned in competitive minor hockey because of the incidents of altercations. There were no long faces on this hockey team. Somehow, the score was not important.

"It was a hard game," said Matthew Couture, still sweating in post-game reflection. "The team played well. They advanced on their opportunities. Unfortunately, we lost, but it was a good game."

"It's only one game guys," said coach Bowie, encouraging his team in the locker room with praise and promise for the next game.

Outside in the hallway, he found success in a 6-0 defeat. "It's already been a special night regardless of the score," he said. "This is something that doesn't happen very often. It's special in that sense. We've now found a place to play."

Rollie Couture, who risked his good standing as a hockey coach when he formed the Outlaws, echoed those sentiments. "There's more joy and banter in our locker room than any dressing room I've ever been in. And I've been in a lot of them."

The Outlaws had made it, finding joy and camaraderie in a game. They learned that hard work would bring results. They learned to be positive. They learned to be inclusive.

Fun must always be present in an effective environment although the need for it and amount of it diminishes as people grow and develop, and enjoyment and satisfaction become the major emotional issues. When kids are not having fun they move to another activity or completely away from physical activity.

In a safe environment every participant knows the conditions of being a part of the group, whether it has to do with punctuality, or cooperation, or adherence to the intent of the rules of the game. The coach models what is expected. The consequences are logical and clear up front. They apply equally to all.

I have always believed that a group or team should be as inclusive as the situation allows. When Tom Watt, Bobby Dann and I were the first Physical Education teachers at the Toronto Board of Education's new and innovative high school, Monarch Park, in 1964, we agreed that as many boys as possible should have the inter-school sport experience and that everyone who wanted should have access to activity. We believed that excellence did not preclude participation. We proved that to be true, again and again.

In the autumn we had almost one hundred boys practicing and playing on the three age class football teams, as well as many more on soccer, tennis and cross country running teams. While this was happening after school the gyms and weight room were also open for "drop-in" activity.

Supervision was highly recommended but we simply did not have enough staff to coach all the teams and supervise the gym and mezzanine weight room in the fall term. The youngsters had to be responsible for their own and each others safety, if they wanted access. That was made clear. Then with a smile on the corner of his mouth, and tongue in cheek, Bobby Dann stated "The Rule" that no one ever forgot. "This only works if you accept clear responsibility. We cannot be responsible for your safety if we are not here. Clear? So no one gets injured here. Should that happen the rest of you must take him out to the street, put his hands in his pockets and lay him in the Cross Walk," the laughter confirmed their understanding and acceptance. Because of the respect given and the responsibility clearly laid out the youngsters created a safer situation than it may have been with a teacher present. For certain those youngsters felt more emotionally safe than in many situations.

Cross country running had three age class teams with seven runners on each team being permitted for the Toronto Secondary Schools A.A. Championships. This sport had no real limitations of participation because of gym size or cost of equipment, as did basketball and football. Throughout the season any boy could run in the weekly meets but there was a limiting factor. Why would a youngster do this if he was not pretty good at running and stood some chance of making *the team* for the championship race? Running, unlike team games leaves no place *to hide*. The runner is alone and his time is a result of individual performance, not of a team. One can feel pretty naked, pretty exposed and on one's own in racing.

Evelyn Freeman, a former national level high jumper, mother of three and a coach at Grinnell College in Iowa has a story about how the running experience can not only made to feel safer but also can be a part of bonding a team – in a completely silly and fun way. The idea originated with the athletes and has been carried on by them.

"It's a hot day today." When I hear one of the captains recite this comment, I know that whatever workout I had planned for the day is going to be tossed to the wind in favour of the "Naked Mile" workout. Late in September, on a beautiful warm day, the

veteran runners lead the innocent, unaware freshwomen on a journey into Eden. Actually, it's the dirt road mile on the northeast 5.5 mile loop. The team sticks close together for a couple of miles to the entrance of "Eden." At that point the veteran runners explain the tradition of the naked mile and ensure that participation is completely voluntary. My job is to stay out of view of our runners and anyone else who might be in the vicinity, appear to be totally ignorant of the activities and to pick up any runners upon completion of the fun, who may need a ride back to campus. One Naked Mile run in the late '90s was especially memorable.

As usual, I parked my mini-van about a quarter mile beyond the point of the end of the Naked Mile so when the runners catch up to my location they are fully clothed and smiling innocently as if nothing happened. From my location I could see that a farmer was harvesting corn adjacent to the road where the women were to pass by. I started feeling anxious, but what was I to do? Do I explain to him what was about to happen and ask him to leave for a while? I was relieved when his combine headed east away from the road.

What I didn't know was that he then headed back west and parked mid-way along their Naked Mile to unload the corn from his combine into a waiting wagon. I shuddered to think about the reaction of the women as they crested over the ridge and were met by the farmer hanging out by his combine. I began planning responses to inquiries or phone calls from town's folk or, heaven forbid, the athletic director. "They did what? You're kidding! I had no idea! I'll have a talk with them." I felt prepared to deal with the consequences...sort of.

I slid down low in my seat and was glad I was not driving a Grinnell College vehicle with its logo displayed on its door. Here's what actually happened. The women were having great fun enjoying the freedom of unrestricted movement. They crested over the hill and surprised not one farmer, but two. Did they all escape and plunge quickly into the ditch of overgrown weeds to cover-up? Did they turn around and retrace their steps? No, they all kept on running, enjoyed the fun, waving a polite 'hello' to the farmers as they passed by. When they arrived at my car fully clothed I asked how the run had gone and if they had seen the farmers. They recounted for me their experience as if it was an everyday occurrence. I, however, spent the next few days anxiously awaiting a phone call of reprimand, but none came. I suspect the farmers were more amused than offended.

Returning to the more figurative sense of feeling naked in a competitive situation, we all feel this because we are compared to others. It is inescapable in individual sports and activities. Coaches teach that it is important to see others who are good as models of what is possible not as standards with which to compare ourselves. If comparisons are to be made they must be made to how we have been and what we have done, relative to what we want to be and do. This is the concept of "Personal Best."

Previously at Monarch Park, the racers had little idea regarding how good they were. Either they won or they did not. Obtaining an accurate time for every boy, for every race made it possible for every youngster to measure his performance against previous performances, not against those of others. The question was how to do it. A colleague, at another school, Ron Wallingford, had years of experience in distance races and was still representing Canada in marathons. Ron was familiar with a wonderfully simple system and outlined it for me. With the help of a couple of students we began to capture accurate times for every boy who ran every Tuesday. I needed times to inspire youngsters to run, not for the team, or for the school or for anything but personal satisfaction, a way to measure improvement, to see clearly the results of their efforts, but the effect was system-wide. Every participant, in every school, benefited because we compiled the results the evening after the races and mailed a copy to every school the next day.

Accurate, weekly times over a constant course gave me the ability to sell kids on the concept of Personal Best. Now there was a specific, measurable, purpose to training. It was possible for every single boy who wanted to train regularly to measure improvement, achieve "p.b.'s," to discover how fast he personally could run over this challenging course, over a season and for many, over an entire high school career. It was not just being one of the top seven in an age group, nor was it comparing oneself to the best.

As in everything in life, the best show us what is possible, but we need to measure ourselves against our own past performances, and our own, personal dreams. In the process we have that most rare of opportunities, to test the limits of our inherited abilities in an emotionally and physically safe environment.

Don Steen is a retired physical educator who lives in Vancouver and is a life-long coach. He tells the story of Dusty, an exceptional athlete, whose father chose to create the safest possible environment.

Let me tell you about my friend Dusty, a nineteen-year old sprinter. Watching him, most would not see anything but an average sprinter until you realize that he is blind and that the same man is always in the adjoining lane running with him stride for stride. That man is Larry, Dustin's father and guide runner.

Exclusion from physical activity starts early for blind and visually impaired individuals. Whereas most children learn by copying the actions of other children and adults, blindness is a unique disability in that you can't copy what you can't see. Eighty to ninety percent of all blind or visually impaired students are relegated to the library while their sighted peers take part in physical education, a sad pattern of exclusion that for most lasts a lifetime. During his school days, Dusty rejected suggestions that he take study hall while his sighted classmates took physical education, a situation that I'm sure challenged his teacher. When Dustin decided he enjoyed running enough to join a local track and field club, he was virtually ignored by the coaches. Exclusion is the most significant factor in preventing the majority of blind and visually impaired individuals from being active.

As Dusty's coach I've strived to give him what I've tried to give every athlete I've ever coached, a well-structured training regimen coupled with the power to believe in himself. Yet I have also received a great deal back. Like no other athlete, Dusty has taught me that coaching goes beyond "Here's how it's done. See?" He's challenged me to go beyond painting word pictures of physical actions, as often I have to physically move him into a desired position. He has challenged me to look at training principles in a whole new light. He has challenged me to be creative and to think outside the box. As a coach, working with Dusty and Larry has been one of my most, if not the most, rewarding experiences.

Vicki Keith, world record holder in a number of marathon swimming events and a ceaseless fund-raiser for programmes for children with disabilities, relates how a damaging experience was transformed into a life time of good.

When I was six years old, like most children I was not aware that I might have some limitations. I had a ballet teacher who felt it her duty to publicly point out my complete lack of talent in dance. When I danced, I could feel the ballerina in my heart pirouetting and leaping with beauty and grace. After my first recital that ballet teacher bound my little ballerina for life. She made some very uncaring and hurtful comments from the stage for all the parents and my classmates to hear.

I left the gymnasium in tears and spent the next couple of recesses in the principal's office while I tried to protect my pride and stand up to the ridiculing of the other children who had been in the gym to hear the ballet teacher's mocking description of my efforts.

I left dance for good that day but I learned some valuable lessons that I take into coaching every day of my life.

Sport and activity are not about winning or being the best. They are about enjoying the process, learning about your abilities, focusing on those abilities, and striving to be the best that you can be.

When eight year old Ashley Cowan walked onto the pool deck her first day of swim practice and told me she wanted to swim across a lake, I didn't look at the fact that she was a quadruple amputee and assume she could never do something like that. I certainly did not tell her that it was hopeless and that she could never swim a lake, after she jumped into the water and swam only half a length of the pool flailing away until she was completely exhausted. Instead I created a niche for her, a place where she could explore and learn, a safe place for her to strive under positive reinforcement and caring direction.

The rest is history. Ashley developed the endurance to swim across a lake. It took eight years of training but she did it. On September 7 2001 Ashley Cowan swam the twenty kilometres across Lake Erie while the world watched and learned that nothing is impossible if you set your mind to it.

Not only did Ashley accomplish the dream of swimming across a lake; along the way she became a national level competitive swimmer in sport for the disabled and learned about having a dream, setting goals and striving to accomplish what she set out to do. You never know the potential of a child standing in front of you. Just because they don't have the "body type" or what is generally perceived it takes to be the best, never count them out. See into their hearts and give them a safe place to learn.

Vicki's story and what she learned from her extremely negative experience with her ballet teacher reminded me of a man I saw speaking on television. His handsome and confident face filled the screen and his strong, clear voice captured my attention. As his story progressed about being a Vietnam veteran who had spent years imprisoned in North Vietnam in what was literally a bamboo cage, the camera pulled back and revealed a wheel chair, and the fact that he had no legs. He described how, while being rescued, the helicopter was shot down close to the American base and he lost both legs in the crash. He spoke of lying in the hospital coming to grips with what had happened and what he now faced. He realized he had the option to get bitter or get better. He chose the latter. In many situations, few as dire, in all of our lives we face the same options. Coaches choose, and support others to choose, always to get better.

Vicki has accomplished some remarkable work with dedicated individuals. Harry is another dedicated individual who graced Vicki's life.

After months of encouraging and cajoling, Harry appeared on the pool deck for his first swim practice. He was a non-swimmer, and was quite apprehensive in the water. Although most swim teams would not take a non-swimmer, our swim team was new and different. It was the first swim team in the area for young people with physical disabilities and everyone was encouraged to participate.

I had put aside time to work one on one with interested young people, so Harry and I began to work together. Harry was an incredibly determined young man who would set his mind to accomplishing a task the refuse anything but the very best from himself.

In mid February Harry had his first swimming lesson. For March break the team traveled to Cocoa Beach, Florida for a leadership training camp. Harry, who could now swim on his back if someone was in the water with him, joined us at the camp. That week, he swam 200 metres on his own with his teammates cheering him on. By June, Harry had mastered swimming on his front and during our 24 hour relay fundraiser, Harry slid into the water during one of his breaks and swam for an hour and a half continuously.

The following season, during one of his first competitions, Harry made a mistake that I am sure every swimmer has made at some point in his or her swimming career. He forgot to pull his goggles over his eyes before the race. Once the race had started, it was too late. After scraping his shoulder and back along the lane rope a number of times and swallowing more than his share of water Harry completed his race. While I lifted him out at the edge of the pool, which just happened to be right in front of the stands filled with parents, I wondered what Harry's comments about the race would be. You never know what a teenage boy is going to say when he is frustrated or upset. I needn't have worried. He looked up at me with a huge grin on his face and said..."Well that was a learning experience!" *As his teammate Jenna says about being a part of the team,* "I have learned that no matter what I have to go through in life, I know I CAN DEAL WITH IT!!!"

Peter Jensen, Corporate Trainer, psychologist to Olympic athletes and a wonderful teacher of coaches tells us how a very wise rowing coach shows his charges the process of getting better in a safe and reinforcing environment and how that is always relative to their own abilities.

I met Bernard years ago when he was probably in his early sixties. I have never forgotten his way of demonstrating reach, possibility, to the young rowers under his care. He told me that when they first came to the club, before they set foot in a boat, he would take then into a nearby grove of trees. He instructed all his young charges to find a tree to climb and stand at the bottom of it. He gave them the following instruction, " I want you to climb as high as you can in your tree. When you are as high as you can go I want you to call me."

When a child called he would walk to the bottom of the tree they were climbing and call up to them. "That's excellent, Jimmy, now listen carefully, I want you to go up one more branch and then come back down to the ground. Have you got that Jimmy? One more branch and then right down to the ground."

To me, this is brilliant. He didn't tell everyone go up this high or this many branches. He let them tell him what they were capable of and then he asked them to go a bit further. He made it clear that that was all he was going to ask them to do. He instilled in them that they could and would stretch, go a bit beyond what they saw as possible. He did this by way of experience, not words.

Sometimes an athlete with phenomenal talent is held back because of concerns off the field. Regrettably, financial concerns plague too many athletes and students and can harm their performance. Elliot Kerr, the founder and President of Landmark Sport Inc., tells how removing that concern made a real difference.

Rob McMillan and David Hearn are two of Canada's most accomplished golfers and aspiring PGA Tour players. They currently play on the Canadian and Nationwide Tours. We have secured what I would call "reasonable" sponsorship income, but not actually enough to offset the cost of a complete golf season. Such financial stress could affect the quality of their play. At the beginning of last season I talked with each player individually and said that he need not worry about money. If the worst happens and he does not earn enough prize money to get through the season I would take care of all his financial needs.

Each golfer had a solid 2002 season. Rob won an event and David was Rookie of the Year. The safe environment I provided, not just financially, but emotionally as well, enabled them to realize their potential. Each year is a building block in professional golf and this was a foundation builder.

Coaches do everything possible to remove obstacles that can interfere with concentration and focus on the task at hand. The also teach powerful, very useful lessons, and change a very negative cultural belief by honouring mistakes and failures. By creating the norm that mistakes and failures are essential to learning and growth they transform emotionally dangerous situations into safe ones. Coaches know that we need to constantly attempt new activities, new skills, new ways of thinking and doing things. In this process we must certainly make mistakes and sometimes even fail dramatically. If we do not we are repeating what we can do easily and no significant progress is ever made. The key to all mistakes and failures is to learn from them. In an emotionally and physically safe environment that is the norm.

Seven Keys to Creating a Safe Place

1. Value each person as an individual – always!

2. Have clear, logical rules of individual and group conduct.

3. Create an inclusive environment based on enjoying the process.

4. Model and create honest, respectful and consistent relationships.

5. Ensure communication from all coaches is consistent.

6. Emphasize that mistakes and failures are essential to learning and growth.

7. Be certain that smiles, fun, humour, and laughter are always present.

2 Best Practice

POSITIVE VALUES

Best Coaches model and teach positive values.

"In matters of style swim with the current. In matters of principle stand like a rock."
~ *Thomas Jefferson*

I was fortunate to have parents who talked about, taught, and modeled values essential to success in life. The cornerstones of their values were honesty and integrity. Honesty was discussed often and while I doubt I heard the word integrity during my childhood, I witnessed integrity in practice. It was lived every day. Promises were kept. Words were backed up with actions.

Values were taught with bits of inspirational poetry, aphorisms and favourite family expressions that my parents had acquired from their parents, and from their "readers" in the one-room elementary school where they had taken their entire schooling. Their education was another matter. Both my parents loved to read and learned as much as possible from every situation and person they met.

Reading, learning and education were family values. However, there was a strong sense of utility behind these. "Useful" was a word I heard often. The most useful person was one who took responsibility for his own life, was grateful for what he had and did whatever he could to help those "less fortunate." Reading, learning and education were first about character and then about "making a living."

Earn what you desire was a value that shaped me in my approach to life and working with people. It was related to opportunity and all the potential benefits. My parents taught me that opportunity was everywhere, that "anything's possible" but the benefits had to be earned. No one owed me anything. Nothing was free. The price was work or effort. "Ye shall reap what ye sow" was the guiding principle. That was as true for success in school as it was my chores around the house or later for work as a fishing guide in the family business. Opportunities were there for all of us. Those of us willing to do the necessary work benefited.

Steve Friesen is Head of Health, Physical Education and Athletics at St. James Catholic High School in Guelph, Ontario. Steve is currently involved with Health Canada and the province in facilitating the offering of health and physical education classes in our schools. Steve learned an important value in his first year of high school.

I was going to run the 800 metres and had about four weeks to train but did not take the training as seriously as I should have. I believed I could just waltz through the event. I wasn't used to losing and hadn't yet figured out that commitment and disciplined work could be really valuable.

My coach was Doug Andrews and he was always on me about my rather lame approach to training. Now I know that he knew what was going to happen. Race day came and I was ready to win, or so I thought. There were about twelve runners in this event one of which would later become an Olympic calibre racer. At the start I burst into the lead and held it for about 600 metres; then the roof caved in! My lack of commitment and training came through. I slowed down dramatically and every runner passed me. On that final turn I was in last place. To me this was unheard of! I can still remember the feeling I had at that time. I felt humiliated. I wanted to crawl into a hole right there on the track. Instead I quit. I stepped off the track and lay down on the infield as the others finished the race.

What happened next I shall never forget. Mr. Andrews was standing over me eclipsing the sun with his body. With the sun behind him his face was shaded but his voice was clear. He said, "You never, ever quit. You finish what you start. You never quit, Steve." To this day I can still see his face and hear those words.

I have always carried that lesson with me. It is the first thing I tell every team I coach. It is the story that defines our team character. We may not be better than some teams but we will never be outworked or out-hustled. The teams I have coached have always played like that. On my desk is a little rock from a motivational company and inscribed on it are the words, "never, never quit".

Coaches know and teach the value of commitment and the meaning of commitment in a deep personal sense. Doug Andrews did just that for Steve at a most "teachable moment." The youngster had quit the race for no other reason than it was getting physically uncomfortable and his own way of seeing things caused him to be embarrassed. I am certain that the conversation that ensued dealt with the reality that first and foremost Steve had quit on Steve. Yes, he did have a commitment to teammates because he was taking a spot that someone else might have had, but the person Steve let down most was himself. Coaches know that perseverance is a useful quality to possess. Nothing of real value comes easily to anyone.

Teamwork, the idea of supporting one another to get the job done was both taught and modeled every day in my family. "Many hands make light work," "pitch in," and "two heads are better than one" were heard and seen daily in everything from road building, cutting and hauling firewood, to washing dishes after the family and all the hired help had been fed. Another related value I saw demonstrated was cooperation in a larger, community way. People came together to support each other in projects that required many "hands" such as harvesting. After getting the job done at one place they all showed up the next day at another. I also saw the benefits of collaboration with regard to the miles of road we built ourselves to the fishing camp. Upgrading and general upkeep was difficult and time demanding work. The entire process was made easier and completed much sooner by my father, working with the local paper mill, that needed access to wood lots in the area. They agreed on who would do what based on resources. In the end, both benefited.

Years later I built the first foam rubber landing surfaces for high jumping and pole vaulting in the city of Toronto by collaborating with a foam rubber dealer. I got what I needed, foam rubber chunks, by agreeing to haul away the dealer's scrap material. Over a decade later in collaborative deals with the University of Toronto, the U of T Track Club and the Canadian Track and Field Association we created the first ever "shared-coach" situation in the country. This was the beginning of eventually developing broader and more significant relationships to create the first High Performance Centre for track and field in Canada. Collaboration makes possible situations that could never be achieved alone, and everyone wins!

Glen Hoag, a member of Canada's national volleyball team from 1981 to 1987, and now the Head Coach of Paris Volley, tells the following story:

Our season was going well as we reached the beginning of the 1999-2000 European cup competition in early December. The format was two pools of eight teams, with the top two teams of each pool going to the Final Four in Athens, Greece.

We were very well prepared for that match, physically, mentally, technically, and tactically. I insisted on playing well, on "doing things right" and staying focused on our game plan, instead of playing " with nothing to lose," as many French teams do when meeting the Italians.

The Italians were missing two of their stars: Spanish player Rafael Pascual, voted best player in the world in 1998, and Russian middle blocker Rusland Olikver, one of the best players in the world in his position. We ended up winning 3-1 at home in Paris, which had put us in great shape to finish in the top two teams. Our goal of making the Final Four was almost a reality.

Our last match was at home against a Russian team from Belgorod. They were third in our pool just behind second place Cuneo (the Italians). A win or loss had no serious consequences for us; we would still be in first place. But for the Russians a 3-0 win meant a second place finish and a trip to the Final Four.

During the week prior to our match against the Russians, some of our players and management were talking about us losing on purpose to let Belgorod finish second and that would keep the Italians out of the Final Four. The Russians made us an offer: " Let us win and we will let you win at the Final Four". I started thinking about all this and I was disappointed with some of my players and our management's attitude. I felt that some of the players had the same block that many French teams had towards Italian volleyball, that they are unbeatable.

I consulted my captain, Canadian setter Kent Greves. Kent was disappointed and didn't want any of it. He said if we were going to lose purposely, he would not play. We decided to have a meeting with the coaching staff and the players, but without members of the management. Everybody expressed their opinion and the discussion was frank but short. The decision was unanimous. We would go for it and meet the Italians face to face on neutral grounds. That day the team changed.

We went on to beat the Russians 3-0. We beat Cuneo, with all their players available, in Athens at the "Final Four", 3-1, in a hard fought match. That year our team won all the competitions it participated in and made French volleyball history by doing so.

This experience was crucial to the team. The following season Paris Volley won four titles, including the prestigious Champions league and the European Supercup, beating the Italians in Italy!

For coach Hoag and his team there was a higher value than winning. Honesty and integrity and "the game" are much higher values. Coaches honour and teach these principles. I recall speaking to a group of physical educators and coaches early in my career and addressing values in sport. I had not written this in my notes but heard myself saying, "The only thing of real value that any of us take away from sport is who we become."

That value had been instilled in me when young and had never been directly taught. What had been taught were honesty, integrity and playing by the rules. In the early 1980's when Gord Stewart went to train in California with a large group of decathletes and talked with me about the drugs they were using, it was not yet an issue for either of us. They did not make any sense in the exploration of personal excellence. A few years later when steroids became a banned substance and it was obvious that many performers were using them, I knew the position I would take: do not cheat. The public stance that I took had been determined decades ago, thanks to my parents. In Canada we witnessed the negative impact revealed at the Dubin Inquiry, not just on the lives of individuals but on the entire sport of track and field.

Recently I was traveling to a coaching education seminar with my long time friend and colleague Barry Bartlett, a leading educator in the field of Athletic Therapy. We were discussing our athletic and coaching experiences and reflecting on early lessons. Barry talked about a life changing moment when he was a young man playing professional lacrosse. His team had won the National Championship and was celebrating at the hotel. Everyone was congratulating everyone else and the celebrants included not just the team, but all the supporters and even other guests in the hotel. Barry got to bed late and when he finally wakened the next day, showered and went down to the lobby, he found himself alone. The lobby was filled with guests coming and going but not teammates, and no one noticed him. The recognition and excitement of the previous night had disappeared. In the long quiet walk he took Barry realized what coaches teach all athletes, that there is only the moment, and it is to be fully experienced. Then it passes and there is another moment. The lesson is clear: Value the moment.

The "Championship moment" is to be savoured and then let go. To live fully and to be successful we need to be in the present moment doing what that moment offers and demands. In a different way, in a different setting Barry came to realize what Glenn Hoag and his charges learned, that winning and success in any form are of the moment, but what we become in that moment is forever.

In my family, responsibility was a daily reality. My father modeled that value. Although he was head of the family and owner of the business he never acted as if this was a privileged position. His actions always showed that he saw it as a responsibility. My father believed that he was responsible for the family welfare and those who worked for him, while in reality people worked with him. His sense of responsibility caused him to despise healthy adults who did not work hard to make their lives better. At the same time he did whatever he could for their unfortunate children.

For men and women in responsible positions in the community respect was taught, even demanded of us as children. It was made clear they had earned respect by their efforts and conduct. We children, too, had to earn respect from others with our actions. We acted with good manners and respect, yet when required we stood against the crowd on a principle. Quality work was expected. It wasn't enough to just get the job done. The principle applied to whatever we did.

Frank Dick is one of the most respected coaches in the world with respect to training theory and understanding the entire athlete development process. Repeated success has earned that respect. Frank tells the following story:

Winning can be a lot of things but it only has real meaning when we achieve our purpose within the framework of our core values. I suppose it is like reaching our destination whilst living every moment of the journey within the Highway Code!

The scene was in Rome, September 3, 1987. Only a year before, Daley Thompson had taken European Gold in what had been the toughest quality, in-depth competition in Decathlon, two weeks after winning the Commonwealth title. Since then, he'd had a persistent injury, which compromised preparation. Nevertheless, Daley was determined to continue and compete to his highest standards.

"Are you sure about this, Daley?"

"Frankie, if you never try, you never know".

After Daley ran 10.67 seconds in the 100m we knew it would be very hard to win a second world title. Splashing through a flooded lane to 48.61 seconds in the 400m ended a brutal day, physically and emotionally, and ended all hopes for gold. Yet every one of the team's supporters stood in the rain, cheering their champion, recognizing to his challenge, sharing his struggle.

Following the pole vault the next day, he walked into the tunnel. "Frankie, I want you to buy two tickets for the Bahamas. One for you and one for me. We'll leave now".

We were laughing. Sometimes you cry when you are laughing. "Don't look at me when I'm crying". I looked away. Coaches must keep their emotions in the middle of the road. Never too high or too low, you must be an emotional stabiliser.

Daley was going to be a father for the first time in a few months. "Daley, when this baby arrives there will be times when medication is required. Sometimes there will be one last drop of medicine in the teaspoon, and the baby will have to finish it"

"Fine for babies Frankie, but I'm me!"

The "me" that is Daley is about winning, in whatever arena he chooses to compete. If it was not to be for a world title, then what was it to be?

Two people provided the answer: Jayne Fredericks, the world class American heptathelete, arrived in the tunnel, "How are you doing, Daley?"

"Well, you know!"

"Listen, what you're doing is incredible... seeing it through... people out there can't believe it... they thought you'd... you know".

Andy Higgins arrived in the tunnel. When I saw him he was radiating the sort of energy that comes when someone you believe in touches the reality of their potential. "Daley you have done a lot of great things, but nothing approaches what you are doing out there".

What I was saying to Daley, who I feel privileged to call a friend, was that he was making a statement to the entire world, and especially the world of decathlon, that a poor performance and a personal disappointment is not a reason to quit. The decathlon, and in fact all of sport, is about experiencing the challenge and Daley was demonstrating exactly that. He had come to Rome to struggle for the gold medal, and it became clear on the first day that it was not to be. Yet he persisted, felt the disappointment deeply, and he finished. I was moved because sport is about the struggle, the struggle "with" one's worthy adversaries and against one's own weaknesses.

Decathlon is Greek and means "ten struggles." Every decathlete knows, what all of us come to know if we are fortunate, that the struggle is always with ourselves, within ourselves, and for ourselves. To become who and what we are capable of we need to be challenged. Thus we need the worthiest of opponents. Nietzsche, the German philosopher said, "That which does not kill me, strengthens me." This is the extreme, but he made the point well. Even children need to be challenged. When left to their own devices, they naturally seek out challenges. When they respond to challenges with excitement it is because the environment is emotionally and physically safe.

At home, we discussed laws and rules, made sense of them, and acted on them. It was important that as children my brother and I not only knew how to act but why we did something. My father, even more than my mother, understood and lived by the intent of the law or social rules. I am certain now that his attitude and actions, particularly discussions concerning the intent of a law led to my understanding why the rules of a game or sport were so important. They are intended to make clear the nature of our relationship in any given challenge. As I write this I am reminded of all the card games and board games we played as a family in which the intent of the rules was made clear. This experience taught me to live with the childish disappointment of not getting the cards I wanted or landing on a "snake" when I was hoping for a "ladder." The satisfaction of winning was sweeter when earned by clever play or persistence. In these games I learned that success is a process. What looked like losing and failures were opportunities to learn more and become better at the game.

Tom Kinsman, is a former National Team gymnast, coach, and sport administrator. He is the father of one daughter and a closet jazz musician. Tom tells the following story:

A small group of male gymnasts were in a close battle for the gold medal on rings. Just before the group performs, they each get one warm-up turn on the apparatus. In that warm-up session one of the leading gymnasts broke his leather handgrip (different from losing your grip). For those who do not know the sport, the handgrip is a leather band that goes from the top knuckle of the fingers over the palm of the hand and fastens to a strong strap around the wrist. In high-level gymnastics these handgrips are absolutely necessary to withstand the powerful forces generated by the giant swings these athletes perform. Without them the gymnast slips off the rings at the bottom of the swing. This gymnast would not be able to compete. One of the coaches of a serious competitor asked his gymnast to lend his handgrips to the disadvantaged athlete. The athlete with the borrowed grips went on to win the competition.

There were many athletes and coaches present who thought this gesture of good will was a ridiculous thing to do. After all, competition is competition. When asked, the coach did not think it was good will but, rather, an opportunity for his gymnast to go head to head against an important rival. He and his gymnast wanted to go head to head with their opponent and find out who was the best gymnast, not who was the best equipment manager. They wanted the victory to be based on skill and virtuosity. There is no jury for this one, only a personal philosophy of what you think sport and competition is all about. Someone said, "It depends on what's at stake." I agreed. The foundations of sport are at stake.

It is not about winning, it is about playing fair and when victory is sought, you win on your strengths and merits. These values, so important in sport, resonate in the business world. Richard Peddie graduated from the University of Windsor in 1970 and immediately joined Colgate Palmolive in sales and marketing. From Colgate, Koolaid and the Hostess Munchies to the Pillsbury Doughboy and Toronto's world-class SkyDome to TSN and The Discovery Channel and now to the Leafs and Raptors, Richard has spent his entire career proving that bringing a consumer and customer focus to three different industries results in success. Behind all the success was a commitment to positive values.

When I became President of Pillsbury Canada I was aware of an almost legendary reputation to uphold. We had a number brand names such as Pillsbury, Dough Boy and Green Giant that every Canadian knew and respected. I wanted to be certain that the entire organization knew and lived our Core values. The first value is 'Quality is Essential'.

In the mid 1980s one of our biggest selling products was cream style corn in fourteen-ounce cans. Corn is a seasonal product and comes available in late summer every year, once each year. No more. We purchase it and process it, a lengthy and complex procedure from removing the kernels from the cob to the final roasting in the cans. We produced about 500,000 cases that year.

At the end of the season when production was complete the young brand manager, Alan Oberman, came to me and said, "We can't sell this years production of cream corn."

I was shocked and asked, "Why, what happened?"

Alan explained that in the final roasting process, because of a mechanical problem the cans were not rotated and were overcooked on one side. When I questioned him whether this had significantly altered the taste, he replied that it had not, that it was only very slightly off.

And then he added, "But we can't sell them, it would be compromising our most significant value – Quality is Essential."

This was a real moment of truth, for me and for the organization. The implications were huge but I agreed with Alan and we did not sell them. The cost of just safely destroying half a million cases cost us two million dollars. Lost sales were millions more.

We went immediately to our distributors and explained why there would be no cream corn this year and that we would be back with our usual quality next year. The impact on our share value and profit was definitely noticeable that year, but the next year we rebounded to an entirely new level. Over the long term, the health and well being of an organization is dependent upon living it values. Integrity paid off. It always does.

Coaches lead by example. They model what they expect. They know that the strongest statement they will ever make is who they are. I learned that at home from my parents. My parents lived this precept. They never asked anyone to do anything they themselves would not do. They worked side by side with hired help at the fishing lodge. I never saw my father stand back and direct anything. I did see him stand with a group and discuss a plan or a strategy and then make it clear what action was needed. He then pitched in and got things started. An observer would have had difficulty in determining who was boss among the working group. Many times I saw a group of men achieve something that individuals could not accomplish on their own. My father would always say something like "We did it!" and everyone would feel proud and act as if they had never doubted it could be done.

Erik Little is a parent and a world recognized expert in dealing with the trauma experienced by airline workers following a tragedy. The sensitivity and awareness that make his work possible are illustrated in his story of an important value that he learned as a youth in sport.

There can be no pleasure found in high jumping on a cold, windy, rainy day. Groups of us huddled under sheets of plastic and rain gear. After a few practice approaches it was obvious that landing (splat) in a soggy, cold foam pit simply added to the chill that was creeping up from our wet, squooshy feet.

As the event started, the obvious discomfort and mishaps of the first few jumpers were jeered and ridiculed by those of us risking a start at a higher height. Three or four of us were particularly vocal and obnoxious. The mocking and scoffs became a distraction to the extent that no one wanted to stand alone to jump.

The official stopped the event for a moment, gestured and called us all in to the centre of the takeoff apron. Looking at each of us he slowly explained that we all needed to co-operate to get the event over and done with. He would do what he could, and asked that we do our best. OK? OK! He looked each of us in the eyes for agreement. Then the event was restarted.

After that moment I noticed that, against the rules, he had jammed the bar between the standards so that the wind (or a grazing body) wouldn't blow it off. He used a towel and the backside of a rake to mop up puddles that formed in the takeoff area. Names were called quickly in the sequence and a word of encouragement was offered as the result was recorded. While there were no records set that day everyone had a chance to jump their best and we all set personal records for jumping in miserable conditions.

At the end, as we were stuffing shoes and wet T-shirts into gym bags and then dispersing, I wandered over to the official. Embarrassed, I apologised. I was thankful that he had cut off my brat-like behaviours. It wasn't a great day, but...thanks. He peered out from under the yellow poncho hood and grinned. "Good, for every person who takes the time to says thanks I know there are ten others who meant to..."

Harvey Singleton had represented the country as both an athlete and an official at the Olympics. Here he was at some piddling little track meet giving back to the sport he loved. "Thanks" is such a small reward for his contribution, yet he was humble and grateful. It was one of those moments confirming that life's lessons are given to us in small but well-packaged boxes. He found a way to reach out and coach.

I could see how uncomfortable I was saying "thank you" in a heartfelt manner. I didn't know how to recognise and praise others for things that made a difference. I continue to be shy with gifts. Yet, I could be quite snippy and aloof when others overlook my efforts or avoid praising my ventures. I rejected others and myself in the same breath.

I am sure that in the track meet of life there will again be times when conditions are cold and miserable, times when I wonder if the rules have changed or I'm standing in the wrong stadium, times when I wonder if quitting is the better option. Perhaps I'll be able to reach out and speak a message of "thanks" to those people who have been patient with me as I sort myself out. I know now that for every time I do say "thanks" there were ten - no - one hundred time that I meant to!

Some time ago I was invited to address the faculty of the Ivey School of Business at the University of Western Ontario on the principles of coaching. From the beginning of my presentation one person did his best, by posture and facial expression, to show this was not only beneath him but a waste of his time. A "jock" obviously had nothing to say that might be useful to him.

When I finished and the host asked for questions he was quick to say, "This is all fine but it has been all about sport, specifically about individual sports. Business is a team endeavour." He took the opportunity to make a statement, to "put me in my place," to illustrate the limits of my thinking about coaching. He could just as easily have asked an exploratory question such as, "so how does this apply in a business setting which seems to me to be a complex team situation?"

I pointed out that in "individual" sports there was always a significant support team behind the person and that in "team" sports each individual still had to do his own part. There is a wide range of increasingly complex skills, as games get more intricate. Basketball demands a greater ability to see a whole situation and interact with others to achieve a goal than does doubles tennis. Yet in each situation it comes down to an individual developing and then being able to execute the required skill set. It is still an individual activity that demands ways of interacting with others as part of the skill. We see this so clearly when a highly skilled team player is unable to play and the ability of the team is immediately diminished.

To point out the team nature of an individual sport I spoke of David Steen's courageous gold medal performance at the World University Games in Edmonton in 1983. David had performed well in the 100 metres, long jump, shot putt, and the high jump. As he stepped off the high jump surface onto the grass infield to move to the rest area to wait for the 400 metres, he stepped into a hole hidden by the evenly cut grass, and sprained his ankle. By the time the trainers got to him it was already swollen and painful. They brought him to the medical area, elevated the leg and iced the ankle. The doctor examined it and said that there was no collateral damage. It was only a sprain, though severe, and the doctor suggested that David was finished for this competition. David believed otherwise and convinced the two trainers and the physiotherapist to do what they could in the hour he had before the 400 metres because he wanted to run. In the end they taped the ankle and David ran a fine race.

The result was more than a good performance time and many points that left him in good standing in the meet. The ankle was more swollen at the end of the race. Once again the trainers and the physio worked on the ankle and also in "warming down" his legs and hips because he could not jog and his legs were laden with the waste products of an exceptional effort. While the leg was elevated and ice secured to it his legs were massaged intensively. Following the instructions of the medical support team David spent the night with his leg elevated and constantly iced.   He had a minimum of sleep and little rest.

There was new medical staff on in the morning and two new trainers and another physio took on the challenge of protecting the ankle from further damage in the first event of day two, the 110 metre hurdles. It was still swollen and quite stiff although when taped and moving around it loosened up, and David ran a good flight of hurdles. At the finish line the medical crew were waiting and helped him to their position, massaged his legs, iced the ankle and re-taped it in a different configuration for the discus throw. The same routine followed the discus, the pole vault and the javelin. At this point it was clear that David could win if he beat the Soviet athlete by about fourteen seconds in the 1500-metre run. He needed to make up 100 points. However, among the top decathletes in the world David was the strongest 1500 metre runner and we knew his Soviet competitor could not run with David, when he had two good legs, that is.

David was determined to claim victory; he had endured too much to give it away now. He asked that they not tape him at all because it was only straight ahead running with no take-offs or twisting motions. He wanted to run free. And run free he did, winning by a comfortable margin and setting a new World University Game record. At the end he needed all the medical help he could get. Over the two long days a massage therapist, four different trainers, two physiotherapists and two doctors attended to David as well as his coach. Back in Toronto were five other specialist coaches who worked with David in the various disciplines of the decathlon, and of course the staff of the medical support unit as well as a chiropractor. An individual event? Not by any stretch of the imagination. This is the best example I know of the old adage, "I must do it alone and I cannot do it by myself."

Carl Georgevski has been involved in sport all of his life from the entry novice level to the elite. He has enjoyed the opportunity and privilege of representing Canada as a coach at the 1988, 1992, and 2000 Olympic Games. There are times when a brilliant coach will forget the important values, but, when reminded, no mater the source will integrate the lesson.

My wife and I have been blessed with two wonderful children, a girl, who is very competitive, athletic and artistic, and a boy who participates in all types of physical activities, who is not at all competitive. Our daughter plays soccer, basketball, volleyball, the flute, and is just starting the cello. Our son plays whatever game happens to be in season with his friends.

Some time ago a father of one of our son Brett's friends asked him if he wanted to play hockey. When Brett said he would try, my wife and I were torn. Many times we had tried to talk him into playing a team sport while another part of us knew that this might not be a great experience because Brett has suffered from coordination and vision (depth perception) problems. Wanting our son to experience the fun, satisfactions, and joy of being part of a team, we went out and purchased all the necessary equipment for him to start playing house league hockey, at the age of eleven. I should add, our son is not a skater.

On the first Saturday of evaluations, Brett couldn't stop, couldn't turn, and he couldn't skate backwards. While every other child was on his third drill, our son was just finishing his first. Tears were pouring out and running down my cheeks. This was the last place I wanted to be, I felt like running onto the ice and just hugging him. Our son is a very sensitive individual.

A flash back raced through my mind of one of his first cross-country races. I remembered waiting for him near the finish line. As the other children ran past, I kept looking for our son, the top third of the field went by, then half the runners ran by where I was standing. At this point I started walking back in the direction of the on coming runners. In the distance I saw Brett kneeling down with his arm around another boy's shoulder who was in obvious pain. My competitive side came out of me as I hollered "what are you doing? Get up and run"! He looked up at me with an expression on his face that is still implanted in my mind, and he said "Dad, I can't leave him, he is hurt and crying and his friends all ran by him" I learned a great deal about, and from, my son that day.

At home we always talk about the journey or the process that one goes through in sport and life. We discuss the human side of sport, the challenges one faces, and has to overcome, and the respect we must have for our fellow competitors. We make a point of talking about the values of sport. Sport has the potential to offer everything that we will ever encounter in real life. Sport can teach us about the intrinsic rewards of hard work, dedication and commitment. Sport can teach us how it feels when we win and everyone wants to be our friend. Sport can also teach us how it feels when we lose and we are often left all alone.

After the practice while I was helping Brett take his skates off, I said, "Son, I have never told you to quit anything in your life, however, if you want to quit playing hockey, its OK with me". He looked down at me and said "Dad, we will talk about this in the van". On our way out to the van all I could see were the images of our son falling, struggling, and awkwardly trying to keep up with the other boys on the ice. I was trying to convince both of us that it would best if he quit. My feelings were all over the galaxy, was it my ego that wanted him to quit? Was it the over protective parent in me?

In the van I was still trying to encourage him to quit. Finally, he spoke up and said, "Dad, I don't want to quit, I know that in few months I will be better than I am now, and I know that I will learn a lot by playing". Although my brain heard my son, my gut didn't. I phoned my friends who had kids playing hockey. Most of them suggested that I pull him out. I then called one of my old coaches whom I have known since I was fourteen, who replied more like a Zen Master than a former coach and friend. He asked me if I still handed out The Rules of the Game to my University of Toronto Track and Field Team. He suggested I get a copy and bring it to the phone, and read Rule # 18. Rule # 18 states, "Always take the growth choice, never the fear choice." WOW! This hit me like sledgehammer. My eleven-year-old son had made a conscious decision to take the growth choice and here I was, taking the fear choice.

Brett is now in his second year of hockey, and aside from the early morning practice, he loves it. He is improving every time he steps on the ice. His coaches and teammates are supportive, caring, and very encouraging. On the weekend we were in Boston, where he scored his very first goal. I am so glad I listened to him. <u>*Do not be afraid of failure; always take the growth choice, in everything you do.*</u>

Debbie Muir is a corporate consultant who lives in Calgary and was Canada's Olympic Coach for synchronized swimming. Debbie was the personal coach of Olympic Gold Medallists Carolyn Waldo and Michelle Cameron. Debbie shares a classic example of teaching best what we need most to learn.

One of the roles I played as head coach of a club was to "coach the coaches". I had one young coach who was in charge of our twelve and under A Team. One day she asked if I would come and observe a couple of her practices because she was having problems getting the swimmers to do what she wanted them to do. She just couldn't figure out why they couldn't get what she was asking them to do.

After observing, I realized she was a brilliant technical coach. She had the best way of describing how a technique should be done, using great descriptive words and painting clear pictures. She came up with some innovative drills that would teach and train the technique. They were so good I borrowed them for my top swimmers.

So what was the problem? I listened and watched. I quickly realized that there was no encouraging feedback given to the swimmers. It was always, " no, like this" –" no, like this" – " no, like this." Even when I could see an improvement she did not tell them it was better. This was a very unmotivated, unhappy group of swimmers.

The problem was the coach saw things as either right or wrong. There was no in between. I pointed this out to her and we discussed the importance of the role of positive feedback and encouragement that any athlete, let alone young ones need. I gave her an "assignment" to do over the next ten practices – mostly as an experiment to see what would happen. One thing for sure things couldn't get worse. The challenge was to only tell the swimmers what they were doing well over the next ten days – NO CORRECTIONS – only what was good.

She thought I was crazy and was sure it wouldn't work because how can you get better if no one is telling you what you're doing wrong. She did it though and about five days into the exercise she phoned me to tell me how amazed she was. She could not believe the transformation in her team – they hadn't improved as much in six months as they did in five days. She was stunned that by telling people what they were doing right could make such a dramatic difference in their overall performance. The team went on to win every competition they had that year.

I decided to try this with one of the teams I was working with. I called it 'Special Thursday' and on Thursdays I forced myself to only tell them what was good. The first time I did this it made for a quiet practice. I was so used to looking for mistakes, I couldn't notice what was right. It is quite incredible the effect this can have on morale, level of effort and ultimately overall performance

One of my favourite sayings is: "Success is the by-product of an encouraged person."

Positivism is an important value in any successful family, school, or organization; and it is a hallmark of all successful people. Positive attitude and positive values, assure whole person life long success.

Seven Keys to Modeling and Teaching Positive Values

1. Make time to clarify values – for yourself and the group. Model the values.

2. State that honesty and integrity are the foundation of everything.

3. Coach long-time group members to model all group values.

4. Act respectfully and coach your group to do the same.

5. Clarify and reinforce values whenever appropriate.

6. Make learning, growth and education a high priority.

7. Take ethical stands regardless of popular opinion.

Best Practice 3

GRAND POSSIBILITIES

Best Coaches see the grand possibilities in all situations
and see people as they can be, just as Michelangelo
could see his *David* in a block of uncut marble.

"If a person has a talent and learns somehow to use
the whole of it, he has gloriously succeeded, and won a satisfaction
and a triumph few men ever know."
~ *John Ruskin*

At my high school in Dryden, Ontario, two coaches, Harry McMaster and Keith Humphrey, were responsible for my introduction to organized sport. They changed my life. They saw me as the athlete and leader I could be, they created opportunities and pointed me in the right directions. At the University of Toronto it was the coach, Kirk Wipper, who recognized my special talent for wrestling even though I had never wrestled before. He insisted I could make the team and that I would eventually be an intercollegiate champion. Despite my fears and hesitation, Coach Wipper convinced me to try, and he was right.

I was mentored by a number of fine coaches, and through the articles and books they had written, educated by many more. Several years later I became involved in "club" track outside the school system and apprenticed to one of the best coaches in Canada, Fred Foot of the East York Track Club. Because of his success with local athletes and world-class performances, which culminated in the winning of an Olympic medal, I knew he had a lot to teach me. At the same time I was also mentored by Hal Brown who, like Fred, was a gentleman and who had been a great athlete and coach of Olympians. Each coach in his own quiet way believed I could coach at the highest levels. What they saw in me became a reality.

In the pantheon of great coaches, Fred Foot holds a special place. Bruce Kidd was touched and motivated by Fred Foot. Bruce went on to become Canada's premiere distance runner in the early 1960s, winning the Six Miles at the 1962 British Empire and Commonwealth Games, as well as many other major championships. His Canadian junior 5,000-metre record of 13.43.8 set in 1962 still stands. In 1961 and 1962 Canadian Press voted him Canada's Male Athlete of the Year. He is now Professor and Dean, Faculty of Physical Education and Health, University of Toronto. Bruce describes how Fred Foot transformed his life.

I first met Fred Foot in the summer of 1958 at the East York Track Club, where he was the head coach. I got there through the encouragement of John Grabb, my coach at Malvern Collegiate, who felt that he could not take me any further. He said that Fred was the best in the city. I was not turned away but I was always on the margins wondering whether I belonged. I had just turned fifteen, and most of the other runners were in their late teens and early 20s. Most of them were national, even U.S. and international champions. Sprinting was the focus of the Club at the time so I was always at the back of the pack. I was not sure that Fred even knew my name and when he referred to me at all, it was always as "the youngster." But Fred had created an atmosphere of such ambition, excitement and comradeship that I kept on going back.

That fall, when the sprinters scaled back their training, Fred announced that he wanted to see whether he could train distance runners. He had been inspired by the performances of Vladimir Kuts at the 1956 Olympics where he had been the Canadian coach. The group was much smaller then. We often trained in the dark at East York or Riverdale Park with Fred shivering despite his long wool coat, calling out the times with a flashlight. The older runners distrusted his experiments with over distance intervals and hill circuits, so I became his 'guinea pig' or co-conspirator. We tried longer and longer workouts, no two exactly the same, and I just kept getting stronger. I loved it. Here was someone who shared and affirmed my deep but inarticulate and underdeveloped love for running, someone who gave me more and more ways to do it. In those moments before and after workouts and during the brief intervals between runs, he talked to me about the world of competitive running. While my coaches and teammates in other sports strategized about teams on the other side of the city Fred challenged me to think about racing against the rest of the world. It was a heady experience. At the end of the fall, he entered the entire group in the Canadian cross country championships in Hamilton, the first time the EYTC had ever competed in anything off the track. He gave me such confidence--I had such trust in him--that I followed his plan, took the lead far earlier than my teammates and I thought wise, and won the race. It was the first of many such triumphs.

I can't remember how my parents, siblings and friends saw the change in me, but I remember that fall as transforming. I began it as a bored, unfocused teenager and came out of it a self-disciplined young adult with an appetite for taking on the world. Working with Fred, trusting his judgment, and achieving something I had only previously dreamed about was one of the most satisfying experiences I have ever had.

Fred had an immense impact on my life as well, but there were many other coaches over the years that shaped my life. They were from all sports, all over the world. The more successful I became, the more I had opportunities to travel and meet coaches from almost every country in the world. I learned something significant from each of them. I learned a great deal about strategies, tactics and training planning but the most important lessons were about the human side of coaching. Working with people is what coaching is all about. To coach is to support people to accept the gifts they possess, to help them face and move beyond personal limitations, to help them express their gifts in ways that create deep personal satisfaction for them. None of what I learned about the human side of coaching was taught in any structured way.

Recently, in a phone conversation with Greg MacNeill, the founder and publisher of *Elm Street*, and previously, *Recipes Only* and *Home Makers* magazines, we discussed the coaching process. Contrasting coaching and teaching Greg said that he had read somewhere that, "the most important lessons in life cannot be taught." At once I felt the correctness of that statement. I feel that truth at a level of understanding that is hard to articulate, but it has to do with learning by being in the presence of those who live lives worthy of being modeled. I once heard Jim Rohn, the successful and wise speaker on human performance, say that we will become the average of the five people we spend the most time with. The numbers may vary but the essence of the statement is true.

It was the stories told by my mentors that instructed me and made the difference for me. Stories were told during training to make a point to the athletes, to entertain and inform on long trips to competitions, to socialize over food and drink at sporting events, competitions, clinics, celebrations, and dinner at the coaches' home. Stories were so commonplace that for a long time I never gave them a second thought, but they were always a factor in my life. Stories made a difference by inspiring me, educating me, creating perspective, or simply entertaining and keeping alive all the fun and passion for life, for people, and for education and sport. The stories told of exceptional performances, of magnificent achievements, of grand possibilities made real.

At one level sport is simply physical "play." At another level it is highly competitive and demands commitment to a discipline that provides endless personal challenge. At the deepest level it is about mental, emotional, and spiritual growth. This is always obvious to the best coaches. They honour and cherish the process while they assume the responsibility of working with people. They rarely take themselves or the activity seriously. They do see the value in taking the commitment to the activity seriously because they see a future of positive and rewarding possibilities in engaging in the activity. Coaches convey emotion behind the idea that it is a rare few of us who are given the opportunity to explore the limits of our abilities, regardless of the discipline, and they inspire us to do the required, disciplined work.

Coaches know we must be conscious of what we say and then check for understanding, especially with critical information. Red Auerbach, coach of the famed Boston Celtics of eleven NBA Championships in thirteen years said, "It is not what we tell them, it is what they hear."

My friend from university days, Morgan Dever, is a retired high school principal and coach. He tells a great story of seeing immense possibilities in a youngster and the lesson he learned when he made an assumption about a boy named Danny. Morgan, like all coaches, has a great sense of perspective and an equal readiness to learn as well as laugh at himself and with others.

In September, as high school re-opened and we began a new football season, one of the men with whom I coached senior football was delighted to find in his grade eleven Phys.Ed. class, a lad, Danny who was 6' 5" and 265 lbs. and fit. When Danny was asked if he would be interested in coming out for the team he said he had never played but would like to try. That bit of information did not get relayed to me.

I was delighted to see that he was as big as described, and also to feel the strength in Danny's handshake at the beginning of practice. In warm-up he was fast. His combination of physical assets indicated to me " offensive tackle."

" OK, I want offensive and defensive teams here. We are going to work on our passing patterns. Do up your chin straps gentlemen; this is going to be live. Danny, I want to see you at right offensive tackle. This play is a 56 roll out right pass. The quarterback will take the ball, drop three steps and roll to the right to give the receivers more time to get deep. Your job is to roll with him and protect him from the pass rush."

The quarterback was a nimble lad and avoided the rush long enough to run out of bounds. Danny was lying on the field not far from where he started. I had not seen his actions so I asked him what happened.

Danny said, " I followed him back there and got down to roll but he just ran away out there and I couldn't roll that fast!"

In that moment the bit of missing information became apparent and I burst into laughter. I pointed out to Danny and the team that I was laughing at myself and the silly situation I had created. As eager young coaches we do make assumptions about clarity, especially of language. We assume, sometimes wrongly, others understand us.

We have all done what Morgan did. We have seen the possibilities but failed to ask the key question: what is your experience with this activity? We have mis-communicated with jargon and assumptions. We all start out as beginning coaches. We have all made mistakes similar to Morgan's with Danny. We have failed to look deeper, to ask more questions, and to get the whole picture before we made a decision. When we can laugh at ourselves for making these mistakes, we send a strong and positive message to those we are coaching.

Phyllis Ellis is a mother of two, a former Olympic athlete in field hockey and now works with a wonderful project called SeeyouinAthens. Hers is a great story of a first coach, not only seeing a grand possibility but building the confidence to pursue it and providing the support to stay with the long process.

In the winter of 1962 I was four years old. My mother, an ace tennis player and golfer, was sitting with me and we were watching figure skating on television. I loved the music and the movements but best of all, at the end of the programme, the beautiful girl in the beautiful gown received a medal, a bright gold fancy medal, which was placed around her neck. My mother looked at me and out of nowhere said then, as she still does today, "You can do anything and be anything you want to be."

I danced around the house for a few days completing each performance with my own ceremony, a walk up the stairs to my imaginary podium. Then one day my mother presented me with spectacular white figure skates and sent me off to the rink in the schoolyard behind our house.

A boy from my neighbourhood helped me tie my skates and I was up in no time, circling the rink playing music with my mother's words in my head. As the night began to blanket my private Olympic stage, my mother came to take me home.

We walked back through the snow and I remember knowing that with my mother around I could do anything and be anything I wanted. Years later the Olympic field hockey pitch was far from an ice rink but the dynamics of competition and the rewards are the same. The affirmation from my first coach carried me through many challenges and conflicts and, yes, celebrations and joys.

I look forward to passing on the strength of my mother's convictions and encouragement to my own. I celebrate my greatest coach and role model through my daughter's growth now as an aspiring Olympian.

Coaches develop the desire to share what has been experienced. They tend to create other coaches. Phyllis' mother did just that. She supported a life of full participation at the highest levels possible for Phyllis who is now doing the same for her daughter. Coaches know that every one of us is capable of opening that door to personal excellence for another and inviting and inspiring them to come through it.

It was from the very best coaches that I learned about commitment and perspective and the power of the human spirit to develop the immense potential of the human being. Coaches develop character, which is essential to all long term, whole life success. All who saw the drama and scandal around pairs skating in the Salt Lake City Olympics do not need to be told what character is. We witnessed it daily by Jamie Salé and David Pelletier. They knew that theirs was the best performance and that the gold medal belonged to them, yet, at times, it appeared that the self knowledge of their victory was all that was important. The opinion and accolades of others was not that important. Win, or lose, character always carries the day.

To be successful, coaches know they need to spend time in the presence of successful coaches. None of us instinctively know talent when we see it, nor do we automatically have a sense of grand possibility. These are acquired from others who do know, by witnessing their actions and hearing their stories, in person, on the radio, television, movies or reading them in books and magazines. Coaches acquire these bits of wisdom, the stories, store them in memory and use them to create successful experiences for the people with whom they work, and, incidentally, for themselves.

Coaches know that the essential stories are rarely told in structured settings. The most powerful and engaging philosophy session I ever attended was a chance meeting with an old fisherman on the beach in Trout Creek, Newfoundland. I greeted him with, "Hi, great weather isn't it?" He responded that it is always this way after a few stormy days. I asked only a few questions as the afternoon wore on and he talked about our relationship to the environment, about life in general and the value of all things on this earth including each of us to others. I knew for certain from his accent and the situation that this man had minimal schooling. On the other hand, his education was extensive and his wisdom pure and simple. When I least expected a great lesson in life, it came my way.

Tom Watt is a lifetime coach who, at heart, is an educator. He taught and coached at the high school and university level before moving on to the National Hockey League.

After an eight year career as an NHL Coach, AHL Coach, director of professional scouting and player development with the Toronto Maple Leafs, I took a head coaching position with the junior Sudbury Wolves of the Ontario Hockey Association for the 1997-98 hockey season. It was the only season that I coached junior hockey and I thoroughly enjoyed it.

Major Junior Hockey has had a reputation for not looking after their players outside the hockey arena. This was not the case in Sudbury under Todd Lalonde, a young and caring general manager. All players attended the same high school and a designated school counsellor called Todd immediately, if a player was late or truant. The player then reported early the following morning, before they went to school, to run with Todd around the mezzanine of the Sudbury arena. Offences were seldom repeated.

The Wolves had one overage player, Jason Sands, who had completed his grade twelve in Ontario and was not attending school this particular season. During a practice session, while skating around the ice before the regular workout began, I questioned Jason about his plans for the future. A skilful, feisty but small player, Jason was twenty years old and had not been selected in two previous NHL drafts. His future as a National Hockey League player was in doubt because of his size.

While on the road after a playoff game that season, my phone rang in the middle of the night. It was Mrs. Sands. In a trembling voice she explained that her husband, Jason's father, had just passed away suddenly. She asked to speak to Jason. My toughest moment as a coach was to go to Jason's room, awaken him and try to be of some comfort after giving him the terrible news. The team got Jason back quickly to his family in Kingston and without him we were eliminated the following evening.

Talking to him later, Jason explained that he wanted to play for a few more years in the East Coast Hockey League where he had some connections. That didn't impress me. Playing in a professional league that offered little security and a low salary might be fun for a few more years but offered a limited future.

Major junior players in Canada are ineligible to play college hockey in the United States. That is an N.C.A.A. rule. However, I pointed out that he was eligible to play in a Canadian university. Some universities in Canada allow admission after grade twelve. I suggested that he play university hockey, earn a degree and then continue to play wherever the opportunity arose. Canadian University hockey is very competitive and many schools have excellent programmes. Jason had not been aware of this possibility and seemed quite interested.

The good news is that Jason Sands was admitted to St. Thomas University in Fredericton, New Brunswick, where he had an outstanding four years of hockey and schooling. In the 2000-2001 season St. Thomas Tommies won the Atlantic Coast Conference Championship and qualified for the National Championships in Kitchener, Ontario. Jason was the team leader and one of only three players nominated for Canadian University Player of the Year!

In 2001 Jason graduated from St. Thomas University, Jason Sands, BA, fulfilling the potential I saw in him. He is now playing professional hockey in Salzburg, Austria.

"Anything's possible," my father always said. It was his reply to questions from people in all kinds of situations. In his heart he believed it because he did everything possible to make it real for himself and my mother, my brother and myself, and for all his clients. Over time, I, too, came to believe that anything is possible.

My father built several successful businesses. When I was a boy my father sold his general store in a rural community in north-western Ontario and built a fishing and hunting lodge twelve miles south of the Trans Canada Highway near where we lived. The road south was only four miles long and ended at an abandoned mine. We built eight miles of road ourselves through the boreal forest!

Growing up, I was fascinated by sport and adventure and I read everything I could on those topics. During that time it was believed not possible to climb Everest, run the mile in under four minutes, high jump seven feet, or putt the shot over sixty feet. Academics and sport journalists wrote endless authoritative articles about why these things could never happen. But within a few years they had all happened! The myths of impossibility were shattered!

I read of Bob Matthias, who, as a young teen-ager suffered from rheumatic fever. As he recovered his doctor encouraged him to compete in track and field to regain overall strength and health. He did so well that his high school coach encouraged him to enter the 1948 U.S. Olympic trials because they were in a nearby city. He made the team, and only weeks later, at age seventeen, he became Olympic decathlon gold medallist. He repeated that spectacular performance in Helsinki in 1952! A year later I saw <u>The Bob Matthias Story</u> in a theatre in International Falls, Minnesota, and was moved to tears. His story and the feelings associated with personal achievement as well as the ability to overcome physical and personal obstacles never left me.   It was the genesis of International medals for a number of young Canadian men and women in decathlon and heptathlon, Jill Ross (Pan Ams), Dave Steen (Olympic), Donna Smellie (Francophone Games), Greg Haydenluck (Pacific Conference Games), Michael Smith (World Championships) and Catherine Bond-Mills (Commonwealth). But then again, as a child I heard my mother say many times, "Great oaks from small acorns do grow."

Michael Smith is from Kenora, Ontario. He now lives in Calgary, working in the financial industry and does commentary for CBC Television's coverage of major track and field events.   Retired from athletics, he is still the Canadian Record Holder in decathlon.

I hold the term Coach in high regard. Coach best describes what a number of significant people have been to me in my life. On several occasions, quite often unbeknownst to me at the time, I have been fortunate to be the recipient of Great Coaching. My original coaches were my parents. Their approach was subtle, just coaxing rather than outright formal instruction. They were covertly inspirational, pointing me in a direction to instil a great sense of confidence. This helped me know one important thing: If I want to do something, I can try it, in a safe and supportive environment. If I enjoy it I have the opportunity to pursue it as far as I like. It was the confidence my parents instilled that gave me the peace of mind to pursue a great challenge.

In the summer of 1985, just before my last year of high school, Andy Higgins came to my home in Kenora to visit with me and my parents to determine whether I had any interest in trying the decathlon. Andy was the Canadian Olympic coach at the time and I was excited to hear what his thoughts were on the subject of decathlon. We proceeded to talk for several hours where he spoke of world travel, Olympic Games and being the best of which I was capable. It was a lot to absorb. We finished our time together and then Andy left, returning soon after though only for a moment with a few small pieces of paper on which was a hand written note in point form. The note was a map, a map of the direction that Andy thought I could pursue, not to find a prize but to experience a journey.

I was excited, and moments later, at the age of seventeen, I was considering moving 1700 km away from home to Toronto to pursue a career in decathlon. I now realize that the path laid to make the decision had been started, groomed and taken care of a long time before. I moved from one positive environment in Kenora to another at the University of Toronto, always being supported, challenged and stimulated in a positive way.

Andy's thoughts on the note correctly predicted a path towards the World Junior Championships, World Championships, Olympic Games and my succession towards being one of the best decathletes in the world. I will always be thankful that he opened a special door and invited me in to explore.

To this day I still have a number of "coaches," some old, some young, and I continue to learn from them all. I still have several varied and different types of activities and passions to pursue, always with the knowledge and confidence that I can have a lot of fun in trying.

I had read of Glenn Cunningham, severely burned as a child, who became a world class miler, and Wilma Rudolph, polio victim, told she'd never walk normally, who became an Olympic gold medallist as a sprinter!! There were so many other stories of magnificent human achievement that no one believed possible - until they happened. I feel like Shakespeare did after reading Chapman's translation of Homer. "Much have I traveled in the realm of gold." Every story challenged my heart, inspired my soul and shaped my thinking about what was possible, and what I personally could do, in spite of my doubts, fears, and insecurities.

Because I believed "anything is possible" it became a reality many times in my own life and the lives of many men and women I taught and coached. I saw it all around me. I went to university with George Stulac, one of the most amazing Canadian athletes ever. At home varsity basketball games, on a signal from the swim team manager, George would rush down to the pool to win an event, and then change back into basketball gear and get back into the game at the next break. He played football only one year and was an All-Star. George represented Canada at two Olympics in three sports! Swimming, basketball, and decathlon!

Vicki Keith's story is a wonderful example of a coach making the appropriate intervention at the appropriate time. The impact the intervention had not only on Vicki but all the lives she has touched has been significant. Vicki is Canada's incredible marathon swimmer who, in one summer, in only 61 days swam across every one of the Great Lakes, raising almost one million dollars for programmes for kids with disabilities at Variety Village in Toronto.

I knew what I wanted to do with my life. I wanted to be a world-class marathon swimmer. I had been talking about it for years to anyone who would listen. As I am sure everyone has experienced, when I told people about my dream, I received a myriad of responses. "What, are you nuts?" "You can't do that...that's impossible." "What makes you think you can do something like that, you're not even that great a swimmer." Or "Cool, go for it." I got all sorts of responses; everyone had an opinion.

You will always find people who don't believe in the impossible and will try and knock down your dreams. You will also find lots of people who encourage you from afar. But when I told that swim coach what my dream was he said the words I needed to hear, "Vicki, Shut up and do it. I have heard you talking about this for years, it's time for you to stop talking about it and get busy and do it." But then he went further and he said, "I will come along beside you, support you any way I can, but it's time for you to stop talking about it and get busy and do it."

That's what I needed, someone who believed in me and my dream enough to step beyond encourager to supporter. With Bob Boadway's support, within three months I had completed two world firsts. I had swum twelve miles of butterfly in open water, and I had swum for 100 hours continuously in a pool. Bob's words sent me off into a very successful career as a marathon swimmer.

What a gift to give someone: the gift of belief and support! Without those words I often wonder if I would have talked forever about my dream, then realized only too late that I had spent my life talking about my dream without taking action.

I had "bought" that dream of discovering what I could really become and achieve and with typical adolescent doubts and fears lived it as best I could all through high school and university. In university, through my coaches, the dream became focused into clear goals that I had been supported in believing were possible: be a good football player, a successful basketball player, an intercollegiate wrestling champion, and a good student.

In my graduating year at University of Toronto, simply doing what I loved to do, I proved to myself that more was possible than almost everyone believed. And, yes, I did this in spite of a part of me that also did not believe. What happened that year changed me forever as a person, and as an educator and coach. Based on my experiences of academics and athletics I came to believe that my dream was possible.

I committed myself to the necessary and disciplined work. That year I played on our college football team as quarterback and running back. Before the season ended I was getting ready for the wrestling season in which I was silver medallist in the

Intercollegiate Championships the previous year, and beginning practices two evenings a week with a Senior "A" basketball team in suburban Toronto. When football was over it was wrestling every day, and two evenings a week after training, with my friend and classmate, Bob Miner, I drove thirty minutes to basketball practice. There were weekends when I both wrestled and played basketball on the same day. And, yes, I created the necessary time to study.

In early March I won the gold medal in wrestling that had eluded me the previous year. In mid April I wrote a final exam on Friday, flew to Sault Ste. Marie that evening, played my share in our victory at the championship game on Saturday, flew back Sunday and wrote two finals on Monday. I graduated near the top of my class. From that year forward I knew that all of us are capable of so much more than we ever imagined.

I had "known of" this possibility because I had read about achievement from the time I was a child and it had excited and inspired me. Now, from personal experience I "knew" it. This was real. It was anchored in every cell in my body.

When I first began teaching at Northern Secondary School in Toronto, I used stories with the youngsters in my classes and those who became members of the sport teams I coached. I told all kinds of stories to illustrate what was possible, to inspire, encourage, inform, and educate them. What I saw then was repeated throughout my career working with people. The single most important element in learning and performance is self-esteem and self-confidence, not just the belief that this dream or goal is possible, but that it is possible *for me*.

I was given the Senior boys' basketball team to coach because no one had volunteered to coach a Senior team for five years! No coach, no programme. With rare exceptions, that is always the situation in schools. It is the coach who creates the interest, shows the way, and lays out the possibilities for the kids. I saw that all around me, all over the country, for all the years I was in education and sport. It is still true today. There I was, in 1961, a rookie coach with only four youngsters from the previous year's junior team and only two with any real athletic ability! None had any self-discipline nor were they team players.

I went to the hallways and talked to every tall boy I could find. Four committed themselves to the idea of being part of something special and investing the time to become a basketball player in one season. A football player also showed up who was very athletic and very quick. Another boy, Bobby Holmes, was reputed to hold some kind of Canadian record in track and field. Bobby was about five feet ten inches tall with an athletic build and red hair down to his shoulders. (This was 1961!) When we talked I discovered that a few years earlier he had set a National age-class record in the triple jump. I convinced him to come out for the team, to get fit for track season. I told him I could help him jump far again. It was a remarkable winter. Boys became young men, learned skills, became fit, began to believe in themselves and each other and, together, became one of the top teams in the city!

A few weeks after starting Bobby rushed into the gym late for practice and his new brush cut said it all. It was his emblem of a new attitude, a statement about being a part of the team. We lost our first four games and then won the rest of the season. We made the play-offs and lost in the two-games total points semi-final by two points, to a Riverdale Collegiate team, coached by Doug Scott, whose story appears later. A week later, Riverdale won the City-wide Championship game by 26 points.

I came to know a good deal about all of these young men and, in particular, discovered that Bobby Holmes was an exceptionally bright young man from an educated family who had arrived in this "tech" programme because of an adolescent brush with school administrators and the law. It was nothing more than a "brush" and it had all been related to a bad attitude. With a diploma from a tech programme he was not getting into a Canadian university, but I knew that an exceptional Scholastic Aptitude Test score and his athletic ability might get him into school in the United States.

I contacted the track coach at a few schools and arranged for Bobby to write the SAT exams. By the time we heard back from the track coach at the University of Oregon, Bobby had already been offered an academic scholarship on the basis of his outstanding SAT scores. He trained a bit with the track team but became so absorbed in the academic programme, he soon dropped track. He graduated early with extremely high grades and won a graduate scholarship to Brown University.

Coaches do what I did with Bobby. I saw a young man as he could be, not as he was. Coaches invest the time and effort to open a door to another world. In that other world Bobby Holmes found his milieu, the place he really belonged. Basketball was just an experience he needed to learn what he needed know to move to where he needed to go. Coaches know that people's lives are entrusted to them for only a few hours a day for a few years and that greater things exist beyond sport for all of them.

I was coaching at the East York Track Club in 1967 when Ian Watts limped into the stadium. Wearing faded jeans, a T-shirt and a shy smile the quiet spoken youngster was just another kid interested in high jumping. He had jumped only 1.65m and walked with a significant limp. He sat on the grass and took off his jeans revealing a pair of faded blue gym shorts and an underdeveloped left leg. Ian was not self-conscious about his disability but I suspect he picked up my discomfort. I never saw him again that summer.

In June of 1968 he showed up again and this time I had something new to show him, the Fosbury flop technique. I had traveled to California for the NCAA Track and Field Championships and had taken movies of Dick Fosbury's new back-to-the-bar high jump style. I knew this was the future of high jumping. Ian loved it. It was fun and different. Later as I came to know Ian better I discovered he was born with two club feet and had undergone a series of corrective surgeries. As a child doctors told him that he would never walk normally and never be able to participate in sports.

Ian became a regular member of the small group of high jumpers I was coaching and demonstrated a love of training and jumping that fit right in with Carl Georgevksi and Erik Little who were from my Monarch Park high school programme. The three became close training buddies and my greatest challenge became keeping them from doing too much. I did not always succeed.

Years and competitive seasons went by and they all became young men, stronger, technically better and jumping higher. Gradually Ian's limp became less evident and by 1972 he ran as rhythmically as anyone in the now growing group of jumpers. He was able to perform single leg hopping exercises with the ever stronger though still much smaller leg. In 1973 Ian became the first Ontario athlete to jump 2.05 metres and a year later the first to clear 2.10 metres.

"Never walk normally, and never participate in sports." Never? Never has only one place in our vocabulary: never let anyone place limitations on what is possible for us. Ever! The word 'never' is the twin sibling of the worst and most limiting four-letter word in the English language: 'Can't.' Do not use either word with regard to your own capabilities. If you believe you are limited, or believe there are real obstacles to achieving something you would truly love, then ask yourself, "Where did that belief come from? Who told me that?" Right now, re-examine that negative, limiting belief and change it to one that is more positive for you – and is of your choosing! And when it comes to grand possibilities in any aspect of your life here are four useful "why" questions:
Why?
Why Not?
Why Not Now?
Why Not Me?
Simply fill in the space after each with your dream of a grand possibility for you.

Alison Korn, was a National Team rower and an Olympian in Atlanta in 1996. She lives and works as a freelance writer in Toronto. She shares how her coach helped her and her team see the personal and team grand possibilities in the moment.

The last few hours and minutes before the Olympic final can be agonizing. Part of you wants time to stand still so you don't have to deal with the stress of it all. But at the same time you want the clock to speed ahead so you can get out there immediately, show the world what you can do and bring a merciful end to the pressure of waiting.

We had a team norm of always pre-planning how we would spend that block of pre-race time. The night before the race we'd meet and set a schedule of times for when we would start the warm up, thirty to forty minutes before the race, when we would visit the bathroom for the last time, when we'd meet with our coach, when we would arrive at the lake, what time we'd get the bus to the venue, when we'd eat breakfast and what time we'd wake up. This way there was no stress or worry about being late or confused. On the big day we just followed our pre-planned schedule.

The pre-race meeting with our coach, Al Morrow, was always a comforting, uplifting ritual. We would gather in our team tent and he would talk about the course conditions, such as wind direction or waves, and how they affect our lane and different sections of the course; he would advise if we should adapt our technique in any way to compensate. He would mention the other crews' strengths and weaknesses. He would give us a few simple concepts to focus on together, to ensure everyone was on the same mental wavelength.

However, the pre-race meeting before the Olympic final was different. Al didn't go over too many race details because we'd rehearsed and reviewed them many times already. Instead he spoke about how everyone in our crew, the eight, was special and how we each provided a unique and essential contribution to the boat. Starting with our coxswain, he went down the boat and said something complimentary and sincere about the character of each one of us.

He thanked us for being there and for giving so much to the sport and to him as a coach. This was very moving and most of us started crying. Then we laughed at the absurdity of weeping just before we were about to go out and have the race of our lives.

Al said how proud he was of each of us, how he admired us, and that he would always be there for us, even after rowing, and that we could always call on him for anything. Then he said something simple like "Have a great race," and left the tent. He looked like he was choked up too.

We wiped our tears, looked at each other and burst out laughing. Someone said, "He does this every Olympics!" We all felt about ten feet tall. Walking out of that tent together we knew we were going to have a great race.

We confidently approached our boat, carried it to the water, and rowed away from the dock with purpose. After a punchy warm up, the 2,000-metre, six minute race was aggressive and painful, taking us beyond our fitness and power and drawing on our guts and heart. Together we won the bronze medal.

Al Morrow is the consummate coach and knows that all he can do is help the athletes prepare, to be as ready as possible, physically and mentally. Then, it is their race. He knows that we cannot control what the other competitors do. All we can control is what we do. His talk to the eight was a reminder that he believed in them, that he saw the immense possibility in them, and saw them all as special women. This was significant because an Olympic Championship race is all about character. Then again, so is every challenge of any significance in all of our lives. Coaches know that and support its development and expression in every aspect of the process. Sport, in the greater scheme, is never the most important life situation demanding character.

Harry Neale, a commentator with Hockey Night in Canada and a former NHL coach, is an intelligent and creative man who sees possibilities that many never see and he is prepared to act on them. Harry shows us what is possible when you believe anything is possible; the highly improbable and definitely non-traditional become worth testing.

The Vancouver Canucks, the NHL team I was coaching, was losing to the Whalers, 3 – 1 in Hartford with about ninety seconds left in the third period. We had played an uninspired game by our standards and I was upset and searching for something that would startle the players and get the undivided attention of the team.

I pulled the goalie, which was not a unique move, and with 31 seconds left we scored to trail by only one goal. The bench stirred slightly. The players were coming awake. However, when I left the goalie on the bench with the goal empty for the ensuing face-off there was more activity and some questioning stares from the players. With fourteen seconds remaining we scored again to tie the game. The bench was now alive, to say the least.

With the game tied at 3 – 3 and fourteen seconds left, I yelled at the goalie to remain on the bench. We were going for the win! Half the players yelled at me and seemed to be questioning my sanity. The other half stared at me and debated my hockey mentality. I gave in and yelled at the goalie to get back in the net. The game ended in a tie, and heading into overtime, I had the undivided attention of a group of very alert players.

To make the night complete we scored early in overtime for an incredible win. One more coaching hunch accompanied by a bit of bizarre chance taking worked. It doesn't always happen that way. Some of the players even suggested that it was my strategy that set up that win for us, another rare experience for an NHL coach.

Coaches always see the "glass half full." They see possibilities and opportunities where others often see problems and limitations. I often heard growing up, "nothing ventured, nothing gained." At the same time coaches do not take undue risks. What did Harry Neale and the team have to lose? He certainly achieved the one possibility he saw, he got their attention.

Erin Woodley a member of the 1996 Synchronized Swimming Team to the Atlanta Olympics tells us how Sheilagh Croxon got her attention – by laying out a truly grand possibility based on seeing Erin as she could be not as she was.

In fifteen years in the sport of synchronized swimming, I had many coaches, and all of these women gave me valuable instruction in some way. Sheilagh Croxon gave me my dream.

My first memory of Sheilagh is of her coaching a team of older swimmers at our club. I was in a younger age group, and apprehensive of moving up, as Sheilagh seemed to be very demanding! Eventually I did move up and Sheilagh became my coach and mentor for the next nine years of my life.

I had always struggled with my nerves during competition, but far more time is spent practicing than competing, and I learned to live with the awful feelings and the sometime disappointing results that came with competition. Despite my terrible nerves, I experienced success by representing Canada on our National Youth Team, and leading the Ontario Synchro Team to a gold medal sweep at the Canada Winter Games in 1991. At this point I felt I had reached my potential as an athlete, and made the decision that I would stop synchro when I went away to university. My life changed forever when Sheilagh challenged this decision, by asking me, "don't you think you could be on that 1996 Olympics Team?"

I had never thought of myself as Olympic material, the Olympics seemed to be something for other people, better athletes, certainly not me. I clearly remember my response; "Do YOU think I could be on that team?" Sheilagh definitely believed I could, and yes, it would take a lot of hard work, and she believed I could do the work.

With her belief in me, and a few words, Sheilagh inspired me to dream of being an Olympian. She also helped me make that dream a reality by demanding excellence from me on a daily basis and helping me to confront my weaknesses. It took thousands of hours of hard work, for both Sheilagh and I, but we did make that team, together.

Coaches know that all any of us can do is our best. They know that few of us have any sense of what "our best" really is. We have a great deal of potential and are unaware of its immensity. Al Morrow knew that this team of young women would discover they were capable of more effort than each of them and all of them as a team believed. Harry Neale was depending on the same belief and that was all Sheilagh Croxon asked of Erin. It is the underpinning of all successful programmes. None of us can ever do more or better than our best. The challenge is to discover what our best is.

Gerry Swan, the long time Head Coach of the Valley Royals Track and Field Club in Abbotsford, B.C. claims to be fortunate to have had the opportunity to inspire a large number of boys and girls to strive for excellence in running and to become good people. Gerry tells us a story of seeing a grand possibility in a young woman, the vision he shared, and the journey that proved the truth of "The only limits are, as always, those of vision."

It was September 1975 when I first had a chance to talk with the eighteen year old freshman at Simon Fraser University, where I assisted in coaching middle distance runners. She was about to take part in her first practice as a member of the Clan track and field team. There was good reason why I would take the time to engage this young woman in conversation. I had watched this tall, slender athlete with the long, graceful and fluid stride compete with good success in high school. I knew her training consisted of mainly over distance runs at a modest pace and she had come to believe herself to be best suited to the longer distance events.

I believed she had the talent to become very good, and my conversation stressed the future she had as a runner. The talk turned to the type of training she might do to become good enough to take part in meets at the national and even, perhaps, the international level, at 800m and 1500m. "But I have little speed she protested and am not sure that I could succeed at the 1500m distance let alone in the 800m event."

Speed for a middle distance runner I assured her, was less a matter of being born with it than a matter of building it over time. My talk probably won the day because it was addressed to a bubbly, enthusiastic person with a receptive mind, who in addition, was an intelligent and idealistic individual capable of listening and reflecting on these future possibilities. Whatever the reason, coach and athlete formed a partnership that would last for 15-years and allowed us both to become part of the world class running scene.

The road to success is not usually easy and this journey was no exception. There was a long and systematic learning curve that both coach and athlete had to master. What could she endure during a training session, and what did I need to learn to become a competent coach of a world-class athlete? The 1500 metre event for woman was a relatively new event in the 70's and every step in designing a programme for a female middle distance runner was a tentative one.

There were the set backs of course. After a very successful first year that saw her cut seven seconds from her 800 metre time and run 2:09 and reduce thirteen seconds from her 1500 metres to run 4:22, it took another three years before any further improvement was made on those performances.

Then there were the inevitable injuries and the struggle to regain form after long layoffs. And there were failures. The first attempt at a senior national championship was one of those character builders that saw her place last in the 1500 metres. Then she was humiliated to tears by another coach's remark about her "dismal performance." But step by step and year by year, the partnership began to pay dividends. In the fourth year her 1500m time was 2:03 and she won a gold medal in the 1500m at the Pan Pacific Games, and a bronze medal in the 800m at the Pan American Games - at which she was selected to run the 1500m but mistakenly entered in the 800m. There were trips for competition through numerous countries and the opportunity to not only meet, but also become friends with many of the world's best runners of both sexes.

1983 - 1984 was the pinnacle of her running career. At the 1983 World Championships in Helsinki, she set Canadian record for 1500m of 4:05.23 with an amazing performance in the semi-final. Coming off the last bend she had been trapped on the inside and it was not until the last 60 metres that she was able to spring free and surge into fourth place, 1/100th of a second in front of an East German who had been the silver medallist in this event at the Moscow Olympics of 1980. A 1/100th of second meant that the East German was eliminated and she gained the final. The woman who eight years previous had believed she did not have "the speed" to compete at this level!

After the World Championships she competed in Europe establishing a new Canadian 800m record (2:00.02) and a week later reduced her own 1500m record to

4:03.36. There were a few more years of running but injuries and the demands of an adult life finally brought her running career to an end. But by that time Brit Townsend neé Lind-Peterson had at one time or another set Canadian outdoor records for the 800m, 1,000m, 1500m and mile and indoor records at the 1500m and mile. She had traveled the world and competed at every major Games, and established herself as one of the world's best runners of her time.

The vision that an athlete and coach talked about in 1975 was well served. Today Brit Townsend is the Head Coach of Track and Field at SFU, with the same love for running. She is in charge of young runners and is undoubtedly sharing a vision with them in hopes that they may experience similar success and garner the same rewards from running that she had.

When we understand that "anything is possible" and that all of us is capable of so much more than we ever imagined, we approach every situation with an "it's possible" attitude. After 35 years in education and athletic coaching, I left to coach performance in the corporate world. I knew what every coach knows, that performance is performance is performance, regardless of the situation. That the grandest possibilities exist everywhere for all of us, as do the stories of possibilities and struggle and success.

I am no longer surprised at what I see people achieve. I have too many friends and acquaintances who are living well and being productive who were told years ago by doctors that they had only months to live. I have seen far too many youngsters labelled as limited, or failures in the school system, become very successful academically and in life. I have seen athletic achievements that no one else believed possible. Today I am only further affirmed in my belief in the miracle of human possibility and always I am in awe of the power of the human spirit.

Seven Keys to Seeing Grand Possibilities

1. Read widely and become familiar with the history of possibility.

2. Do everything possible to associate with successful people.

3. Create and share a compelling vision – believe others into a new reality.

4. Make every effort to really know the individual person.

5. Ask "possibility" questions: "Have you ever thought of...?", etc.

6. Share a magnificent intention, create plans, goals, and objectives.

7. See people as they can be and support their confidence to be who and what they desire to be.

Best 4 Practice

SIGNIFICANT CHANGE

Best Coaches begin always with
the expectation of significant change.

"To know even one life has breathed easier because you have lived;
This is to have succeeded."
~ *Ralph Waldo Emerson*

When Jerry Osborne said, "coaches change kids' lives," he was absolutely correct. Coaching begins with an expectation of significant positive change, and that expectation sets it apart from all other endeavours. Coaches understand the growth and development process as they create the necessary safe environment. Coaches know that long-term success is only possible when built upon a solid foundation of positive values, and they model those values. This is what coaches teach. All coaches, in whatever medium they work are intimate with human potential and have expectations of magnificent achievements as a person and as a performer.

Coaching is a process of thoughtful change and coaches are the most powerful change agents most people ever encounter. Coaches know that the real change must occur within the individual before anything else can change significantly. The basis of this process is greater self-awareness, self-reflection and self-evaluation. With youths, sport coaches are often more influential in the development and reinforcement of attitudes and values than are parents. However with children, the first coaches, parents, set the stage. Parents who coach and all other coaches understand this and accept the responsibility.

Because of the passion coaches bring to the activity and their encouragement for people to be doing what they truly love to do, the learning environment is often intensely emotional. High energy exists combined with high goals, great challenges, and deep personal satisfaction related to the activity. There are two distinct and different possibilities for coaches. They can actively support, or passively condone change for better or for worse. Coaches consciously choose from the beginning of their work to make all change both significant and for the better and they make every effort to learn how to do this effectively.

"If you want the situation to change, you have to change." I had been a coach and educator for three decades and knew this truth when I heard it from Jim Rohn, a legendary motivational speaker. It was a clear statement of a reality I had grown up with but which had never been articulated so elegantly. In the world of coaching I had learned that insanity could be defined as, "continuing to do what you have always done while expecting a different outcome."

Lasting change, with rare exceptions, occurs in small steps. The ordinary person takes the first step, or a few steps, and gives up. Coaches know that the only way to transcend the ordinary is to act in ways that the "ordinary" do not. My parents exhibited that; they took all the required steps and always accepted responsibility for the outcomes of each step. They wanted a life for their family that was different than the poverty they had come from, and that was still too common around us. They were aware that more was possible and they expected positive change to become a reality in their lives. The first step was to simply work hard and persistently. They did what was needed to get the job completed, every day; no matter how long it took, producing the best quality of which they were capable. They were willing to begin, to try, and to continue to try. They expected the same from my brother and myself: Do whatever work is required to succeed.

Coaches know how to make dreams real through a long series of incremental changes. Each change is built upon the previous change, one step at a time, in a planned way towards a clear goal. Coaches know we all have dreams and that for the majority they remain just that, dreams. Coaches help us bring our dreams into the light of day and create a vision of the grand possibility that seems real to us. Then they lay out the significant and magnificent changes and the time and effort required to accomplish each. They point out the small steps and the time all these steps will demand. They inspire us to begin and commit to support the process and us.

That is exactly what coach Bob Boadway did when he said to Vicki Keith, "Shut up and do it and I'll be there to support you." A number of coaches did that for me, starting with my parents. From the mid 1970s to the late 1980s Gerard Mach our Canadian Head Coach did that for a large number of Canadian Track and Field coaches. His belief in world-class achievement and all he did to help make that real for me, and the athletes I coached, changed my life and theirs.

Mike Dyon has run internationally for Canada eight times as a marathoner. He is a partner with his brother Paul in a sporting goods distribution company, R.M.P. ATHLETIC LOCKER LTD., which distributes a number of different brands including Brooks, Umbro, Rider, Airwalk, Ripzone and Powder Room.

The statement that coaches change kids' lives is true, many times over, in my case. As a thirteen year old in grade nine, and weighing ninety lbs, I was fortunate enough to be nurtured by Hugh Cook the high school wrestling coach who recommended that I take up running to keep up my fitness for wrestling. I had many other coaches in my high school years who reinforced all the Best Practices in your book and I can say that every coach changed my life in some positive way.

A major coaching influence came into my life in December 1976. I was in my fourth year of physical and health education at the University of Toronto and had experienced a disastrous fall cross-country season. As any athlete would, I was looking for answers. My younger brother suggested I talk with his coach, Hugh Cameron, who ran a small track club in Etobicoke. Hugh invited me to come to some of the workouts and saw that I had tremendous endurance and a passion for running. We set a goal to establish a personal best over 10,000 metres on the track the following spring. Hugh set an interim goal to run the 30km Around the Bay road race in Hamilton at the end of March.

We ran every day on our own all winter long and on Tuesdays and Thursdays would meet and run long intervals outdoors. Every Sunday, we managed a long run, regardless of the weather. We started out at sixteen miles and added a mile every two weeks. Hugh drove his van along with me and gave me split times. He encouraged me to cross-country ski for fun and to build endurance. Two weeks prior to the Hamilton race,

I completed a 22 mile run and I knew then that I could run the distance comfortably. My interval workouts (repeat miles) in the two weeks preceding the race were twenty to thirty seconds per mile faster than the pace target I had set for Around The Bay and it felt like I was jogging.

Race day came and I finished a strong second. Hugh and I immediately decided to delay our 10km track race to the summer, and to run the Ottawa marathon, which was in six weeks. Three weeks before Ottawa, we did a 28 mile run going through the marathon (26.2 miles) in 2 hours 33 minutes. I eased up training ten days before the marathon, my intervals were even faster than before Around the Bay, and I felt good heading to Ottawa.

The field included the winner of the Around the Bay race plus many other top seasoned marathoners from around North America. Hugh Cameron rode his bicycle behind the lead pack. With six miles to go we both sensed a slowing of the pace, I surged, broke the field open and went on to win the race in 2 hours 18 minutes.

Six months earlier, Hugh Cameron recognized the possibility that I could become a marathoner. He believed in me and made me believe in myself. All the training was geared to simulate the race day, from pacing to drinking water on the Sunday runs. He created an environment and atmosphere for success. Hugh lobbied the Canadian Track & Field Association and obtained an invitation for me to run in Czechoslovakia. At the age of 21 I represented Canada at international meets. I went on to win the Ottawa marathon twice more and continued my marathon career for 22 years finishing second overall in 1999 in Ottawa at age 43.

Because coaches see grand possibilities they begin with significant change in mind. That was Hugh Cameron's approach with Mike and when an even more grand possibility presented itself, even greater change was expected and worked towards, step by daily step over months and years!

Nathalie Rivard has skated on the National Women's Hockey Team since 1992. In that time, teams with which she has played have won three World Championship gold medals. She is an officer with the Ontario Provincial Police, which has always granted her the time to pursue her dreams.

Looking back on my hockey experience, there were many important moments on the road that I chose to travel. My mother, who was my first coach, tells me that at the age of seven, I asked her if I could play hockey. She spoke to my father and they decided "Why not?" They approached our local hockey association in Cumberland, Ontario, and enrolled me in a house league where I met my first hockey coach. Sadly, I don't remember his name but I remember his presence. After talking with my parents, he could see no problem with me playing on a boys team. He too said, "Why not?" At that age, I was bigger and stronger than many of the boys and the house league was a place to develop skills and have fun. Off I went to begin my journey.

Today, I am grateful to my parents, Michel and Mariette Rivard, and my first hockey coach for seeing the value of engaging a child in a fun sport instead of looking at the barriers that are too often highlighted in children's development. I remember scoring my first goal during a practice and thinking that I had just won a championship. I was laughing, cheering and looking at my parents.

My first year at the University of Toronto, 1991-92 proved to be a year of many firsts. I left my hometown for the big city and played in the female ice hockey program led by an amazing gentleman, Dave McMaster. Coach McMaster had captured my heart at a very early age when I traveled to Toronto each year for the Provincials. That same year I played for the Toronto Aeros, coached by Ken Dufton. Mr. Dufton is well known on the National circuit. To my surprise, I was invited to a National Team Selection Camp and was selected for the 1992 World Championships to be held in Finland. Over the next few years I had to re-evaluate my skills because my coaches could see my potential but I wasn't reaching it. In 1998, I decided not to play the season but instead to concentrate on my off-ice training. The evaluation from the National program emphasized working on my foot speed and mobility. I had to be leaner and quicker. My efforts were rewarded when Danièle Sauvageau chose me to attend the 1999 World Championship, also held in Finland. I continued to work under her supervision and was selected for the 2000 Worlds in Mississauga, Ontario.

My memories of my hockey experiences are mainly positive and I believe I grew as a human being because of the interaction with my coaches. I would put many of my teachers in this same category. Over the years, my coaches guided me by offering me their best resources and all I had to do was seize the opportunity.

I would want to say to all coaches out there: "Never under estimate the power of your words." Athletes look for guidance and to them you are their key to success. They need to believe that you believe in them and by treating each player fairly and honestly you will create a powerful and dedicated individual eager to achieve his/her full potential. You are in a position of authority. Use it wisely and you will be rewarded by success throughout your coaching career. More importantly, you will impact the life of people in such a way that they will be changed by you and remember you forever. Winning the gold is not the only indicator of success.

I will always remember the day my father taught me about positive change, using olives! When I refused an olive offered to me at dinner one night, my father inspired, even demanded, positive change. He talked about the wonders of new and different foods from different cultures, how tastes were acquired and that I should never judge any food until I had tried it a number of times. With olives, he said, I needed to eat at least twelve before coming to a conclusion. I didn't need to eat them all now or in the next short while. I just needed to eat at least twelve and then I could honestly say I did or did not like olives. Then the coaches "demand" part came – try one now and don't comment, just eat it. It wasn't that bad, and I don't remember the next eleven or however many it was. I love olives now. I learned that all I had to do was be willing to try, to actually take that first small step and repeat it over time. Fitness, skills and attitudes are very much like tastes, they are acquired over time.

Roy Williams is a retired sports journalist and former international athlete who lives in Auckland, New Zealand. Roy is one of the best all-around athletes of all time in New Zealand representing his country in basketball as well as athletics. He was Commonwealth Games Gold Medallist in decathlon in 1966. He still coaches.

I began coaching Basil Ake when he was thirteen years old. This very athletic and highly intelligent boy had a Maori father and a Samoan mother who had separated when he was ten. He lived with his mother and two sisters during the eight years I coached him.

During this time, Basil became the New Zealand high schools and National under eighteen 110 metres hurdles champion and record holder. He was also an outstanding Rugby Union and Rugby League player.

At age eighteen Basil went to Auckland University to study engineering but in that first year, like too many teen-agers, his priorities were anything but study. He began to party and drink heavily. Then one morning I received a phone call from him. He was in jail having been picked up for drunken driving and abusing a police officer (who had called him a racist name). Basil was calling for my help and asked me not to tell his mother. As it turned out he had failed all his first year exams.

I bailed him from jail. He was given a heavy fine and he lost his driving license for a year. A week after "the incident" I suggested he come around to my home for a talk with my wife, Ngaire and me, which he did. I told him he possessed superior intelligence and athletic ability, but if he continued on the course he was taking he would end up a "nobody" and could be spending much of his life in jails.

"Do you want this?" I asked.
He said, "No."

I then said, "Let's take the time right now to set some goals you would like to achieve by the time you turn thirty." His three main goals were to complete his engineering degree, play Rugby Union for the National Team, the All Blacks, and save NZ$100,000.00 to pay off the mortgage on his mothers' home.

After our talk, with clear goals in front of him and a painful life lesson behind him he settled down. By age thirty he had achieved all but the goal of playing for the All Blacks. He came very close though, playing for the National Under 20 Rugby team, the New Zealand Maori Rugby team, and the Auckland representative team the year it was New Zealand's champion provincial side.

Basil left New Zealand at age 22 to play professionally in England where he completed his bachelor's and master's degrees in engineering. His professors wanted him to continue towards a doctorate degree but Basil believed he could not afford the added years of study. He returned to New Zealand and paid off his mother's mortgage. There he began to work with an engineering firm. Now, at age thirty-nine, he is earning a significant income and is happily married with two young children.

Coaches know they are most needed when life situations are at the worst. It is not surprising that the first person Basil phoned was his coach. He knew it was 'safe' to do so. Nor is Roy Williams it response surprising. While they do not accept actions that are detrimental to our long term welfare, coaches understand our humanity. Roy Williams believed in Basil and the young man knew that in life and as in athletics the coach helped create a sense of possibility, specific goals and a commitment to doing what was necessary to achieve them.

Coaches change our relationship to our performance. They know the real work is with the person, not the activity, and that work is to support and develop self-esteem. Self-esteem is manifested as confidence and it is what most of us talk about when we refer to the ability to perform. The coach's unstated commitment is identical to the Hippocratic oath: "At first do no harm." The very best never, ever, act in ways, or say anything that is detrimental to the learner's self esteem. Never!

Coaches separate the performance from the performer. They teach the performer that "I am not my performance." They reinforce this in all they do. Parents love the child while pointing out that an action was bad, or good. It is never "you are a bad girl" or "you are such a good boy" because of some action. The child is neither bad nor good because of what they do. The child is innately good and loved and needs to learn how to interact socially. It is the same in the classroom or the playing field. Neither high marks nor a high jump make one a better person. Nor does the opposite make one a lesser person. The person is always valued and supported and their performance is seen as and commented upon as just that – performance.

Jamie Hamilton was head coach of pole vaulting at the University of Toronto High Performance Centre and has been a high school science teacher for many years, a role in which he still coaches young people. He tells the following story.

On a beautiful summer evening, at the end of an excellent jumping session, one vaulter was slower at increasing his heights than the others. I had enough experience with people to know he wanted to speak with me individually. He was pleased with his session that day and his training overall. He said he wanted to talk about his future in the sport. He then told me that his goal was to be a member of our national team and go to a major international games. He wanted me to know he was dedicating his next two years to attaining that goal so I could shape his training accordingly.

While I was pleased that he was enjoying vaulting and expecting to continue to improve, his expectation of vaulting high enough to achieve the standard required was unsettling. I knew his physical capabilities and I believed this was an unreasonable goal for him. The next day I brought it up with my mentor, Andy Higgins, the head coach of the program. He agreed with me that the athlete did not have enough leg speed to vault the height required and that holding this as his only reason for continuing to train and vault could only lead to disappointment. It would create far too much performance pressure and obscure all the good things that an athlete experienced and achieved over the course of a career.

Do not kill the dream, but at the same time do not allow it to be the focus of everything that is done. Such a distant and, perhaps, unreasonable goal takes the focus away from the day-to-day experience. Andy felt that one of the most important jobs a coach can do is help every athlete learn to enjoy every day, to find joy and satisfaction in the task at hand. If they did that they would have better training sessions, perform at a higher level in competitions and be more likely to leave the sport fulfilled and happy with their accomplishments.

The athlete did not make the National team but he did continue to vault. When I last spoke with him, he was coaching pole vaulting at a high school and thoroughly enjoying himself. While I know that his athletes have achieved much success at competitions, the thing I feel best about was hearing from teachers and coaches at the same school about how much fun the pole vaulters in that training group experience.

Since that talk with Andy I have embraced that philosophy and have identified something in my work every day to enjoy. I have found it has made for a wonderful ride.

Coaches invest considerable time supporting the development of a young person. Time is an essential requisite, time per session and time over an extended period, because nothing of value is developed quickly. Change is a process, and significant change takes a good deal of time, not days or months, but years. Few can persist for the required time unless there is some satisfaction, some joy, some sense of accomplishment in the daily process.

Modest changes of any kind are easy to bring about with typical teaching and instructing methods. However, the significant change that is necessary for real success is tougher and is often resisted unconsciously by the athlete or performer. Coaches know this and begin with a clear understanding and an agreement with the performer that the most challenging work will be the inner, personal work. Together they take advantage of every "coachable and learning moment."

The coachable moment is that time when, for significant personal reasons, the individual is ready to learn. Success is a good teacher but adversity and failure are greater ones. Strong emotions open us to the possibility for change. Frustration and disappointment are powerful because they are the result of not achieving what we wanted, worked towards and hoped for. Even joy and elation can serve to create openness particularly when something has been done to create success that the performer has been resisting. Affirming the achievement and pointing out the performer's wisdom or courage in doing what caused the outcome is a wonderful way to anchor the learning.

It is the negative experience, the public failure, the great disappointment, or personal rejection that opens the door to significant change. Like all of us who have a degree of insecurity, Rob Pitter, when high jumping, often lost all focus on executing a run-up and take-off. His mind shifted to the height of the bar or what making this height would mean. Rob was a talented jumper whose physical gifts far exceeded his sense of self-worth. He was also stubborn and could only take so much feedback before he began to resist.

The coachable moments came in training and in competitions when he had been jumping well and then, at a "critical" height, his technique came apart and he failed miserably. His immediate anger at himself opened the door to a discussion about what had really taken place. Over the years it became a regular occurrence.

The talk usually began with my questions: "What happened there? What were you thinking and feeling? Where was your focus?" Each question led to the same answer. He was still emotionally involved in the previous jump.

No one can execute a skill at a high performance level without being focused on that particular effort. Lessons from the past are extracted and stored, adjustments are made and the past remains the past. The future can exist only if the present is successful. In competition and performance, as in all of life, there is only now. I pointed out to Rob innumerable times, "there is only one jump." There is always only one jump, the jump that is currently being taken. Whatever the feedback from the previous effort, a slight change needed, possibilities raised because of exceptional performance, the focus must return to executing the only jump there is – this one!

Along the way Rob won two Canadian inter-university championships and set a meet record during one of them. This young man had come into our program as a seventeen year old struggling in grade eleven. When he finally completed his Ph.D., he phoned me to say 'thank you' for the one great lesson I had taught him that made it possible to get through the long and challenging doctoral program. "You taught me there is only one jump, the one I am taking now and that truth became the focus of all the work I faced. There was only one task, one assignment and that was the one I was working on at the moment. If I had ever stopped to look at all that was demanded of me and that lay ahead of me it would have been overwhelming."

Sometimes the lesson is direct and clear. On rare occasions it is powerful. It is absorbed immediately. The influence a coach has on a person is far greater than many people realize. The impact can carry into all aspects of life without the coach ever realizing it. The following is a story of one small intervention. It reflects a simple value of mine, involving language, and how it says so much about us as learners.

Brenda Gibson neé Reid is a mother of two, a former heptathlete and always a significant volunteer in her community. Brenda was always able to see what was right when it was pointed out and she possessed the personal courage to act on it. Here is her story of seeing, accepting and acting for a needed change in and for herself.

I began competing internationally in track and field when I was a teenager. I remember the most important event that took place during those competitive years happened in Saskatoon during a Canada-U.S.A.-Great Britain Heptathlon competition. At the end of the day I had scribbled a note for my coach and left for dinner with a few other athletes.

On my return, my coach pulled me aside and showed me how poorly written and badly spelled my note had been. He told me that I couldn't compete at a high level of sport without clear and intelligent thinking, and that sport wasn't a career nor all of my life. It was time I started to get my academic performance up to the level of my athletic performance, the highest possible. The news shocked me. Coach really believed I was capable. I always thought I was simply dumb!

To this day I still spell badly, but I can do almost anything to which I put my mind. It started the very next year of high school. I switched to an alternative school, doubled my course load, and completed two years in one before starting university.

As strange as it sounds, I know that if my coach hadn't said anything to me that night it would have taken me years to realize that I could accomplish just as much off the track as on it. Thanks Andy.

Brenda has a caring heart, bigger than most and a spirit that is indomitable. She achieved what she did while spending a good deal of time with her best friend from early childhood who was living the last difficult months of a life limited by cystic fibrosis. At the same time her father was critically ill, surviving on dialysis and waiting for a long overdue kidney transplant.

Coaches know that challenges can create change. There is something in each of us that loves, in fact needs, challenges. It may be only a very small part and that part may even be a little timid. But it is there. And in each of us it may be of a different nature and related to many different aspects of life. Here a coach does what we all can do for ourselves and those around us, recognize what that particular "something" is and support the using of it to advantage.

Brad Morley lives with his wife, Rose and two children in Owen Sound, Ontario where he teaches English, coaches cross country running, and still runs regularly for the joy of it.

Human beings crave difficulty. A good many of us thrive on it or at least love it. Convincing young athletes of this can be as difficult as convincing someone that there is joy to be found in working through a Shakespearean sonnet or a poem by e.e. cummings. Why would I join the track team if it means I have to hurt two or three days a week? It is because they are demanding that we want to play. The play, so to speak, is in the effort. It is one of life's surprising ironies.

Consider the grade ten cross country runner who didn't mind the hard work of training but never really seemed to race up to her level. She complained bitterly one sunny October afternoon in the nearby park after finishing yet again a few places behind a girl both she and I were convinced she should be beating but had yet to do so. I had to get her to race harder, to suffer more than she was used to doing in races. She balked when I suggested she forget about how long the race was on the coming Thursday and how she was going to finish and not to worry about her contribution to the team. I suggested that instead she just run for as long as she possibly could, despite the discomfort, right on the other girl's shoulder.

"But," I commented, "you know you don't mind hard work, look at the really tough workouts you've done. Staying with her for as long as possible will teach us how we can make those workouts pay off even more. If you have to drop out of the race, fine, do so. It is better to learn something concrete than to have you finish once again a few spots behind her."

The young girl liked the idea of learning something specific about her fitness and she liked the idea of it being ok to drop out of the race. Our goal wasn't to finish but to work extra hard for as long as we could. Oddly, working hard was fine with her in a way that racing to the end had never been. So off she went, and lo and behold, with three out of the four kilometres done, she was right on her competitor's shoulder, and looking pretty comfortable, while her opponent seemed a bit frazzled by this unexpected turn of events. With about 800 metres to go, she went by her surprised quarry and beat her by several seconds. My young athlete finished, smiling, and the first words out of her mouth were, "I've always liked hard work." She had found joy in the effort, and completing the task was a satisfying by product. What she hadn't said was that for some strange reason she had always been a bit afraid of racing.

A simple concept like changing the definition or changing the label of a thing and tapping into whatever part of the brain it is that likes challenging work had turned this young woman into a better competitor and a slightly wiser person. As well, her willingness to try something new and tougher had made me a bit wiser and a bit humbler in the face of both the power of language and the power of a young athlete. I still think of her when I introduce my poetry unit to my grade nine classes.

This is a wonderful story of a young girl achieving the success that she deserved because she had the talent and did the work. But wait! Look again, this is a story of many things that coaches do all tied into one situation with one athlete. Brad Morley saw that the youngster was afraid to compete because she might "fail." He saw that she did not compete and, in her own mind "failed" by not running as well as she knew she could! Coach Morley used what he knew about her to the advantage of the youngster. He shifted her focus from the "outcome" that created fear, to the process she loved, effort, running hard, challenging herself. He then took away the last possible fear of loss of worth by making it acceptable to drop out of the race. With nothing to fear she was free to explore her potential, something that makes life rich for all of us.

Here a coach found a way to get the youngster to focus on the process, to engage freely in challenging her willingness to endure, which he knew she found to be a worthwhile and satisfying act. He used the power of language, and in this one race significantly enhanced the girl's self-esteem.

Coaches do this in every situation, while parenting, in the classroom, on the playing field, and, yes in the corporate world. They help individuals understand what is getting in the way of possibilities and they find a way to move beyond it. As my friend Peter Jensen, constantly reminds us, "what's in the way is the way." Mr. Jones did that for me in my final year of high school. I had arrived fresh from a one-room elementary school in the bush. The teachers had been, with one exception, less than adequate and I arrived in grade nine with no real understanding of grammar. After four years I was barely surviving in French.

Mr. Jones had come to Dryden that fall from a large collegiate institute in Toronto. Within days he took me aside and said that my background in French was going to keep me from passing the provincial exams and getting into university unless drastic measures were taken. I was shocked when he said that my only hope was to meet every day for an hour after school, to bring the basics up to the required level. The same applied to my friend George Marks. When we told him we practiced football and basketball after school it was his turn to be shocked. He was surprised we had not heard the message about the seriousness of our situation, and then he "got it."

The teacher who cared enough to make the offer to help saw that sport was important to us. He realized it was a basic motivator that we both needed. He accepted and worked from this knowledge. We found times to meet and Mr. Jones invested hours in teaching. There is no doubt that had he not arrived that year, had he not seen my situation and spent the time with me, I would not have passed those demanding exams and University would have been out of the question. Like all coaches Mr. Jones saw our current situation and also saw us as we could be. He laid out a path and did what all coaches do; he was there to support us every step of the way.

Change must begin where the youngster is. Coaches know that no matter what the envisioned long-term possibility, they must assess all aspects of the youngster's current state and start from that place. A beginner is always a beginner. Age and experience will determine the rate of progress but coaches know that the first steps, the foundation upon which all learning is built, are critical. This is as true for attitudes and beliefs as it is with skills and competencies.

Tom Bourne, who organizes Little League baseball in south Florida, and coaches a team every year, offers some questions for youngsters to ponder, questions that cause kids to think and that shape attitudes towards work and self-discipline and getting ahead in whatever they do. Questions of this nature, in a coaching environment, become internalized as a sort of personal challenge.

What are my dreams worth?
Is a little sweat and effort and sometimes being uncomfortable too much?
What if everyday someone else, somewhere else, is trying to make himself a better player?
What if we are trying out for the same team-same position?
Why would I not try everyday to make myself a better person and a better player?

Ken Bellemare is a former coach, Director of Athletics at Dalhousie University and now is a facilitator of change in the world of business and sport administration. Ken tells how a professional athlete, in another country cared enough to support significant change in a young athlete.

When I was an aspiring high school football player I read an article in Sports Illustrated about Raymond Berry, a receiver for the Baltimore Colts of the NFL. This outstanding pass receiver had to overcome a great deal to even make the team. He was not tall or big, he had bad eyesight requiring him to wear contact lenses, he was not considered fast and he had a chronically broken finger on one of his hands. What I remember from the article is that you always had to have a positive outlook no matter what the odds were of you succeeding. You had to be willing to work harder than other people. With these two things you could make up for a lack of size, height, speed and superior talent.

I learned that prior to the start of training camp Berry would review films of the games from the previous year and chart out every play. He listed these plays in consecutive order on a large poster. He would then take this poster to the field and by himself in full gear he would play the game executing all the things he would do from his position at full speed. He would go back to the "huddle" where the poster was, to get ready for his next play. I was so inspired by the article that I wrote Raymond Berry in care of Sports Illustrated. To my great surprise he wrote me back within a couple of weeks, a hand written five page letter. He offered some great tips on how I could improve my play. His advice had little to do with the skills but concentrated on attitude. I finished my football career as a starter for my university football team and entered physical education to become a coach. Raymond Berry had a hand in my career choice.

Coaches understand that continuous learning and development require continuous challenges. It is not just our muscles that adapt to a particular challenging load, our entire being does the same. Whenever anything becomes easy we can be sure we are no longer learning and growing.

Tom Enright is President and CEO of Canada NewsWire. He remains active in many associations and organizations. He believes it is important to give back to his community. Tom says, "The smartest move of my life was to marry my wife Linda. She continues to make me want to be a better person. Our two amazing children, Matthew and Courtney, remind me constantly what it is like to be both young and old." He tells us how he was started him on a journey of significant change.

It changed my life. I know that sounds like a cliché, but it is true. It began while I was employed as a manager at the Toronto Stock Exchange in the late 1980s. At that time I witnessed an extraordinary event, the metamorphosis of a person who would become my boss, coach and mentor. He transformed himself from a typical businessperson and focused on his own career, to a coach who saw what could be accomplished by freeing people to attain their personal bests.

I remember his catch phrase to this day, "Let Eagles Soar." Through his change process he came to realize that by surrounding himself with the right people (eagles) and working with those people to help them understand what they were capable of accomplishing (letting the eagles soar), we would together achieve amazing results.

I was lucky enough to be chosen to be one of his eagles. And so my journey began. The first step was to understand who I was. I had to come face-to-face with my own strengths and weaknesses. I needed to understand what motivated me and what I was passionate about. This was not an easy journey as I admitted to personal behaviours and discovered things about myself that did not thrill me. This understanding of myself was not limited to just the work environment but also included the personal side of my life as well. My coach guided me through this self-examination in a completely non-threatening way, which is difficult to accomplish in a business setting.

What freedom this exploration created for me and what power it provided me! Suddenly I could make better decisions because I knew how I approached problem solving and what personal strengths I could rely on. I found that I could overcome my natural weaknesses by involving others who were strong in areas where I was weak. Because of the confidence I had gained in reaching a better understanding of myself, involving others in situations because of their strengths did not threaten me. I knew that by assembling the strongest approach possible by combining our strengths a maximum result would be possible. In time I was able to overcome some of my weaknesses.

I understood what motivated me and what I wanted out of life. For me this was not money but a sense of making a real contribution to the growth of the Canadian capital markets. This created an excitement in me about my job and created a passion in me for the pursuit of this goal. It has been a part of my reason for being, every day since then.

The journey also taught me that we face many choices in life and that there is always a right choice or an easy choice. The right choice is usually the harder one but it is the path of superior performance over the longer term and must always be the choice taken even though the easy choice may offer short-term gain. I came to realize that I was capable of achieving far more than I previously thought and I saw this applied to other people too.

With my new understanding, my mentor and I were able to create a common language that allowed us to communicate effectively and efficiently. By understanding who and what I was, we knew how to approach issues and situations in a way that created the best possible outcomes. My mentor never manipulated me because that would have eliminated the bond of trust between us and jeopardized the long-term success of our journey.

We agreed upon a course of action that would guide my development to the next levels of performance. This included developing my life skills, the skills on which we base our decision making and our perspective. In my case this lead to the discovery of my first management credo. Attitude + Quality = Profit.

I will let you judge how well the eagles soared. Within ten years of embarking on this extraordinary journey my path took me from my position as a manager at the TSE to President and Chief Executive Officer of Canada NewsWire. I know this was possible because of my coach.

When I was only a boy my grandmother told me, "you must choose what you really like to do in life and at times you must choose to like what you really need to do in life." Success and happiness depend on our passion for the activity or job or career. I always felt that I would be teaching and coaching even if I wasn't paid. I loved the challenges and I thrived on the feedback that I received watching people learn, change, and grow. It is still the most deeply satisfying work I do.

I first discovered the satisfaction of this work when I was only thirteen. My father had me act as a guide taking guests fishing to the smaller lakes. It did not matter that I could catch walleyes. What was important was the guest could catch them. My first coaching job took place in a boat with adults. There is a subtle difference between a fishing-bait gently touching a weed or a rock and a walleye's "nibble." I faced two challenges: Teach that differences and teach to deal with the nibble. We invested many minnows in the learning process but I was always amazed at my patience. I loved it.

I learned the other side of my grandmother's dictum. There were days when it was windy, rainy and cold, and it was plain hard work to control the boat, deal with snags and catch a limit or not! This was doing what I needed to do, and I learned to like that as well. The lessons I learned were useful for everything I have done since.

I had learned the key factor in this process from my parents in so many varied tasks and skills. We all learn best by doing. Confucius said, "I hear and I forget, I see and I remember, I do and I understand." Coaches support the "doing" process, and they know that for achieving what we are capable of it must be done with full awareness of what is being experienced.

Coaches know that significant change demands energy from them and the learners over a long time. They know that any deeply ingrained faulty skill will get worse before it gets better. Performers must be willing to take a step back to be able to take greater steps forward later. It is never easy and coaches prepare learners for this challenge in the beginning.

Barrie Shepley was Canada's coach of Triathlon at the Sydney Olympics where Canada's Simon Whitfield brought home the first gold medal of the 21st century. Barrie is the president of a corporate health consulting company, Personal Best, and does motivational work with corporate and school groups. He can be contacted at: Barrie@personalbest.ca.

I've always believed that thinking about something intensifies the effect of it. Think about pain and it will intensify. Think about a great friend and you will feel warm all over. After twenty years of coaching thousands of athletes, my upcoming fortieth birthday made me decide to prepare for and enter my first ever Ironman Triathlon. For this a 2.4 mile swim, 112 mile bicycle race and 26.2 mile run must be completed in under seventeen hours. To me the Ironman symbolizes human possibility. It is a journey with many ups and downs and no guarantees.

Soon after my decision a number of friends joined the challenge and within a week we were a group of 24. With six months to train for the event, every training day would be important. One of the pure novices was 58-year-old Larry Karasiuk, a successful businessman who loved a great challenge. We learned quickly Larry's challenge couldn't have been greater. On January 2nd we had our first swim lesson and discovered he was terrified of water. He spent that first day learning to blow bubbles!

Supported by my belief in what is possible, and by their dreams, the group worked hard toward the goal of an imaginary finish line in Klagenfurt, Austria. For Larry, one lap in the pool turned into two laps, and four laps turned into twenty. Early in May Larry called to tell me he had swum 152 straight laps of the pool, 2.4 miles! Swimming in a pool is one thing. Swimming in open water is quite another. In two weeks of swimming back and forth in front of the beach, Larry made another major step toward his ultimate dream; he swam across our small lake.

One of the group, Gary Black, fell in a bicycle crash three weeks before the race and broke his collarbone. A true team player, Gary came to Austria to support the rest of the group even though he wouldn't be able to race. I met with the group the night before to talk about final strategies to get us all through the race. The odds were against us. Half of our team had never competed in a mini-triathlon and yet tomorrow we would attempt an event that would take eleven to seventeen hours of non-stop performance. I asked Gary if he thought he could make it through the swim one-armed. I was concerned about Larry making the 2hr 20 minute swim cut-off time and I thought that Gary could help by swimming next to him. "I'm not sure, but I am prepared to try" he said.

Race morning saw 2000 athletes standing on the small beach looking into the sun. The 7 a.m. cannon started our final test. While I had high hopes of training properly for the race, the hundreds of visits and days spent with my mother in her last months and final days of her struggle against cancer had been a much higher priority. As I dove into the lake, I knew that I would have to give a Herculean effort. I hit the shore at 1hr and 50 minutes, ten minutes behind my target time, and I worried about Larry making the cut-off.

Crowds cheered madly as I rushed off to gather my bicycle and start the first of three 60k hilly bike loops. With a picture of my mom taped to the side of my bike, I cycled away and hoped that I had enough to hit the finish line. Within minutes a long-lasting hip problem showed signs of getting serious and part way up the tough 6k steep climb I was in such pain I could not continue to pedal. I got off my bike, limped to the top of the mountain and knew my day was over. The stress of the past few months and the strain of losing my mother just days before, finally started to flood in. I sat and wept for a very long time. I gradually became aware of the people and the athletes speeding by on their bicycles.

The pain was intense and I took three anti-inflammatory pills. Minutes later a medical van arrived and the paramedics gave me a shot to freeze my hip. Despite my profound disappointment I knew I still had an important role in helping my teammates achieve their dreams. I saw the one I was most concerned about. Larry was standing on his pedals trying to loosen his back as he rode past. My novice swimmer had gotten out of the water at 2 hours and 16 minutes, four minutes under the cut-off, and now was going to have to ride faster then he had ever ridden in his life. "I will be here next time you come by," I hollered. The next challenge was to make the ten hour cut-off at the end of the bike ride. I knew I couldn't pedal up hill but I believed I could pedal on the flat and downhill surfaces and be of some help to him.

In the two hours I waited for Larry to complete the loop I reflected on my mother's life. We often talked about "getting more of what you think about." Instead of feeling sorry for myself, I would focus on helping a great teammate. When Larry came by he looked fatigued. The increasing heat and elevation changes were really striking at the heart of this courageous guy. I told him I was going to ride beside him for the next 50k and see how fast we could go. In spite of being fatigued and sore, he increased his cadence and gear ratio and sped toward his last 80k. Many others had already quit. Larry was in last place and pedaling harder then he ever had. As we approached the hills on the final lap I said, "You're on your own buddy, dig deep," and turned and pedaled back to the finish line. There I waited anxiously until at nine hours and 57 minutes, with three minutes to spare, Larry entered the transition zone.

We now had every athlete in our group out on the run course. The youngest and fastest athletes crossed the line in daylight just over ten hours after they began. Over the next six hours I watched old and new friends smile as they crossed the finish line fulfilling a magnificent goal. Among them was my beautiful, and supportive wife, Caron. With less then an hour to go, in the dark of night, I watched 58 year old novice athlete Larry Karasiuk step across the Ironman Austria finish line, pause for a second and raise both arms in the air!

In less then five days I had witnessed and experienced three of the most powerful mental achievements one could imagine, my mother waiting to die until I got home, Gary Black doing the entire Ironman swim with one arm, and Larry Karasiuk completing the Ironman in under seventeen hours. What is humanly possible? Anything is possible if we think about it enough! I will think a lot about these three, and their memories will make it very difficult to ever have a down day!

Grand possibilities are not just for a select few, for Olympians or Honour students or the fortunate or wealthy or gifted! When we expect and accept significant positive change, magnificent achievements are possible for every one of us. All we need do is be clear about what we want, ask for the required support and make what we want that which we think about most!

Seven Keys to Beginning with an Expectation of Significant Change

1. Model that learning, not teaching, is the active process.

2. Believe that you and all others are capable of significant growth.

3. Understand that significant change is a process that takes time.

4. Begin, now, where you are, with what you have – people learn best by doing.

5. Make clear that success demands hard work in all activities and in the person.

6. Support people in doing what they love to do; and loving what they need to do.

7. Dream big. Set no limits – "Anything is Possible."

5 Best Practice

LEADS FROM THE HEART

Best Coaches lead with caring, passion and concern
for what is best in the long term.

"I've learned to lead more from the heart than from the mind."
~ Richard Peddie, President Maple Leaf Sports and Entertainment.

Coaches care first about the person. Coaches are passionate about possibilities and they care deeply about people. Coaches inspire others to follow and understand the process because they have been inspired in their time. Coaches lead by touching the hearts of others with grand possibilities, possibilities that are in the best long-term interests of the individual.

Coaches inspire with a vision of power and clarity that we, as their students and charges, sense it as already achieved. Coaches invite us to follow the noble path towards the possible. We walk this path with coaches because they know that the journey will be challenging and satisfying. We feel in our hearts we will be safe, and sense that this journey, this quest is ours. The coach's vision clarifies an aspect of our own dream as the coach engages us in that first great journey, which is inwards. We begin to discover our own complete dream. With care, the coach helps us create our own vision which over time becomes ever more powerful and clear.

Coaches know that inspiration is a clear message from the heart and soul that touches the hearts and souls of others. Inspiration comes from knowing oneself and the humanity of others. Coaches appeal to the very best in people. It can be a speech to the entire group or a quiet conversation with a few, or with an individual.

The process of 'the very best' is simple. Act with respect and dignity and do the right thing while you continue to grow as a whole person. Set aside time each day for study or learning a new skill, mastering a challenging discipline, or becoming a better parent or manager. The process is simple although coaches make it clear that simple is never to be confused with easy! They help people understand that it is rare that anything worthwhile is easy to achieve.

Kirk Wipper saw me as a championship wrestler in my first wrestling class at University of Toronto. As he quietly told me what he saw, he added that I could achieve it as part of "a really great group of men." In a few simple and sincere words he created a marvellous vision for me and invited me to become part of an exceptional group. His vision gave specific direction to my dream of athletic excellence, and the "great group of men" held promise of a worthwhile journey.

When I went to Kenora in August 1985, to invite Michael Smith to move to Toronto and become a decathlete, I knew football and basketball coaches had already approached him. I had come to believe that Michael was an independent and rather private person. I talked about what was possible for him and how we could assure it. We had already demonstrated our programme with David Steen. He improved the Canadian record in decathlon by hundreds of points, earned a Commonwealth Games silver medal in 1982 behind world record holder Daley Thomson, and gold medals in 1983 at both the World University and Pan Am Games and placed eighth in the 1984 Olympics. Then I said, "Michael, decathlon is your opportunity to compete with, and be among the best in the world, and it is the only situation in which you can take total control of your destiny."

All this could be achieved in a world-class university, making education his highest priority. He could have it all, if that was what he wanted. It was all possible.

The facts of the situation were aimed at his head, his logic, because he was an intelligent young man. The idea of competing among the best in the world was aimed at his heart, while the notion of controlling his own destiny and being able to discover how good he could become was directed at his soul. Not only did I outline a vision of grand possibility, I wanted to touch and begin to give shape to an unfocused dream of grand athletic achievement that existed deep within Michael. It is a dream that exists within everyone who loves sport. Coaches help us discover our dreams and express our talent.

Victor Lopez is the head coach of women's track and field at Rice University in Houston, Texas, whose heart still resides in his native Puerto Rico where he invests much time and energy in coaching and sport development. Victor tells the following story.

In 1962 I was looking for concrete directions about where I would go in life and I did not have a clue what I wanted to do. I met a man who would not only change my life forever, but also inspire me to become the human being and the coach that I am today. Positive values and principles were already instilled in me by my parents, yet for some reason they were not able to make me commit myself to the discipline of attending classes and pursuing a university career.

I was having too much fun as an eighteen year old teenager. I was a musician who started playing professionally at age thirteen. I was way ahead of my peers in street life. Academics were not a priority although in those rare times, when I applied myself to schoolwork, I was pretty sharp.

Then, out of the blue came this man to my high school. I fell in love with him immediately and he became like a father, not just for me, but also for a bunch of us who needed that type of father figure outside of home. I do not know what makes young people reject the good advice and counselling they get from their own parents. I guess they want to get their freedom and fly away from them since they have been under their wings too long. They do not listen to them. This does not mean that they don't love them, but for sure, around that period of time, we feel that what they tell us is not what we want to hear.

The man I am referring to was our high school physical education teacher, who, after spending more than thirty years in another high school on the other side of the island, came to our hometown to be close to his grandchildren. The man was friendly but strict and had an aura around him of loving care, class and seriousness. He was very committed to education and to developing and guiding his students. His classes were organized and inspirational. He showed us that there was another side to physical education besides playing on the field. He showed us the history and theory behind movement and the values behind being involved in sport in a serious way. He was a master at this which was the reason for his success at his previous high school in all the sports he coached.

There was no question in my mind that I wanted to be like him. We became so close that I used to talk with him all the time. I became sort of like a son to him. Instead of going to my home for lunch I used to go to his home. He inspired me to talk about great sport heroes, politics, national historical events, values and principles. I probably learned more from him about civics and ethics than from any of my teachers in all my years in school. The funny thing is that he was not educating me in anything different than my parents were. Perhaps a factor was that my coach/teacher was able to spend more time with me than my parents because they were so busy working hard to provide for us so that we could lead a decent life. I spent two class periods a day, then varsity practice and then walked home with him to his home and spent three or four hours more with him there.

The man not only made sure that I graduated from high school but made me a pretty good volleyball player and the top junior sprinter in 1962-1963 in Puerto Rico. In the summer of 1963 I made my national team and toured Central America. I was undefeated in the 100 and 200 metres that year. All along he told me that I could get a scholarship to a university in the USA to run track and become a great sprinter. However, I wanted to be a coach like him. I received seven scholarship offers in 1963. In the spring of 1964 I left Puerto Rico for the University of Houston, in Texas.

I am now a veteran in coaching with thirty-two years of experience, thirty of them at the university level and my last twenty-four at Rice University. I have been able to pay back my coach/mentor by helping other young people to develop their talents.

I do not regret one minute of the life I have chosen and I doubt that anything else would have fulfilled me. Sometimes I wonder why I have been blessed with so much happiness and so many positive experiences. My answer is that I have made of the profession a religion inspired by one of the most outstanding human beings that has ever existed, my high school coach.

Coaches know that we all have dreams, most of which are unfocused or buried under fear and doubts. They know that only our dreams can move us towards who and what we can be. To help us clarify our dreams and bring them to the light of day and focus them, coaches ask questions. "Why are you being like this?" "Why are you doing what you are doing?" "What is it you are doing when you feel your absolute best?" And they have more questions, "Why are you not doing that all the time?" "What is your dream?" "Why not focus your dreams into a clear and compelling vision?" "Why not begin to examine and toss out the doubts and fears that you never asked for in the first place?" "Why not begin to live your dreams today?" Coaches inspire us to ask ourselves: Why? Why not? Why not now? Why not me? Then, because they care, they support us in acting on our answers. Never forget, coaches always listen. That caring and support is exactly what a number of coaches did for me and I, in turn have done for others. There is no other reason for our existence than to become who we were meant to be and express our special talent and support others in doing exactly the same.

Asking "why" questions are the key to achievement and to success. It is truly magnificent what we can do when our "why" is big enough and clear enough. I attended a business seminar in downtown Toronto on a wet, cold March day when the speaker asked who among us would join him in a walk to Mississauga City Hall about thirty kilometres away. Right then, dressed as we were, not a hand went up. He then asked the same question, adding one inducement. "What if there would be a guaranteed one hundred thousand dollars in cash for all who made it?" Every hand went up!

We will endure and overcome almost anything if our "why" is powerful enough. It is important to understand that the money was not the real motivator. The real drive, "the why," was what the money could buy. Every one of us has a dream that we can achieve, or move closer to, with a windfall of money. My question is: What is your dream, and does it mean enough to you to get a 'coach' and begin to act on it?

The perceptive sportswriter, Jim Christie of the Globe and Mail, tells the story of Max Birbraer and his coach, Paul Rosen.

There are precious moments in the coach-athlete relationship, moments when a skill is imparted and properly executed, moments when the competitive fire is kindled, moments of triumph that have nothing to do with the scoreboard and everything to do with the spirit.

Such are the moments that bind Paul Rosen and Max Birbraer, each man in his way an outstanding athlete, each in his way a mentor and coach. Rosen, from Thornhill, Ont., had been an AAA-level hockey player in his mid-teens when one day in 1975 his right skate caught in a rut. His leg twisted savagely and the bones in his leg were shattered into about fourteen pieces. Doctors patched him together like a jigsaw puzzle and he returned to the game he loved but for the rest of his career on skates, the leg and especially his knee would be subject to constant abuse and pain.

But Rosen had a passion for the game. He learned every job there was in hockey, from player to coach to scout to manager. He helped to put together a national team for Israel, has coached three different teams for that country and is coach of the Canadian standing amputee hockey team.

In 1996, in Belgrade, Yugoslavia, Rosen was Israel's assistant coach when he encountered a young Kazakhstan-born player, Max Birbraer. Rosen recognized talent, Birbraer was a strong skater and the top scorer for the Israeli junior team, but also saw Birbraer's lack of opportunity. His coach played him up to 56 minutes a game, but even with that ridiculous amount of ice time no one with hockey connections would ever see him playing in the Middle East.

Rosen persuaded the boy's parents to allow him to be Max's guardian and brought him to Canada in 1997. He mentored him, trained him, found him places to tryout and to play. Ultimately, all that raw talent Rosen had seen came out. Max blossomed as a Tier

Two Ontario junior scorer and was a third-round draft pick of the New Jersey Devils in 2000.

During Max's rapid rise, Rosen's old injury came back to haunt him and his knee collapsed. Doctors told him there was no alternative but to have a knee replacement operation. He did that, but an infection set in, so serious that it might have cost Rosen his life. Repeated operations failed to get the problem under control, and the ultimate solution was to amputate the leg above the knee.

It was traumatic, depressing. He'd been worn down by eighteen surgeries over two years and the infection that had death looming over him. Paul Rosen had been robbed of the zest and will that had been important in his life.

Sometimes, when you unwrap a devastating hardship you discover an opportunity at the centre. Rosen needed help. Max Birbraer saw it was time to switch roles from student to mentor. Max made it his duty to return to Rosen what he had been given by the Canadian, a chance at a life through sport, a spirit to compete, a will to live.

Rosen had been a goaltender in ice hockey and ball hockey. Birbraer decided to use that aptitude and began grooming Rosen for goaltending in a sit-down version of the game, sledge hockey. It's a high-speed Paralympic sport, played in sleds, which Rosen didn't like at first. But Birbraer, unwilling to give up on his friend, shot pucks at him. Former Washington Capital Mike Marson, who runs a Tough Hockey gym, was enlisted to work on Rosen's fitness and attitude.

"I love my family, but this was something they could not help me with. The thing I needed was something I could only get from Max," Rosen said. "There will always be a bond between us. He may not have got to where he did in hockey without the things I did but I might not even have survived if not for what he did for me. I had no will to fight on."

Something clicked. "I didn't take to the sledge game ... but after the third or fourth game, I just said to myself: `You've got to get over this, man. You're alive.' "

He learned a different set of skills for the sledge game. "The biggest difference is that any puck that would hit me in the stomach in able-bodied hockey could hit me in the face in the sled," he said. He developed a lightning-fast glove hand.

After three training camps, Rosen made Canada's fifteen member national sledge-hockey squad. At age 42, he figured he was the oldest rookie in the history of the Paralympics. He played at Salt Lake City, where Canada placed fourth and vows to keep going through to the 2006 Games in Turin and, "if Vancouver wins the 2010 Winter Olympics I can think of no sweeter dream than to finish my career with a gold medal at home."

Coaches understand that if they want the best they need to appeal to the best within people. The appeal is made from a perspective of reality, which makes clear the challenges, the setbacks and the disappointments possible as well as the satisfactions and joy. The appeal is not only to the vision achieved, but the joy of the journey itself.

Catherine Garceau was a member of the bronze-medal-winning Canadian Synchronized swimming team in Sydney, in 2000. She tells this story of her coach, Sheilagh Croxon.

As a member of the 2000 Olympic team, I am grateful to have had the privilege to experience such a wonderful journey under the guidance of Sheilagh Croxon. Having joined the centralized programme in Toronto as it was established in 1998, I was a member of the Centre of Excellence team for four years.

A stern and nurturing head coach, Sheilagh excelled at the technical teaching and was also an outstanding motivator for the team. Never accepting less then perfection, she demanded more from all of us, even if she knew we were doing our best This was what brought us to our successful bronze medal performance in Sydney.

After frustrating setbacks, I remember many meetings with Sheilagh freeing me from the drama I was creating from failure. Always finding a way to leaving me inspired, her belief in my abilities as a synchronized swimmer and as a good team player encouraged me to stay positive and keep charging forward. Sheilagh sees seeking personal growth as a sign of strength. This allowed me to see that pursuing mental training was not only crucial to my success with the team, but an experience I could take with me later in life.

Although I attribute my success in making the Olympic team to my strong work ethic and my increased mental toughness, I do feel that Sheilagh was the one who opened my eyes to that possibility. She pushed me beyond the limits I had set for myself. She guided me towards finding enough confidence to be able to trust in the work I was doing.

As I embark on a new journey, the journey of life beyond synchronized swimming, I value the relationship I have built with Sheilagh and continue to go to her for advice and support. Through our growing friendship I hope to give back as much as I got, whether it be over breakfast at Cora's or lunch at the Yellow Cup Café, I can always count on a meaningful and enjoyable exchange with Sheilagh to brighten my day.

Sheilagh touched Catherine's heart with the grandest of visions and cared enough about her as a person to do two key things: guide her towards "enough confidence," and push her "beyond the limits I had set for myself." This latter is a greater act of caring than many understand. Coaches know that the greatest life-long burden a person can carry is the gnawing regret of "if only." I know how hard, both mentally and physically, these women trained and it would have been easy, many days, to say "enough." It is often that little extra, in all things we do that really matter, that makes the difference. Sheilagh knew that. It would have been both unfair and uncaring to allow them to work so hard for so long and not to have done the extra that was required to make the difference. The "extra," which they believed, at one level, they could not do, they did. It guaranteed that no matter what happened they would never doubt they had done their absolute best. They could do no more. No regrets, ever.

Not all coaches appear in person, nor are all stories about sports, but they are about victories. We met Doug Scott in Best Practice Two. Doug is an educator, coach, volunteer, father and friend. He has a doctoral degree in education and has been a college dean of students as well as an organizational consultant. Now 70, he lives in Toronto and is enjoying growing up with his ten year old son. This is his story about victory over cancer.

In February 1978, I had a nodular malignant melanoma surgically removed from my upper back. Biopsy showed it to be dangerously deep and advanced. Chances of recurrence were high, with key vital organs the most likely recurrence sites. Survival potential would be slim beyond eighteen months. Ten months later, a monitoring chest X-ray showed a tumour on my left lung. I was devastated and despondent. My only hope of survival, would be that the tumour was single, isolated, and self-contained, a rare occurrence. "You might be one of the lucky ones," my chest surgeon replied when I asked him the chances of that. That was my first ray of hope. More was to come.

In Los Angeles, a friend told me about The Center for the Healing Arts, where they had reserved for me a packet of articles on holistic practice and healing, and an audio-cassette tape for cancer patients by Dr. Carl Simonton on relaxation, meditation, and mental imaging. I picked them up immediately and began the Simonton programme. It was the Simonton tape - supplemented by the articles and books on the power of the mind/body connection and of doing all that you can to support your treatment, survival and recovery that constituted the major "coaching intervention" for me.

The audio-tape was voice-directed by Dr. Simonton himself, which provided great credibility and confidence for me. In it he explained, simply and briefly, the function and power of the immune system. This was followed by a relaxation induction, then a mental imaging exercise visualizing strong, aggressive, active white blood cells surrounding and containing the tumour. I had seen my tumour on my chest x-ray, so I knew its size, shape, and precise location. My "Simonton" exercise repeated faithfully three times per day, plus my daily three mile run up the road of a nearby small mountain, my very healthy diet, combined with my readings of articles, helped me build my "holistic" strength - mind, body, emotions, and spirit, and to return to Toronto prepared and determined to go through all the cancer detection tests free and clear, to have successful surgery, and to go on with my life with new resolution, all of which I did.

In the 25 years since then, whenever physicians, cancer/melanoma specialists or dermatologists hear about my survival, they respond with disbelief and awe. They often refer to this as a medical miracle. This length of survival for a metastasized melanoma to the lung is unheard of in their clinical experience. The part my holistic approach to that health crisis 25 years ago played in my physical survival - or whether I was simply blessed with a phenomenally strong and effective immune system that kept the tumour and cancer cells contained and in check, is a subject of some speculation and debate.

What I know with certainty is that the "Simonton" coaching, through his book, Getting Well Again, and his audio-tape provided me with inspiration, direction, technique, confidence, and positive expectation and determination. Dr. Carl Simonton saw the possibilities in people and in the new holistic approach that he helped pioneer; one which celebrates inner strength and possibilities. His book and audio tapes made his work and dedication available beyond his personal patients. For a number of years after my own ordeal and recovery, I did volunteer work passing this information and approach on to cancer patients.

I had the pleasure of meeting Carl Simonton a few years after my cancer ordeal and found him to be a courageous and passionate professional who cared deeply about helping people mobilize their resources to battle cancer and to do their very best to overcome it.

Coaches, in their hearts, know what is humanly possible and it is more "unbelievable" than most can accept. They know that the process of achieving these grand human possibilities starts in the heart. Carl Simonton is a deeply caring doctor.

Peter Warren is a retired physical educator and school administrator who spent his entire career at Riverdale Collegiate in Toronto.

In 1970 I had the pleasure of coaching a talented football team. One of our captains, our quarterback, usually led the warm up drills. In the quarter final game he injured his throwing arm. During practice the following week while preparing for the semi-final game, I told him not to throw or use his right arm extensively. One night at practice while leading the warm up drills he asked the players to do twenty push-ups. He waited for them to start but they only watched and waited for him to lead the way. He proceeded to get down in push up position and do twenty one-arm push ups using his left arm! The team followed his lead and we went on to win the championship. Some men lead by word and some lead by example!

All great leaders develop other leaders. It is no surprise that young men in Peter Warren's programme at Riverdale C.I. tended to lead by example. Always quiet and soft spoken, Peter has always been there when someone was needed to show the way. Peter was like that when I first met him in 1956. He continues in that way today.

Mike Badour is married to Mary-Ellen McIntosh and they have three incredible boys, Carter, Cameron, and Ryan. A successful transformational executive, now with Canada Post, Mike is a true believer in "Coaches change Lives."

I had the opportunity to coach one of our managers, who blamed everyone else for his problems. Our systems didn't work, our management team was not supportive, they want us do more work, this strategy does not work, etc. You know the type. I offered that it does not take a particularly wise man to stand on a soapbox, and point fingers. In fact it is easy to do. Our value as leaders is to provide solutions, instil confidence and lead by vision regardless of our conditions. As one would expect, his team was combative, they were last in our metrics and the overall morale was not good. I explained that the results of his team were a direct reflection of his happiness as a leader. He had to make a choice of changing the way he led, or changing where he lead. I suggested he could be a strong positive leader and that I would be there to coach him should he decide to lead here.

He reflected and took the challenge of changing the way he led. He committed to excellent leadership and being open to coaching. He read all about leaders, practiced what he learned, and not surprisingly, his team changed. They became collaborative, competitive and leaders in our organization. Such dramatic successes take an immense amount of day-to-day effort. When asked about the key difference that made him and his team successful, he selected two: His personal commitment to learning and change, and growing out of that, time spent communicating.

Previously it was evident that this manager's lack of commitment had been transferred to his team. Instead of creating an environment of opportunity, he created mundane positions; instead of possibilities he had created problems. The end result was a poor experience for all. His change to leading positively, with passion and caring, in both speech and actions, created an immediate turnaround.

The change was time spent focusing on what Robin Sharma calls "the worthy," communicating. The manager previously had spent 5% of his time communicating with his team. He changed that to 30% communication. No wonder the turnaround was so dramatic. Simple things that are tough to do but they are leadership.

Coaching is based on relationships and we need to spend time with people to create them. We need to let them know we really care about the work we both do by expressing our passion for it. We need, by listening to them and acting for them, to let people know we care about them as individuals. The old cliché, "People don't care how much you know until they know how much you care" is a great truth to remember.

Victor Lopez's high school coach had the influence he did because he spent a lot of time with the youngster, first in what engaged him, the sport and then in conversations about life and possibilities. Coaching is effective in "changing lives" because a good deal of time is invested in being with a person, communicating and caring.

Mike Badour saw the possibilities in his manager, made clear the options and offered full support if the manager chose to make the growth choice. That is leading from the heart, seeing people as they can be, caring enough to let them know the possibility and the alternative, and supporting them in the challenging process of achieving the possibility.

Tricia Clarke is a former intercollegiate basketball player who founded and coaches the Charisma Cowgirls, a basketball experience for young women that is run from a community centre in downtown Toronto. Tricia's programme works with the whole person.

Getting all the logistics in place for this new programme was an interesting task, but no challenge. The first real challenge arrived at try-outs in the name of Diana, the essence of what my programme is all about. She was new to Toronto and Canada and felt isolated. She reacted to each emotional stressor with verbal explosions. She was not a skilled basketball player but she tried her hardest, even arguing with the coaches and other players in loud, aggressive ways. When team selection time arrived I was uncertain about what to do even though I knew Diana deserved a chance. She was going to need attention and support; but don't we all? I named her to the roster and began the process of getting to know her.

Diana is a remarkable young woman. She came to Canada to be with her father who quickly kicked her and her sister out of the new family home. Diana decided to live in a shelter temporarily until she could get on her own feet. In a short time she moved into an apartment with her sister and continued to practice, work at two jobs, and go to school. That experience alone would have broken the spirit of the average teenager, but Diana was not average.

Over the summer she continued to work out with the team and position herself to be ready for the try-outs in the fall. Diana's deep determination was her great asset, on and off the court. Today she is confident and stable, flourishing in the supportive environment of the Charisma Cowgirls team family and elsewhere. Today Diana speaks of college and starting her own business, and taking risks to achieve her aspirations.

The programme and its coaches had a huge impact on Diana because it gave her the chance to belong to a group of people who became her friends and an extended team family. It allowed her to feel special and cared for. It helped her accept that she was capable of learning new skills on and off the court. She came to feel she belonged and that people liked her and cared for her.

Recently we honoured athletes and sponsors at our first "Girlballers Hall of Fame" ceremony. Diana was one of the four players recognized for her significant contribution to the team during the first two years. She had to rush from work for the ceremony and was shocked to find she was an inductee. I was pleased and amazed to watch her excitement and her big smile as she accepted her award. Nothing is better than watching a young person like Diana actively pursue her dreams and goals as a confident student-athlete.

In an article in the local newspaper, she referred to my associate coach Jason and myself as her guardian angels. In truth all I had done was shed my own fears, and accept the challenge to consider what was best for that unsure and scared young girl who wanted to be part of a team and enjoy the game. Neither of us knew, then, the personal growth journey she would embark upon to become a self-loving, confident young woman.

Graham Daniel, with his wife Wilma, lives in Durban, South Africa. Both are top athletes who represented their country internationally. They now coach athletes from junior to international levels in swimming and triathlon. For more about these coaches and their programme: www.mrpricesport.com.

We continue to have wonderful experiences with athletes of various ages and abilities. The most significant factor about our job though, is that we never have the same day twice. Our "work," if you can call it that, is always a new discovery as we lead athletes down the path to adulthood, to personal growth and to high levels of achievement. The flipside of this is that we sometimes see jealousy of athletes' achievements and ridicule by their non-sporting peers. Success is not admired and respected by everyone - some are threatened by it. This is a part of their development and is a key lesson for committed athletes. They have to place all of their life into perspective.

What is most remarkable is seeing athletes who are overcoming significant obstacles in their lives. One such athlete is a young Downs Syndrome swimmer, Jennifer Higgins who was encouraged to swim for therapeutic reasons. After researching all the necessary background precautions regarding exercise and Downs pupils we accepted Jennifer into our programme. She was eighteen years of age but swam with our junior group. Jennifer progressed fairly quickly and we were able to move on to training. However, she required much attention to swim the strokes according to the rules in order not to be disqualified when competing.

Jennifer was not able to tell us how or what she may have been feeling, she just swam. She did not fully understand the "set instructions" but did all she could with enthusiasm and enjoyment. She continued this to a level where she was competitive within her squad and then went on to swim in the various disabled competitions. For local galas she competed in the normal "open" division. She continued her improvements and ascended the ladder of success to medals at the World Disabled Games. Jennifer was accepted by the athletes as just another swimmer. She was treated no differently and rose to the challenge of being a swimmer. In her eyes, I believe, she saw herself as a swimmer and the same as everybody else. It reinforced what my wife and I believed: Do not "pigeon-hole" or neglect athletes who don't meet our "standard norms." Their achievements can be just as significant as anyone else's.

Lindo (Stanley) Shandu is a young African male who we introduced into our triathlon programme after he showed interest in the sport at our local triathlon. He comes from a background of nothing. To explain his circumstances is superfluous, as he had NOTHING. His father left his mother, his mother worked as a housemaid earning less than R50 a day (the price of a meal) while she had a family to support. A racing bike, shoes, clothes, caps and goggles were well outside the budget of this household. We stepped up and took Stanley on board as a full member of our squad, providing him with all the necessary equipment. He was the only black African in our squad, and indeed in triathlon in South Africa, at the time. His courage and determination to stay with the programme was compounded by the fact that he had to run to school daily (5km one-way) then ride his bike to the training session (12km one-way,) then train and be on a par with his fellow squad members for a full training session. Consider too that his nutrition was sub-standard and we were often sending food home to help with his increased nutritional needs while training and growing up.

The culmination of his dedication was a bronze medal at the South African Triathlon Championships in his age group, in a very competitive field. When asked what his proudest achievement to date has been, he said, "to be the first black African to compete in triathlons." He is paving the way for future athletes entering the sport and as a pioneer has to experience these hardships personally. He continues to train with us and now, with a scholarship, is writing his final school exams and winning events in cross-country and athletics. He is an integral part of our squad and is a major force on the local racing circuit

Gail Donohue is a former National Team synchronized swimmer, the Olympic Coach for New Zealand in 1984, a sport administrator, and a mother of four. Gail is now the Director of the National Coaching Institute Vancouver

Swimming competitively as a young girl, my coaches could make my day or break it. As an adult, I know that my own attitude, the one I choose, will make my day. But at that young age, as I was learning and growing up, it was my coaches who influenced my attitude. I was lucky. I had coaches who taught me how to make my own day and gave me valuable life lessons by which to live my future life.

When I think about it now, I realize the kinds of things my coaches did. I believe the most important quality they had was that they always spoke to me from the heart. Their words and actions always seemed genuine and sincere. I felt that I could trust them and it encouraged me to work harder. I felt they supported me and not just my performance.

It did not matter if I came in fifteenth, last or first. Their concern was that I enjoyed myself. I learned something from the experience and it was another step forward. Whether I achieved a small training goal, learned a new technique, or accomplished a task that I had had trouble with, the achievement was acknowledged with encouragement and genuine excitement. A type of mini celebration, you might say, and I would feel great! These celebrations consisted of words of encouragement that demonstrated an attitude of confidence in me. Sometimes these words were expressed tangibly in a card, written words noting the hard work I had been doing or they spoke of my coach's admiration for the progress I had been making towards my goals.

Other acknowledgments involved hugs, an arm around the shoulder, a warm look with a smile. They also took time to look at me, to look directly in my eyes when they said "way to go" or "you nailed it." I also had choice within my training programme. With *this choice I was more invested in "myself," taking on my own responsibility. This made "celebrations" much more significant.*

There were struggles too. During those times, I felt that my coaches listened and asked questions. They didn't judge me. They didn't try to have an immediate fix. My coaches were patient. They waited and planted seeds of encouragement daily, in small ways. Later, when the time was right, they would suggest a new idea, a new technique or a new way of thinking about the problem. I can see now that they had given thought to my challenge.

In these ways, my coaches' actions motivated me to reach a little farther, to keep trying and live toward my dreams. They helped me learn how to make my day and now live my life.

Will Freeman is the Track and Cross Country Coach at Grinnell College in Iowa. An All-America pole-vaulter while at the University of Florida, Will has coached his teams to 21 Conference titles in 23 years at Grinnell. He teaches sport psychology and wellness at the college. Will is a regular speaker at track clinics nationally and internationally.

I met Walter Welsch when I was a young freshman at the University of Florida. I had been recruited by Jimmy Carnes to pole vault for the Gators. It was an exciting time for this young Kentucky boy who had never even been on an airplane until he flew to Gainesville to go to school.

I was immediately impressed by Walt Welsch, but I wasn't quite sure what to make of this man who always had a story, or a joke (some better than others). What I learned over time was that he would always be there for me. He was by the pit the day I first made 16', the first time I made 17' and the day I won the national junior championships in the vault at the UF track. Walt Welsch was the starter of the meet that day, and I remember him coming by the pit afterward and saying "I knew all along you would win this thing." Just another vote of confidence, and I believed him when he said it. He was a lot more confident than I that day. It wasn't just that he was my pole vault coach at UF, he took an interest in me as a person, and he saw talent in me that I didn't.

I came to know many facets of the man, as a coach, an employer (I lifeguarded for him at a private swim pool he managed), and as a teacher (I took several of his classes at UF). Over the seven years I spent in Gainesville I was part of a special circle of people involved with the pole vault, but Walt Welsch was unique. He always made me feel like I was the most special athlete on the track or in his classroom. I truly enjoyed being with him. There were many who knew more about vaulting, but few who would impact me the way he did. He simply cared about me the person, and not just me the vaulter.

I eventually went into teaching and coaching and I have always tried to measure myself against what I saw in Walter Welsch: teach with passion, care about the person, make time for people, and be a friend. There are no better goals as a teacher and coach. When the athletic experience is over, what is left is the friendship and respect...and thanks. I honour and respect Walt Welsch. I couldn't have had a better coach, or friend. He knew that because I told him.

Make sure you tell those who matter to you how you feel about them. The great lessons we learn cannot be bought with money, they come from the heart. Share it

Will trained with me at the University of Toronto for a year, but he didn't come for my coaching. His heart brought him here for a deeper reason. He had met Evelyn Oljans, a high jumper I coached, at the Florida Relays, and came to be with her. I was best man at their wedding.

I hold you in the same regard as I did Walt Welsch. You were there for me when I needed someone during my year in Toronto. That was a bit of a tumultuous time for me but the image of you as a coach sticks with me to this day. You were knowledgeable, caring, and always provoking me to grow. I thank you for that. You have been a wonderful model for another humanistic coach who has to live in an athletic environment that is loaded with social comparisons and other external motivations that only detract from one's potential and internal experience. It was good for me to have that year at U of T and to see sport done in a healthy manner. We haven't forgotten. Our programme models what you did at U of T and our athletes prosper in many more ways than just as athletes. We coach from the premise that it is about creating stronger people, not just faster runners. It is healthy and it works. They tell us in so many ways after they leave. I thank you for giving us that.

What I gave, had been given to me by many remarkable men and women. I cannot begin to name all who gave from their heart to me, who shared their passion for personal growth, personal excellence and personal achievement. They cared deeply about me, and everyone they worked with. It seemed the natural way to coach.

Julia Warren is the High Performance Director for Manitoba Synchronized Swimming, a coach in the National Team programme, she is Head Coach of the Junior Team in 2003, a graduate of the first class of the National Coaching Institute Ontario and a passionate leader of young women.

I will never forget the look on their faces. Barrelling towards me, soaking wet, a little slimy from the gelatine that was dripping down their necks, and delirious with excitement... "Oh my god", they shrieked, "that was amazing, Jules, we get it!"

This was a team I had not intended to coach, a team I took over at mid season. They where low in confidence, to say the least, only moderately skilled and very negative about themselves as a group. Actually, they were not really a group at all, and had little belief that it was possible for them to succeed nationally.

There was so much to do and so little time in which to do it. I decided to focus on three keys - process, accountability, and pushing for a moment of unison that would be so powerful it would be fun to perform. I had to get them to believe they could improve by ten places to be in the top ten in Canada. I believed there was only one way to do it: expect the highest standard of behaviour and performance as individuals and as a team, both in the water and out of it.

They did not want to accept responsibility for poor behaviour, failure to follow through, or less than useful behaviour towards each other. I was aware that each time I confronted them there was the potential for someone to not be able to handle the feedback and throw in the towel. Yet somehow they took it and they kept coming back. Just when I thought they might break they would make the next performance jump and gain confidence. They almost grudgingly kept rising to the expectation that they could compete with the top teams that they could perform to a high standard of excellence.

In the lead up to Nationals we had enjoyed some success but had one rather disappointing meet in our home pool. It was a challenging setback to have one month before the nationals, but I knew I had to continue to push for quality, accountability to our daily practice objectives, to encourage the girls to treat each other with respect, and to support commitment to the season's goal.

It was a never-ending siege - Jules, why do we have to do this? Jules, this warm up is too hard, Jules, are you sure we will ever catch up to the others? And I refused to be anything but positive. Yes, Yes, Yes!

They were so unsure that all of this was worth it. They doubted they could do it. I knew they could and I expected only the best from them. In the end that is exactly what I got. In five months this group of girls became a team, and the number three team in Canada.

They felt the power of striving for the highest standard as a team. They felt the rush of accomplishment and the reward of seeing their work come together. They loved every minute of that championship performance. They had become a team of young ladies each of whom had, only months ago, believed they could not trust the others to go the distance. But they did. First they learned to trust themselves, individually and then they began to trust each other. They let go of the fear of losing, and stepped up to what was expected of them and performed. It was magic for me as a coach; pure magic to hear "Thank you so much, we get it...."

And I learned a valuable coaching lesson: You do get exactly what you expect.

Yes, you always get what you expect when you lead from the heart. Coaches see the grand possibility for the whole person and in the end it is the person who matters. It is the heart of a coach that really challenges the heart of the learner, which is why it is felt so deeply, and felt to be safe. It is a rare one of us who has not experienced or witnessed something similar to what Julia just related.

From another culture, a half world away, Graham Daniel has the same thing to say. Cultures are different, habits are different, situations are different but the human heart is the same in everyone everywhere.

One experience that has been a lesson for me, as a coach, happened after we held a "Back-to-Basics" training camp. We took the athletes in to the mountains and gave them tasks and challenges to complete in very trying and difficult circumstances. While the whole scenario was controlled and monitored the athletes felt hard-done-by, but they survived and made it through the week. The tasks had little to do with their actual sport but to this day the athletes still refer to that camp with fondest memories. The lesson for me was that when the work is the most difficult, it is also the most rewarding. Athletes need not fear hard work and coaches need not fear giving their athletes hard work, because they will rise to the challenge.

Hard work and challenges are essential to our human nature and people thrive on it when it is felt to be in their best interests. Kids choose this all the time when left to their own devices. They also choose it in situations, in fact we all do, when we sense that the challenge comes from the heart of the leader be it the parent, teacher, sport coach or business manager. If the passion, for whatever the challenge, is about our experience, our growth, and our satisfaction, and not just that of the leader, we will attempt "the impossible dream." Coaches lead from the heart and that is why they change lives and achieve grand possibilities with and for people.

Seven Keys to Leading from the Heart

1. Express your caring about people.

2. Be passionate about the activity or competency.

3. Show that whole person health and happiness are most important.

4. Act with courage and conviction regarding what is best for the other.

5. Celebrate successes. Support experiencing the joy in the process.

6. Create circumstances if they do not exist – act boldly.

7. Express feelings honestly and appropriately – and move on.

Best 6 Practice

KNOWS THE PATH

Best Coaches know the path and understand
that success is determined by the individual's willingness
to learn and grow as a person who performs.

"...if the path has a heart it is your path."
~ Carlos Casteneda

A s coaches we see grand possibilities. We see individuals as they can be. We lead with passion and care, assuming the responsibility for positive change. We know the path to personal excellence. We know how to support people to move them safely and effectively towards that grand vision. It is never straightforward or easy. The path of excellence is always challenging, but with wisdom similar to that imparted by Castaneda, the best coaches know the value of and support choosing a path with heart.

Coaches know the outer path, the path our talent must follow to become all it can be, the path of student, athlete, artist, artisan, educator, businessperson, scientist, whatever our talent and our heart must express. Coaches are effective teachers who bring all we need to learn to move forward. When necessary they access other experts to complement their own strengths.

Philippe Voissard began coaching in the Laurentian University swim programme in Sudbury, Ontario before he even graduated. His coaching and life philosophy have been influenced significantly by the Toltec teachings, an ancient tradition of whole person self-actualization. Since 2002 he has been teaching English in South Korea. He tells us about working with a key issue on the path of personal success.

Often, my swimmers would focus so much on the outcome of a situation (winning/losing, getting what they were hoping for or not getting what they were hoping for) that they would not be able to focus on the moment and the task at hand. At these times, they would be filled with fearful thoughts and feelings of inadequacy that would sometimes paralyze them and irrevocably lead them to underperforming. To overcome these ineffective feelings, I would remind them that the only thing they have is THEIR BEST. This means that after you have accounted for all the things you control and the ones you do not control in the battle you are facing, you do your best with the things you control and forget about the ones you do not control, because all you have is your best.

Doing your best in this context means that when you look back on your actions you will be proud of yourself. You will not regret or be ashamed of a single action regardless of the end result. Only you can be the judge of the quality of your effort. You know when you have done your best and you also know when you have done less than your best.

When you look back at your performance, you will gain knowledge about it that you did not have before. You must take the challenge, do your best, review your performance and apply what you have learned in order to move your best to another level.

You need to perform at your best effort to learn what you need to learn. Do your best at all times with the knowledge you have available at the moment. You will find out that your best becomes better with practice.

Coaches know the inner path and all its potential obstacles. We know that it is this path on which the greatest challenges will arise and the greatest possibilities exist. Coaches know that mental/emotional limitations will be encountered long before we come to limitations of our talent. They have seen the impact of limiting beliefs, doubt, fear, loss of confidence and faith in the plan, and failures of courage and will. Coaches make it clear from the outset that these are our greatest obstacles and the source of our greatest learning. Success is possible if we are prepared to accept reality and commit to the process.

Harry Neale, now with *Hockey Night in Canada*, shares a revealing story from the period when he coached the Vancouver Canucks. Faith and will can get blurred when we must do what needs to be done repeatedly, often when we are tired or at less than our best. This is life on any path of excellence.

I was faced with the reality of 80 to 100 practices a year and that interest and energy are tough to maintain. I decided to split our team into pairs (excluding the goalies) and challenged each pair to plan and execute a practice of at least 60 minutes made up of nine to twelve different drills. Each pair had to give me a written practice plan the day prior to their assigned session. I promised a portable color television to the two players who ran the best workout.

I scheduled the first player led practice session in early November and assigned about two a month at convenient times during our schedule. The programme was a huge success. Each practice got better, more intense, and more competitive as the season wore on. The players loved them.

As a bonus, I learned many new and useful drills for future regular workouts. I often referred to the drill by the names of the players who had first used it during their session. Executing a drill that came from their teammates seemed to create renewed enthusiasm. Being identified with the drill always pleased the named players.

The entire team learned to plan and execute a meaningful practice, which is not an easy task. For these highly paid and widely recognized athletes, the little presentation ceremony in which the television was awarded was a highlight of the season.

Interesting how a bit of whim improved our season. Years later when I would run into many of these players it was rewarding to hear how they remembered this aspect of the season as being interesting, useful, and fun.

Coaches understand that no matter how passionate we may be about our talent, music, academic pursuits, athletics or anything else, it is not our life. It is an aspect of our life. Our life is our relationship with ourselves and with those closest to us. Who we are is far more significant than what we do. And here is the paradox: When the emphasis is on personal development through self-awareness, the talent, performance, success, and what we do, become natural outcomes. Coaches teach us early that the more important the goal the more important it is to focus on the process, on self-awareness and to act on that awareness.

Through his coach, Pat Bolger, one of the very best wrestlers and judokas in the world, journeyed on a voyage of discovery inside his mind. To Pat's surprise and delight he discovered inner strengths and wisdom.

This incredible life lesson was given to me in my very first World Championships of Wrestling. I was nervous in anticipation of the draw to see who I would compete against. The most advantageous draw obviously would be to fight in the first two rounds against inferior countries allowing a gradual building of confidence for the "hot shots" in the championship. The "luck of the draw" as they say, was not with me that day! I drew the ultimate hot shot of my weight class, the World Champion!

By the end of the first round I had been totally dominated. I did not score one point! My coach advised me that this Russian champion was only human, just like me, and that I could beat him. At the end of the second round I still had not scored on him. I was experiencing a mental block. The concept of "beating the World Champion" seemed so large I was totally intimidated and inactive.

Anticipating the third and final round, my coach said, "Pat, all I want from you is one takedown! Take that Russian down once for me! This narrowed my focus to something totally realistic and attainable. The concept of "beating the World Champion" at this early stage of my career seemed insurmountable, but the coach's suggestion of this small step of achievement seemed real to me, and therefore 100 % achievable! I took the Russian down with relative ease. I did not win the match but it left me with the distinct belief that if I could do it once, I could do it again and again!

In my competitive career, whenever I allowed myself to be influenced by the reputation of an opponent or event, I became intimidated and lost. However, when I focused on a step-by-step plan of attack, I won! Why? We have all heard the familiar phrase "When you truly believe, you will succeed. "So, why not break down the unachievable to small fragments of success that ultimately led to victory?

Years later, in the World Judo Championship, I fought the Olympic bronze medallist who was from Russia. He fired me through the air with his favourite technique dropping me on to my right shoulder and causing it to separate. Fortunately, adrenalin flow was such that I felt little pain. I was focused on the particular position my opponent happened to be in and not on his obvious dominance of the fight. It was a position that left him vulnerable, prompting my counter attack. At that precise moment, time seemed to stand still remembering that lesson of focus and belief. My counter attack was enough to win the match! Thanks Coach!

My very good friend, the late Jack Donohue, the legendary basketball coach always told his players that it was more important to be a good person than a good basketball player. He pointed out that they would be a person a lot longer than a basketball player. And he meant it, and they believed it, and of course their human qualities made them better players!

For the last 28 years Steve Konchalski has been Head Coach of the St. Francis Xavier men's basketball team in Antigonish, Nova Scotia. Steve was assistant coach to Jack Donohue with the Canadian National team from 1973 to 1988. He has coached at three Olympic Games, (1976, 1984, 1988) and has won three CIS National titles with St. FX (1993, 2000, and 2001).

The Men's Olympic Basketball Qualification Tournament in Montevideo, Uruguay, in May 1988 marked national team head coach Jack Donohue's last summer with Team Canada. After 17 successful seasons (the longest serving National Coach in Canada) during which time his teams qualified for three Olympic Games, Coach "D" was planning retirement and was down to his very last game. Our opponent was Uruguay, in Uruguay, in front of 12,000 rabid and emotional fans, a team that had beaten us in the first round.

This was not only Coach Donohue's last game, but also the last for several of our veteran players. We had two opportunities to qualify for Seoul, but the night before we lost a heartbreaker to Puerto Rico at the buzzer after letting a substantial lead slip through our fingers.

We had a day off before that final Uruguay game and had an early morning practice scheduled. As the players dragged themselves onto the bus, the question ran through my mind, how was Coach Donohue going to bring this team back up and make them believe they could win this one last game in the most hostile of environments?

When we got to the gym I found out. Instead of a typical pre-game preparation type of practice with scouting reports, walk-throughs, and so forth, Jack ran his charges through a full hour of "fun" drills, shooting competitions, dribble-tag, and big men vs. little men. All were designed to put the tough Puerto Rico loss behind us and remind the team of the times we had enjoyed together over the years. By the time we left the practice facility everyone was laughing and smiling and very up-beat!

Over the next 24 hours some amazing things began to happen. Players began posting messages to the team on the trainer's hotel room door. Letters and poems appeared expressing how much we cared about each other and how no one could prevent us from achieving our goal of qualifying for one last Olympic Games!

The game itself was a blur. Canada took a commanding early lead, which resulted in the out-of-control crowd hurling objects onto the court and creating havoc. Nothing could stop us that night. The biggest challenge we had was leaving the gym without getting hurt by the debris.

We were now off to one more Olympics! The unique strategy employed by the Master Coach was successful in creating an atmosphere that allowed the team to put the devastating loss of the previous game behind us and brought out all the qualities of togetherness that he had been building over many years.

As Coach Donohue used to say, "Coach people not players."

As I was preparing this section, I witnessed one of the most magnificent athletic performances ever by a Canadian. I watched with a lump in my throat and, at times, moisture in my eyes as Mike Weir won the 2003 Masters Tournament. The next morning I read his comments about his incredible shots over the last few holes when he had to make every one of them to force a play-off. "I kept reminding myself this was just a putt. That a six iron is just a six iron." And as the world saw he succeeded admirably in doing just that, keeping his focus on the process.

Deryk Snelling is a legend in coaching circles. Between 1964 and 1996 Deryk coached 75 swimmers to Olympic teams and they won 23 medals! And he says, "but most of all, the great thing is and has always been the fun and challenge offered me. Deryk now works with Swim Canada as a mentor to developing coaches.

Three one-hundredths of a second was the difference between first and second place. For Mark Tewksbury to consider Olympic gold in 1992 in Barcelona, he would have to increase his speed by only .03 of a second.

Mark was swimming well for many years before winning Olympic Gold. In fact he was ranked no worse than fourth in the world in the 100m Backstroke, for over five consecutive years prior to Barcelona.

After the 1988 Seoul Olympics where Mark had won Silver, leading off for Canada in the 4x 100m Medley Team, we didn't feel completely satisfied as we had not medaled in the individual event. We both came home from those Games with an idea that we must really get tougher and do things much better than in the previous four years leading into Seoul if we were to win four years later in Barcelona.

We went into Russia and trained with the top swimmers in Moscow and in Sakumi at their top National Center down in Georgia. We introduced altitude training in Los Alamos, New Mexico at 7200ft to our programme and trained with the toughest Australian coach Laurie Lawrence and his team on the Gold Coast in Queensland, Australia. In fact, we did everything that we felt would make it possible to win.

In 1990 the World Championships were held in Perth Australia. We felt that we would know better how we were progressing in our goal to win in Barcelona from the way we swam in Perth. The 100m was a great race for Mark and he won the Silver, losing the Gold by a mere .03 of a second, to current World Record holder Jeff Rouse of the USA. From that moment on we left no stone unturned to prepare over the next two years.

One thing we worked on was racing more back-to-back meets where we could swim against as many of the worlds best swimmers as possible. In 1991 at the Pan Pacific Games in Edmonton, Mark again swam in the final of the 100m against Jeff Rouse and was beaten into second place once again. The difference this time though, was that I had worked Mark really hard leading into the meet and he found it tough, trying so hard to win without being properly rested and prepared. I felt that it would be best to do all the heavy work in the year before the Olympics and not compromise at all.

With a year to go I felt really good about our chances after the work we had done in 1990 and 1991, and the main thing was to stay confident, relaxed and fast. We did this by racing hard and doing a lot of world record setting swims in the Short Course meets; Mark broke the World record 6 times from 1990 to 1992 while racing fast with no compromise in the training.

When we got to the Olympics in 1992 everything was set for a great rematch with Jeff Rouse. Mark's heat was good and so was Jeff's. The final was a race of Rouse's super kicking technique and terrific speed, against Mark's fitness and the mental toughness he had built up in the past four years since his first Olympics in Seoul. Rouse led from the gun with Mark staying close and it was in the last 10m that Mark held his pass and had to wait until Rouse started to tire. On the last arm stroke Mark drew even and with a great lunge he was home first by an amazing .03 of a second, an exact reverse of two years earlier at the Worlds in Australia. Mark was never in front during the whole race, until the last six inches.

Those three 100ths made all the difference for Mark and gave him not only a Gold medal but the self satisfaction and rewards due for an unbelievable effort over a very long time, plus a feeling of immortality with the inclusion of his name in Canadian history.

For most of us, for most of the time, Olympic gold is not the object of the quest. In fact, that is true for the vast majority of people in sport, even those who train seriously over many years. Coaches know that the nature of "the quest," the seeking and struggling to achieve a noble goal, whatever it may be, is essential to all of us. Sometimes, it can be as simple as the satisfaction of being a part of a team, of contributing to the success of your friends, and the work required, relative to age and situation is just as arduous and just as rewarding.

Dave Cooper, is a parent, a sport consultant, a tennis pro for eighteen years, a writer and a lecturer on how to get Optimum Sport Experiences and results. For more on Dave go to www.mlsports.ca. Dave tells us how an elementary school coach allowed him to walk the path of belonging and success.

As a young athlete and student I wanted to be a part of my peer group. Unfortunately in grade eight most of my friends were interested in basketball and with me being all of 4' 2" I was a little out of my league.

I decided to try anyway and be around my buddies for the tryouts. For two weeks I rose at 5:30 a.m. and my dad dropped me off at a friend's house to go to 6:30 practice. With thirteen kids trying out and me struggling to get baskets over my taller friends - although being friends they tried to help me score - I knew the writing was on the wall.

Final selections day came and I was called into the coach's office. With sweaty palms and a racing heart I was trying to hold back the tears knowing the "cut" was coming. My coach said, "Coop, I need a team manager and with your commitment to this team over the past two weeks you're my guy. What do you think?"

I was ecstatic. Over the next months I handled all the manager duties, getting practice set up, water, everything that was needed. The real neat part was the coach drove a Corvette and for away games I got to ride with the coach! Well we ended up winning the York Region Championship and were awarded medals on stage in front of the whole school...yes I was the last called up and received mine as well.

I became a Professional tennis coach and a motivational writer. I still remember how my coach found a "spot" on the team for me. He could have easily "cut" me and over time I would have gotten over it - but he didn't, he believed in me as a person and that is what all coaches need to remember.

Mark Tewksbury's quest for swimming gold led him down the path of mental toughness to which Deryk Snelling referred. Pat Bolger traveled the path of greater personal awareness and confidence while working arduously for years to be one of the best wrestlers and one of the best Judokas, in the world! The coach must be familiar with the chosen path of technical excellence, from parenting to teaching to running a business or developing young boys and girls to become men and women of extreme competence in sport.

William Motti lives in Antibes, France, with his wife, Valerie and his nine year old daughter. He teaches sport to elementary school children. He was one of the top decathletes in the world for many years, finishing fifth in Los Angeles at the age of twenty. William loved everything about competition with his worthy opponents and friends. His father was an outstanding athlete and a physical educator. He was a first best coach in every way possible and knew what to do with a gifted youngster. This is the greatest challenge of all, to coach our own children and not be living through them, to need and expect too much too fast. This is the scourge of children's sport. William's father did exactly the opposite, exactly what is needed for all children.

My father was my coach since I started track at eleven. He didn't want me to train hard when I was young, actually up to junior (at age eighteen), to let my skills improve naturally. We trained only twice a week with very much emphasis on doing things right very early to achieve a good technique to be able to improve correctly. He made me practice all the events except pole vault with which he was unfamiliar. At fifteen, I was national champ in high jump 1m94, and javelin 58m84, plus the combined event. At sixteen, I was national champion in high jump 2m08 and discus 47m50, plus the combined event. At seventeen, again in high jump 2m19, shot 17m15, and discus 48m, plus the combined event. At eighteen, my first year as a junior it was the same with high jump 2.22m, javelin 70m38, and decathlon. I tell this just to show that we always worked on technical works and different events, without specialization too early, to keep having fun at the track, to prepare the future career. My father didn't want me to be what he called "old" (tired) too young, so I was active in different sports, like European hand ball, to complete the conditioning I was not doing on the track. In this way, at eighteen, I was able to garner 7800 points in the decathlon, threw javelin over 70m and jumped 2.22m.

My father always insisted on one attempt in the different events as long as the goal was achieved or close. For example, I would long jump and if the first jump was good, I'd stop. He thought it would be a loss of energy and a risk of injury to continue. The jump might improve or not and if not, I wasted over an hour of energy. Doing this a couple of times during a decathlon left me be in greater shape for the other events. In the 1984 Olympics in Los Angeles I did only one long jump and one discus throw, and I broke my record and the Olympic record with 50m92. I already did great, no point to try for more. Not enough chance to do better. It was smarter to rest, while the others get tired running after a score. I did that in many competitions during my career. I applied what I was taught since very young, now I try to transfer all that I learned from my different coaches to the athletes I train now.

Charles Cardinal is Université de Montreal professor agrege, Federation Internationale de Volleyball Instructor, and a Coaching Association of Canada Course Conductor and Consultant. Charles has been an outstanding coach and mentor to generations of athletes and coaches and is an inductee to the Volleyball Canada Hall of Fame.

One year at the Nationals we did not qualify for the Final Four. There was much bickering and finger pointing. Once back home, I wrote this proposal. As we did every year, we got together to wrap up the season. I handed out what I had written and a group session followed which turned things around for the team. The environment became healthier and more conducive to the pursuit of excellence from then on.

Charles wrote three full pages outlining each of the key qualities required to become "National Champion" and discussed it in detail. I have edited it in the interests of space.

To become NATIONAL CHAMPION talent is essential, indispensable, vital. Talent is the corner stone on which athlete development is built. However talent alone will not cut it. It takes something extra, something has to be added in order to experience success in sport.

The will to win must permeate the athlete/team. The difference between wishing for a medal and winning often boils down to your attitude to pay the price to get there. Whatever the situation or context, pushing yourself to the limit of your capacities, never giving up, leaving everything on the court are characteristics of a strong will and a key to success. No gifts to our opponents. If our opponent wants to win they will have to deserve it and extend themselves. The word quitting is not part of our vocabulary. An athlete in the pursuit of excellence will dig inside and give a 100% effort from start to finish.

DISCIPLINE and HARD WORK are evidenced in the ability to focus on the immediate task at hand, day in, day out, and eliminate all distractions. It's the difference between going through the motions and getting the job done right. You play as you practice. There are no short cuts to success. Concentration and selective attention to the confrontation with the opponent is mandatory throughout the game. You must be alert, vigilant, the thinking wheels spinning before every serve. You must be consumed by the role you play on the team. The mandate is specific, go out, focus and do it.

TENACITY AND PERSEVERENCE means, "Hang in there." Keep plugging away. Rome was not built in a day. It's a long road, so build on small successes. One step at a time. Satisfaction comes when you can do easily today what was impossible yesterday. The will to get it right is a trait related to achievers.

ATTITUDE is everything. When life is going smoothly, everything and everybody is beautiful. However when life is rough, who or what is to blame? Do you try to pin it on someone else? Do you try to find excuses for your own performance or are you trying hard to find a solution to the problem/challenge? Attitude is not linked with talent. Success comes when your attitude is a problem solving one.

MORAL COMMITMENT. Once you have mastered basic individual and team skills it's commitment that moulds the team. To win there has to be commitment by every player to a single purpose. A common goal becomes the extension of individual aspirations. There is no number one player, no number eight or nine. The team is a whole. It is not the addition of its elements but a complex and harmonious blend of athletes striving towards victory or our best performance yet. Result is rarely because of a player's outstanding performance but more often a team effort. This requires passion, work ethic, resolve and loyalty to your teammates.

LOYALTY is essential to a team. If you are part of a team and you identify yourself as such, then you don't say anything negative about your teammates. You don't second-guess the coach. Focus on doing your job right. When we recap our performance after the game is the time for constructive criticism and dialogue to find solutions to our problem or challenge. What you see, hear and say in the locker room stays there. It is of no concern to anyone outside the team.

PRIDE. Great athletes want to excel, to be the best they can be. They are proud of their accomplishments. They hurt when they lose a match. They are never satisfied with an average performance. They always seek excellence and push themselves to the limit of their abilities. When you have the right attitude and take pride in your play, you will always be hard to beat. Opponents will have to pay the price to win. They must deserve the victory.

CONFIDENCE is the cornerstone of the mental fabric of a champion. "I CAN DO THAT" comes from building on a series of small successes. What a feeling when you are able to say, "We have done what we set out to do." It takes years of training, hard work, perseverance and a good level of competition to reach this mental state. There is no instant success in sport. Do the work and enjoy the trip of striving towards the Nationals. When you are there and you can honestly say, "I have done everything in my power to prepare for this, I'm focused on my tasks/assignment," then the results should come.

Marian Sweetnam coached the Lindsay, Ontario Lightningbolts Swim Team for eighteen years. In 1989 she was Canadian Swim Coach of the Year and in 1990 and 1993 Ontario Female Coach of the Year. Her top athlete was her daughter Nancy who was a 1992 and 1996 Olympian in the Individual Medley Events. Marian speaks of her belief in and approach to developing confidence.

My coaching philosophy has always been to encourage athletes to reach their potential by setting realistic goals and recognizing the commitment and hard work needed to accomplish them. Achievement of a small attainable goal is reinforcing, while failure to reach too high a goal sets up future failure.

I believe that athletes embrace and enhance their training programmes when they have input into the goal. The coach's responsibility is to support athletes along the path as they climb to success. Success is the greatest motivator of all. Success is achieved in a series of "baby steps" made by setting challenging, attainable, realistic goals, one at a time, climbing every rung of the ladder, to the top.

I believe swimmers should compete in their respective age group, no matter how good they are. I only let them compete at a higher level when I know they have developed the self-confidence to handle the pressure and the skill needed to experience success.

My large club consisted of an Olympian, National and Provincial Qualifiers but the majority were just regional competitors. They all developed skills that they now use in life. They learned that goal setting, commitment, and hard work were all needed to achieve success.

I never suspected at the time the impact this approach would have on their whole lives. I get feedback now that is so gratifying from both swimmers and their parents that my philosophy continues to empower them with confidence to achieve greater rewards.

It is not a coincidence that successful coaches from two different sports tell us stories of what they believe to be the basis of all success: Self-confidence! Without the confidence to go out and express our talent, success is not possible. Self-confidence is the greatest gift we can give our children and all with whom we work.

Terry Gudzowsky owns and operates a private oil company in Calgary, Alberta, and his wife Barb, who owns a fashion design company, continue to provide chauffeur and volunteer services for Chris and Jeremy's activities. Terry has a wide background in sport including as driver on the Canadian bobsleigh team, coaching and officiating at World Championships and Olympic Games. He continues to hold various positions with national and international sport bodies.

I've had the opportunity to coach many sports at many levels and the most satisfying experiences have occurred while coaching my two young sons. We encouraged our boys to participate in as many activities as they wished with the only stipulation being that they maintain their schoolwork. We've taken the attitude that if we're going to haul our kids to the rink, field, court, track, or pool, we may as well be helping out in some capacity. For the kids, the whole experience is enhanced because now mom and dad are involved in their sport. Over the years my wife and I have handled scorekeeping, timing, refereeing, managing, snack supplying, first aid, equipment, and coaching. In addition, we've learned that while countless volunteers are needed, every kid needs and deserves good coaching.

The most important factor to remember when coaching very young people is that your leadership will undoubtedly have a long lasting influence on the child's future. A coach's positive impact can provide life long encouragement to excel not only in sport, but also in other facets of life. Your contact with the child can instil the confidence required to be successful in many other pursuits.

At a meeting of the parents after one practice, we decided to enter the team in a big hockey tournament in Medicine Hat. We all agreed that it would be a fun outing for the kids and it might provide a focus for them as a team; being together for a whole weekend could create closer relationships among them and bring them closer as a team.

The great thing about travelling to a tournament of any sort is that you get to compete against new teams, meet new people, see a new place, and spend a little time away from home. One of the difficulties for organizers of this type of tournament is ensuring a somewhat equal skill level from a variety of entries drawn from an assortment of programmes. Judging by the high calibre of play in front of us, the Rangers were going to have a miserable weekend.

The coaches quickly huddled to formulate a strategy for the game. We agreed we had to keep the players occupied in the dressing room until game time. They did not need to see the games going on! Coaches Ken and Hugh reviewed only a few key details of offence and defence knowing that kids need to concentrate on a few clear tactics. I tried to focus their excitement into good play.

Before the players left the dressing room, we mentioned that this tournament was the first one for almost everyone in the room. We agreed that so far, everything was great, and that if we continued to have a good time we would remember this adventure for the rest of our lives. The players laughed when I suggested that it would be a great story that they could tell their own kids some day. More significantly, we agreed about what constituted a "good time." Even though winning the game seemed to be important, putting out our best effort was more important. We agreed that if we tried our best from start to finish, we would not be disappointed in ourselves, even if we lost the game. We would work hard individually, and we would support our teammates so that they could do the same. We agreed that the Elbow Park Rangers would win the respect of the opposition no matter what the scoreboard said. With a final rousing cheer the players headed eagerly for the ice.

Over the next sixty minutes, the parents in the stands witnessed one of the most astonishing displays of hockey by a group of kids. The Elbow Park Rangers played the game of their lives. Team play, which had rarely been seen before, was spectacular. Every player played his shift with surprising levels of enthusiasm and energy. The bench was alive with chatter, encouragement, and at times, even laughter. The players were having a "good time."

That was the only one the Rangers would win all weekend. But over three days they learned a great deal about themselves and their teammates. Players who had not previously associated with each other became pals. The more highly skilled players now involved the other players in the play. Although they probably couldn't describe it, each player knew that something pretty good had happened. It was a happy bunch that arrived back in Calgary on Sunday night.

After that weekend, the Rangers lost only one regular season game and advanced to the city divisional final, losing in the third game of a best of three series. At the team wind up party, that assorted bunch of unsure kids from October looked confident enough to go out and take on the world. One game in Medicine Hat had changed their lives.

It was not just a trip out of town that made the difference; it was a well planned and well executed trip. It began with a clear intention because the parents involved "knew the path" and when a potentially emotionally dangerous situation presented itself they adapted quickly. By creating a perfect attitude prior to the game everything was changed. The kids were given process goals that were achievable when winning seemed an unlikely possibility. As we have seen already, process goals are the path to success.

George Touliatis has been a theatre producer, director, film and TV actor, restaurant owner, stockbroker and grower of orchids. He has also been a world class sprinter and a student of humanity.

The late Elia Kazan was one of the greatest directors of stage and film in the twentieth century. Some stage and film directors coach actors, some ignore actors, some teach actors and some bully actors. Kazan was a coach, a Great Coach! I observed him working on the movie FACE IN THE CROWD featuring Lee Remick, Andy Griffith, Walter Matthau, Anthony Franciosa and Patricia Neal. He was faced with two coaching issues.

Both Griffith and Franciosa came from the New York theatre and this was their first movie experience. For a theatre actor, the first time in front of a camera can be a daunting experience. In the theatre, actors rehearse, they then set what is rehearsed and finally play what was SET. In the theatre what is called for is the "illusion" of the first time. It must appear that the actors are going through the experience for the first time. In movie acting, the "illusion of reality" by itself won't cut it. The reason is that the camera can read into an actor's mind and thoughts. Therefore absolute reality is mandatory. A film actor must have a visceral experience.

In order to keep Franciosa connected and real, Kazan played tricks with him. Accustomed to the theatre and having everything set, Franciosa was used to having his props in the same place. In one scene Franciosa wanted Griffith to sign a contract with him. The contract was Franciosa's character's meal ticket to the big time.

During each take Kazan had the prop people put the contract in a different pocket in the coat or pants thereby forcing Franciosa to "search" for his prop instead of just patently going to a set pocket and pulling out a prop. The contract became this life-changing item because of the intensity of the search for the prop. This was brilliant coaching because it kept this stage actor connected with himself.

Kazan believed Griffith did not bring enough inner intensity to his character. Being a laid back Southerner, Griffith appeared to have insufficient drive or intensity to satisfy Kazan. He was playing a country singer who was on his way to major stardom. In order to inject an edge into Griffith's performance, Kazan began querying Griffith about the whereabouts of Griffith's wife the night before. After a few mornings of this Griffith began believing that his wife was stepping out on him with one of the crewmembers. The effect on Griffith's performance was profound. He developed a distrust of everyone who dealt with him. Suspicion and disbelief began permeating his character. Kazan had coached these qualities into an actor's consciousness. Kazan's essential approach to acting is that the actor must have the life experience inside him in order to portray this on film. With Griffith he felt he had to inject suspicion into his life so that Griffith actually was suspicious. Granted this was dangerous meddling with the inner workings and life of a human being, but whoever said that acting was anything other than walking on hot coals.

Coaches find the key to enable performers to access what is in them and what is needed in the moment. The key is always appropriate to the individual and the situation. Professional Hollywood acting is not the school play, and commercial/entertainment sport is not kids hockey. The great tragedy of minor hockey in Canada is that the professional models of coaching are far from appropriate for children.

Dick Harding graduated from the University of Toronto in 1956 with a degree in engineering and a record of having been intercollegiate sprints champion for all four years. During that time he was also a member of Commonwealth, Pan Am and Olympic Teams. Dick gave back to sport for many years in various volunteer administrative capacities. He tells us how a different coach in a different activity knew him well enough to access what was within him to get the required performance.

Occasionally at track meets that often ended in a variety of relay races, I would go to Fred Foot and tell him that after all my individual events I really wasn't up to running a 440 leg (expecting, I guess, that he would urge me to reconsider and run) and he would always say "okay, we'll get someone else" which would inevitably make me suck it up and run.

The thing that I learned from these experiences was that there is always something more I can dig deep for when I think I've given it all. This has provided me with some inner strength in various real life situations when the easiest thing to do was to give in and let somebody else do it.

In both these so widely different situations the coach was acting in the best interests of the individual. The lessons were powerful and long lasting.

Louis Mendonca is the assistant coach with Canada's National Men's Field Hockey Team who says he is "totally in debt to his wife and children for allowing him to follow his dreams." Louis funds this passion with his work in Quality Performance at Boeing Canada.

The coach of my high school cricket team was an ex-major in the British Army and just the tone of his voice sent shivers down the spine of the student body, whether you were a cricketer or not. One cold winter morning I was rushing to class, late as usual from oversleeping. Suddenly I heard his thunderous voice, "MENDONCA." Immediately I thought, "Boy, I am in trouble," which was the normal reaction at this school if an authority used your surname. Quickly I checked to make sure I was wearing my school tie and blazer. Everything seemed to be in order, and as I hesitatingly approached Mr. Harris he calmly asked me if I was available to play for the team in the weekend matches.

Thus, at about twelve years of age, I found myself on my high school cricket team, which had produced many world-class athletes and was considered one of the best in the country. Cracking this line-up was indeed an amazing feat, players did not usually represent the school at this level until they were fifteen or sixteen. I was feeling good about myself. I practiced with the team all week and it was tough. The discipline on the team amazed me since I knew the character of the players away from the school atmosphere. I attributed this to the coach's iron fist rule but I was wrong.

On game day I was excited and could not wait to get started. The other team batted first and made a reasonable score. Then it was our turn to swing the willow. I went in at number seven and my mate at the crease was an established player. We played along for a few overs. Suddenly, he hit a ball to a fielder and came scampering down the wicket. It took me by surprise and I just stood there. My partner was run out. I scored twenty some odd runs and felt good in spite of the team's loss. Most of the players were disappointed except me. In my opinion I had done my job; the others did not carry their weight.

It was customary that, after the game, the rookies put away the equipment, which four of us did. No player ever left without saying good-bye to the coach, and the gesture was genuine. Mr. Harris took a few minutes to pass words of wisdom to each player about their performance or the game. When the four of us approached our coach he broke into laughter, and said, "My kids, I need to tell you a story. In a test match, I was at 49 (a score of 50 is an accomplishment) and Tom Dickerson, the star of the team, was at the other end. He ran a risky single, I gave up my wicket for him, he went on to score a century and we won." We all understood the story, especially me.

Over the next few years on the team I learned that Mr. Harris not only volunteered his time coaching, paid for all the teas and lunches during the matches and even purchased equipment for players who couldn't afford it. He was the first one at practise on the first day, which began at 6 a.m., an act that inspired the whole team to be there before him. He personally maintained the equipment. His players had the same respect for the gear and completed regular tasks without being asked.

At twelve, I never understood what contributed to our success. Looking back now, the answer seems obvious. Mr. Harris modeled and created a belief that if we put in the required work, we could accomplish anything. He also instilled in us a deep understanding that our ultimate success would be relative to the amount of individual glory one is prepared to sacrifice for the success of the team!

Bill Crothers became the best in his event in the world, and was silver medallist in 800m in the Tokyo Olympics. Bill says, "what is more important is that my athletic training and accomplishments were training for being a good citizen." For the past fifteen years he has been a member of the York Region Board of Education, the last eleven as Chair, committed to developing good citizens for tomorrow.

The Tokyo Olympic Games took place in October 1964. In the mid-1960s there were virtually no competitions in Canada beyond the middle of August, although that particular year a warm-up competition had been arranged in Vancouver. Unfortunately, the weather was quite inclement and this was before the introduction of all-weather tracks.

In September we trained at Varsity Stadium on the University of Toronto campus in downtown Toronto. I can remember playing a game of golf in Aurora one day and becoming quite concerned that I would be late for practice. I hurriedly left the golf course without finishing the last few holes. I arrived at Varsity stadium a few minutes late, feeling quite harassed and tired, and feeling sorry for myself.

All of our workouts were set by Coach Fred Foot, but some of us, quite naively, felt we could influence the nature of the workout with some subtle suggestions. So when I arrived on the track and started to warm-up I quite calmly suggested to Fred that I was feeling a little tired and asked if we were just going to be doing some gentle 200s that evening. He replied that I should just get a good warm-up and that he wanted three or four of us to run through an easy 800. Nothing hard, just an easy run. What he didn't tell me was that he had arranged with a couple of the other runners to go through a fairly quick 400 metres at race speed, and he had asked one of the quarter-milers in the club to run the last 500 metres with me with instructions that he was not to allow me to pass him.

Fred's instructions to me were to just run along with the pack, and stretch it out in the last 200 metres. The outcome was a time-trial during which I ran my fastest time of the year to date. My only faster time was the previous year while winning the U.S. Amateur Athletic Union Championships. That run set me up for a good performance a few weeks later in Tokyo.

Fred was as good a technical coach as any in those days. He was also a master of knowing how to motivate a runner, even if the runner believed he knew what he was doing. He knew I needed a good run. He knew I was ready to run a good time to boost my confidence. He knew that it would be best if it happened spontaneously, without a big build-up. He was right.

All this happened before there were official sports psychologists. But good coaches in those days instinctively knew their athletes and when the lucky athlete came in contact with a good coach, marvellous things often happened. There were years of training leading up to my first Olympic Games, but I can't help but feel that I owe my silver medal in Tokyo to that day in late September in Varsity Stadium and to a coach who knew more than just how to train.

It is important to note that all of these coaches know the practical path of the activity that is basic in high performance in any endeavour. More importantly, as we see again and again, the coach knows the inner, personal path to both the age and stage of development of the individual and the situation.

Seven Keys to Knowing the Path

1. Make every effort to learn as much as possible about the path of success.

2. Get a coach, for yourself and make the journey – in everyway you can.

3. Work at mastering the skill or competency.

4. Learn the theory, and engage in experiencing your "inner path."

5. Appreciate the mundane process of doing very simple things extremely well.

6. See the positive possibilities in every mistake, disappointment and failure.

7. Love the process and coach others to love the process.

7 Best Practice

CHARACTER

Best Coaches know that to live as a person of character
requires commitment, courage and confidence.

"Everyone thinks of changing the world,
but no one thinks of changing themselves.."
~ *Leo Tolstoy*

Character is like beauty, difficult to define yet we all know it when we see it. Coaches know that character is a quality essential for success and they coach character. They support its development by modeling and teaching all the positive values described in Best Practice Two. The first building blocks of character are honesty and integrity. In games and sport these are straightforward and simple: They are the rules of the game. As a code of conduct they can be thought of as "fair play."

There are many qualities of character, such as consideration for others, thoughtfulness, compassion, generosity and respect. There is also the willingness to make commitments. People of character do what they say they will do. They also communicate clearly and effectively. Another quality is courage. It is vital to be able to face personal challenges and take stands on important issues. I am certain you can think of many more. From all of this grows a deeper sense of self-confidence not overnight, but over years.

Many of these qualities are illustrated in this story from Diane Clement. Diane is an Olympian and the Past President of Athletics Canada, our national track and field body. She models another key quality of character - Diane daily celebrates life.

During the early years of coaching at the Richmond Kajaks Track and Field Club that Doug and I founded, we received a call one day from a Doctor friend in the interior of British Columbia, asking, "Could one of my club's athletes stay with you for the summer and train with you?"

The tiny twelve-year-old girl he sent to us ran in our Richmond Kajak's British Columbia Elementary School Championships the year before and won her event running barefoot. The physician told us that she came from an abusive alcoholic family situation and needed a "normal" family environment. We agreed and she became an extension of our family.

We bought her first running shoes and surprised her with a pretty summer dress for our Kajak's summer party. She competed all summer and became part of our track club family as well. She pitched in with the daily chores, babysat and give us a night out, and invited her new friends to pop over to watch TV or just hang out! She cried when she left us at the end of the summer and we regretted her leaving as well. To our delight, she returned the next summer.

Several years later Doug and I received a beautiful letter telling us that she had graduated from university and was now a social worker, she said how those summer months with us had moulded her life. She said she never knew before what a "family" really should be until those summers with us. She found the courage and confidence to leave her abusive environment and make something of her life.

Over the years she has sent us Christmas cards and on one occasion dropped in to surprise me at my Tomato Restaurant. As we chatted over coffee she told me she had two wonderful daughters but had been in an abusive marriage. Again, she possessed the courage to start a new life with her daughters and move on. This year, after a jog with a friend, we stopped for coffee. In the line-up a young woman turned around and it was her. She had moved to Vancouver. We chatted and caught up with all our activities. She was beaming. She told me she had met the most gentle, loving man and they have been together for several years now and her two daughters had just graduated from university. We both shed tears as she took my hand and said once again, "You and Doug saved my life, I will never forget the values you taught me." That is what coaching and mentorship is all about - it doesn't get any more rewarding than that.

Coaches understand the reward of making a difference. They also understand that a difference made in a person's life impacts on not only the children of the person but all the people she meets. Diane and Doug, like coaches everywhere, cared enough to give of themselves to this child and broke the chain of addiction and abuse. The value to the individual is immense and to society it is beyond measure!

Coaches demonstrate respect for all participants and for all involved, officials in and around the game, parents, support people, and the media. Respect is always there for all they meet. Coaches model respect as they teach every youngster to respect herself and all she meets. This is especially true of opponents in any contest and contrary to the sickness and sadness we see demonstrated every day in commercial-entertainment-sport. Because of this all-pervasive negative influence, coaching respect for opponents and the rules of the game is even more important today than ever before. Respect is a key quality of strong character.

Ian Bird who is now Executive Director of the Esteem Team and a former Olympic athlete in Field Hockey has this to say about his coach teaching respect.

John Haywood was my soccer coach when I was a boy. He expected us to be "good people" first, and the best soccer players we could be second. None who were coached by John will ever forget "The Code" which was given to all players and their parents. It was 20 rules to live by as a member of the MacSween Highlanders. All were memorable because they were talked about and referred to often, but as a Vancouverite, I just love #13: "We play many games in cold and wet weather which really bothers our opponents."

As soccer players individual skills were essential only to playing more effectively as a team. The Code stated, "In everything we do the TEAM must come first. Whatever is right for the team will be right for every individual on it." Another was equally clear. "If you are asked who you are playing for, the answer is, "The other ten guys on the field dressed like me."

John Haywood also taught us to respect one another, our opponents, the game and everything associated with it. The Code made that clear. "Without the referee there would be no game, therefore respect the referee. If the referee makes a mistake you may tell him so, providing you are playing a perfect game yourself."

In so many ways our coach taught us to think about why we did what we did, and what it all meant to us. His year-end letter was filled with subtle bits of philosophy and a whole lot of questions to ponder and the suggestion, "I don't have an answer for you. I want you to find your own answer."

He reminded us that at the beginning of the season he had said, "Success is measured in many ways." He then wrote a page of what he saw as some of our successes. They were all about positive values and ranged from exceptional attendance at practices to "playing with honour" and "no player having to be disciplined by a referee." He concluded by writing, "When we look back at this season and we ask those questions, instead of me giving you the answers, I prefer to give you the question. Ask it, answer it yourself and be happy, for you are a success."

A man of true character who had an immense impact on my life and success as a coach came to Canada from Poland in 1973. Gerard Mach had been tremendously successful as a coach of sprinters and hurdlers and had developed a training system that has shaped much of the world's approach to sprint training. He was the most inclusive coach I have ever met. He taught all of us in track and field in Canada to respect one another and be supportive of each other's programmes. He insisted we could compete with the world and did everything possible to give us the confidence and the opportunities to do that, and we did compete. Gerard modeled commitment and personal integrity and expected it from all who worked with him. Here is what Gerard Mach, one of the most successful track and field coaches in the world, has to say about character.

I am first of all interested to know what kind of person is he or she? Each person has different talents, different qualities. To understand a person you need time. I take a blank sheet and the person, with their behaviour, will write their positive and negative characteristics.

Gerard made it clear what he expected from coaches in the National Team programme and when a coach failed to live up to that standard he dealt with it immediately. He addressed the issue with the coach and gave him another chance to be the person and coach that Gerard believed he could be. What was once an issue became transformed into a lesson. Gerard and the coach could now move forward. He treated National Team athletes exactly the same way.

Coaches support the development of character by clearly stating what is expected of all who are a part of the programme. They consistently model that behaviour and quietly hold others accountable, expecting them to act in ways that demonstrate character.

Commitment is one of the first aspects of character modeled and taught. Coaches teach others the power of committing to the process, not the end result. Coaches know that nothing we do is simple. In some way, everything we do is related. It takes a degree of courage to commit to something new and challenging. It is in the process of living that commitment and confidence is built. Supporting youngsters to complete what they say they will do is a most valuable lesson and a basic building block in creating character and developing confidence.

Coaches also know that any process has many aspects to it. The key is to focus on what we are doing, nothing else, and especially not the desired outcome. The youngster who is focused on getting over the high jump bar misses frequently. The one who is focused on executing the best possible run-up and take-off jumps effectively. Sounds simple and yet this is the ultimate challenge in all games and sport, in fact in all of life. Upon retiring from professional tennis, Pete Sampras was asked what he had learned as a developing player that would be useful to young players today. "My focus was on playing well, not on winning," was the best advice any of us can hear regarding any endeavour.

Sometimes when we are mentally or physically tired, our focus becomes difficult to maintain, especially if it is during some repetitive activity such as running or in the story below, paddling over a considerable distance. Coaches teach us that there are many ways to maintain focus and to re-focus.

Roger Allen lives in Whitehorse in the Yukon, is a member of the territorial government and was an Olympian in cross country skiing. He tells the following story of transferring a lesson from one situation to another.

In 1989 well into the 1,100 mile Mackenzie River Canoe Race, the unexpected happened and changed the race for all for us. The weather was cloudy and cold for that time of year. It was mid-July when we normally experience being suffocated by clouds of mosquitoes and flies. Many of the teams were tiring with long days of paddling and nights made sleepless by struggles with mosquitoes.

On this day, our team, the Aklavik Paddlers were struggling to keep in rhythm and began to lose ground from the front team. I called on my experience as a cross-country skier and encouraged the captain to guide our canoe in behind the lead team. This way we could "draft" in their wake to save some precious energy and use their rhythm and tempo to stabilize ours.

The captain agreed and gave me the responsibility of leading our team through this day. I kept us in second place for most of the day and then, in the last few miles of this leg, we began to pick up the tempo. We moved into first place with a final surge and gained over three minutes on the team that had led most of the day, increasing our overall aggregate lead.

That day the team learned there are many ways to win a race other than leading and setting the pace all day. It was a particularly rewarding day for me as an athlete and team member because what happened fostered a new sense of confidence for each of us in our ability to find a way to succeed and the inner resources to carry out the strategy. The result was that we eventually won this challenging endurance event.

Coaches do what Roger's coach did, they provide young leaders the opportunity to take charge and exhibit their abilities. There is no better way to develop confidence and the ability to lead than delegating responsibility appropriately. Roger passed on this new knowledge to others and enhanced their experience in race strategies, tactics and their ability to persevere under very challenging circumstances. Taking responsibility, accepting leadership and possessing perseverance are all valuable aspects of character.

Coaches develop a sense of appreciation in others for the gifts they have and the experiences they have been afforded. When we understand clearly what we have been given we are left with a sense of wanting to pass this on. Tom Bourne tells us about his way of passing on what he believed was given to him.

When asked why I coach, this is my usual response: I blame it all on my coach, my high school coach. At the time, sport was fun. It was hard work. It was being part of the team. It was hanging with your friends. It was winning. The coach was the teacher you needed to open the door. He had the key.

That was 38 years ago. The words are the same but more recently when I had my own kid, they took on a different meaning. My coach was a teacher and he did indeed open the door and he did possess "the key!" We didn't know it then, but he really did have the key and without that key we didn't get into the gym or the equipment room. We needed that key when the janitors weren't around or early in the morning to get in and change. We needed that key to get the 64 green Chevy! The real key, the key to our future, was the more potent, invisible key.

The coach was always there and he worked us hard. He challenged us. He gave us the opportunity to explore our limits, and we did. To us, growing up, athletics was about winning and winning we did. We never lost in our districts and our challenge became running to stay ahead. Ironically, running became our life and the lessons we learned moulded our life. Winning was fun. We won for us and for our coach.

After high school we went in different directions and to different schools. My coach accepted a teaching/coaching position at the local university and went on to continued success. He coached nationally and was named as an Olympic coach four times. We weren't the athletes then, but we were there. In our way we played our part. Later I came to realize that he too was seeking greater challenges, exploring his limits.

My coach made a profound difference in my life and how I view the world around me. For all those unforgiving, unpaid, unappreciated, unacknowledged, thousands of hours of dedication and commitment, I now give of my time in the same unselfish commitment, a commitment to myself and to my coach.

I had the opportunity to say to my coach some thirty years later that there were another 1,000 kids in Florida that benefited from his dedication and commitment. Kids he never knew in a sport he never coached. **He made a difference and hopefully so will I.** *Besides, it's incredibly satisfying, and yes, it's fun.*

Coaches model and teach the significance of the little things, the details. People of character take the time to say the simple "thank you," to notice an act of kindness or generosity. They perform the thoughtful acts, giving small gifts that acknowledge the contribution of others. Coaches know that a quiet word of recognition, an encouraging comment, or a bit of shared information can have an impact beyond belief and you never know with whom or when.

We met Ken Bellemare in Best Practice 4. Ken lives and works in Vancouver. He tells the following story from his time at Dalhousie University.

We were sitting in the Halifax Forum in the middle of the City Basketball Championships. My son's team was very strong and favoured to beat their archrivals, Queen Elizabeth High School. As with many "sure things" they ended being out coached and losing to the Q.E. squad. About thirty minutes after the game my son joined me in the stands where I was sitting close to the Q.E. coach, Bobby Douglas. Coach Douglas and I were friends so we went over to say hello and to congratulate him. My son was somewhat reluctant but he agreed to come along. We greeted him and chit chatted and my son mumbled "good game" to Coach Douglas. He was in the process of leaving to meet up with his team when he turned to my son and said a few very positive things to him that he had noticed about his play in the game. My son smiled and thanked Coach Douglas and then he was on his way.

The story doesn't end there. Three days later my son received a personal, hand written note from Coach Douglas in the mail, indicating how he had enjoyed their brief conversation and praised him for his maturity in coming over to talk with him. He said he knew how difficult it must have been after losing such an emotional and tight game. He also commented on my son's play, which indicated he was aware of his enthusiasm and his ability. My son is now thirty years old and he still counts the letter from Bobby Douglas as one of his important memories. The words from a respected coach made a life long impact at a critical stage of a young man's life.

David Howes is a partner in an Executive Search Practice in Toronto, and lives in Port Credit with his wife Sharman. They have four sons who are all involved in sports. David was an excellent student and a fine university athlete with broad interests and a great life perspective, which hasn't changed over the years, as we see in his story.

I am not a coach, at least I do not really think of myself as a coach. I still think of myself as an athlete, although I have just turned 50 and there are those who believe I should be settling into more sedate activities.

I have been lucky enough to learn and benefit from the lessons of some great coaching. One lesson is that physical activity should always be a part of our life, just like eating, breathing, and sleeping. I learned this from one of the foremost coaches this country has produced, Andy Higgins. He has taught a lot of people that if activity is fun, enjoyable and satisfying, you'll do it for a long time.

I arrived as a first year student at the University of Toronto when Andy returned as Head Coach for Track and Field. The university can be an imposing place for any incoming student, but Andy welcomed a large group of us who formed the nucleus of a track powerhouse for many years to come. More important than the success, we had fun. We dominated at the provincial and national level for years. In fact, U of T still does. Here is another lesson. If you create and maintain a quality programme, it will continue when you are gone.

Andy's first goal was never about winning. He stressed individual participation, interaction, personal development, and academic and intellectual growth. Winning was merely an outcome. The Track Office became a focal point for athletes and coaches just before the daily workout. It was a place of rich discussion and much humour. We learned that success meant measuring ourselves by our own standards and our own abilities. Of equal importance, was to be comfortable with who we were and how we performed. While this sounds simple it was significant for highly competitive student-athletes, focused on performance. Andy helped each of us find perspective and balance in our lives academically, athletically, and socially.

Andy taught us that when it comes time to compete, we must be ready to make it our best performance because performance counts. We learned that the quickest way to get respect for "our" track programme was to be successful as students, as well as a team. Why else would the university and the Department of Athletics increase their support? We learned how the system works, a great lesson for anyone.

I stated that I was not a coach. However I am a husband and father, so, in a way, I am a coach. I have seen the impact of my "coaching" on my sons. My eldest, Ian, since age twelve, has been a competitive sprint canoe racer with lofty ambitions. I have seen him develop as an athlete and as a person. He has trained hard, raced hard, traveled widely for competition and training, and enjoyed every minute.

As a first year student at Western, Ian watched countless friends in residence succumb to the excesses of university life. He was not among them because he had developed the self-discipline to focus on what was important.

While I learned perspective and balance from Andy, I see it in Ian. I am not sure how it happened. Clearly, a lot has come from Ian's own coaches. How do you learn to get to the start line completely relaxed and focused on performance? Is it taught? Is it intuitive? Is it something you pick up by observing others? My guess is that is a combination of all of these, and that Ian learned what I was taught through osmosis. I do know we have both become better people for the acquisition of perspective and balance.

The greatest lessons of coaching are the lessons of life, finding the confidence to go forward and take your place in society, treating people with respect and dignity because if you don't, you cannot respect yourself. Perhaps the greatest reward is that one day, without realizing it, you discover that you have become a coach, dedicated to the development of others. When you realize what has happened, you have to pause for a moment and thank the coaches who invested their time and energy in you.

Coaches know that the person who is prepared to face whatever is presented on the way to a goal will succeed. They will succeed because they knew it was not going to be easy, that challenges, some of them immense, would have to be dealt with and that they could be overcome. Coaches develop the confidence to face such challenges by supporting us through situations that are difficult and demand courage and creativity of us.

The great marathon swimmer, Vicki Keith, tells us about the courage required to simply get into the pool.

One season a most amazing accomplishment happened to a first year swimmer who joined our team. We had a 24 year old swimmer with arthrogryposis join the swim team. She had never mastered transferring herself and seldom pushed her own wheelchair, partly because it is very difficult for her and partly because there is always someone close by to push it for her. This young lady always has all the help she needs. People close by are willing to give her a hand.

She and I spent a lot of time talking about independence and the advantages of it. I told her that as she strengthens I would help her learn some of life's necessary skills so that she could learn independence and hopefully someday be able to move into her own place.

In the first few months after joining the swim team, she learned how to swim efficiently on both her stomach and her back, but had to be lifted out of the pool with a hydraulic chair lift. One day after many attempts, she managed to pull herself out of the pool and into a seated position on the pool deck. Three months after joining the swim team, she surprised everyone while she was sitting in her wheelchair waiting for swim practice to start. She decided that she wanted to go swimming early, so she lowered herself from her chair, transferred herself to her stomach, crawled across the pool deck and slid into the pool. No one could believe their eyes as she surfaced and a huge smile spread across her face.

OK, getting into a pool may not be a huge accomplishment on most swim teams, but it inspired our entire swim team and all the lifeguards on deck.

Courage is required of the coach, if she is to continue to grow and be more effective. Coaches need the emotional courage to face, head on, the most challenging human issues and support others in moving beyond the pain or grief of the moment. It also takes emotional courage to deal with a troubled, angry, deeply disappointed, or frightened person to whom we have some responsibility.

Here is a story by a coach who has just had a learning experience that has been life-changing for two reasons: She was committed to professional development and had the courage to face her commitment to her client. Anyone can be there when it is easy and everything is going well. Coaches are there when it is difficult because that is when they are needed most.

Sara McIntyre, is a Personal Development coach living and working in Vancouver, British Columbia. The following is from a letter sharing this personal learning experience with a colleague in an advanced personal coaching course.

I have been with a friend at the hospital in the two hours before her mastectomy. Eight months ago we talked about reclaiming her life after two previous occurrences of cancer. She had a great deal of fear about making any long-term plans in case something got ripped away from her as it had twice before.

Then a few weeks ago she called to let me know that the cancer had appeared once again. I cried after that call. She let me know that she was not willing to give up our talks but I had many questions about my ability to be with her. Last week she asked me if I would video tape her at the hospital before surgery. She's been documenting her process over the past five years and I agreed without hesitation.

This weekend I stepped further into my confidence as a coach. When I left the class on Sunday I was ready to be with her, and this morning I told her I was there not only as her videographer but also as her coach.

At the hospital my friend bounced between contemplative and feisty even while her family was so clearly uncomfortable being with her under the circumstances. She kept telling jokes to the doctors. One laughed. By the time she was taken into the operating room her family had long gone, unable to bear the situation. I stayed with her until she went through the doors. She reached for my hand as they wheeled her away thanking me for being there. I told her I loved her.

I am sharing this with you because I learned I was able to be with her the whole time. I didn't have any compulsions to distract her or make jokes, I just stayed and kept breathing and looked right at what was going on. Before I left the house to meet her this morning I had a moment of fear that she might not trust my ability to be there because I hadn't been as fearless in our relationship as I know I could have been. She might not know my strength. From now on I am going to lean into my clients with my full weight so that when they need to lean on me, they know how strong I am. I am not going to hold back.

These coaching skills are so powerful. They allow us to stand in the fires where others fear getting burned. As her coach I have touched the compassion and the humanness that this situation brings up. I am committed to staying open to these experiences regardless of what I think I believe. I don't want to be shielded from the pain because I know, now, how to handle it. I'm seeing that with this job comes so much more of life than just my own - if our purpose on earth is to have experiences then we are indeed the blessed ones as we witness and share experience with our clients in their lives. We coaches have such a huge purpose!

Coaches understand that the development of human qualities and character is no different than physical endurance. You must begin at the level of the person and move forward from there. Development starts with small seemingly insignificant matters.

When I was coaching track and cross country running at the high school level I taught the youngsters that it was important to train every day regardless of the weather. In fact, the worse the weather, the better for us. We were preparing to be able to compete in the worst conditions because there would be a day when we would need that training. We gained an advantage training on a day when most of our competitors were not. People of character do whatever is required to achieve their goals. Difficult? Yes. Sometimes uncomfortable? Yes. Rewarding? Definitely. Coaches support that kind of learning in others.

Evelyn Freeman neé Oljans was a national level high jumper in our University of Toronto Track Club programme. She met and married an American pole-vaulter, Mike Freeman, moved to the U.S., worked on a graduate degree, and became a teacher and coach at a small mid-west university, Grinnell College. There she has experienced much success. Here is her story of how mental and emotional preparedness for the worst pays off.

Monmouth College hosted the Midwest Conference cross-country championships on November 2, 1991. The weather was perfect—cold, windy and snowy. Although it may not sound like ideal weather, for our Grinnell team, it was. All week long we had prepared for inclement weather. We practiced in the rain, running outside instead of staying warm and dry indoors. The rain had turned to snow, but the weather was a challenge that we, as a team, were prepared to handle. We went in with the attitude: 'Let the snow bother our competitors. We'll use it to our advantage.' Our pre-race team cheer up to then had been "We're good enough, we're smart enough and gosh darn it, people like us." For Conference we changed it to, "We're warm enough, we're strong enough and gosh darn it, we like this weather!"

The wind blew in vindictive gusts and slapped our faces raw with clouds of sharp snowflakes. Bundled in scarves, socked hands, tights, and strips of torn T-shirt covering their faces the team ran in slow packs across a barren airport runway and onto a trail through a lightly wooded area. Groups of Grinnell supporters huddled along the paths urging Grinnell on with shouts that turned to clouds of frozen steam. Sam, one of our runners, passed out. We knew competition was going to be tight. Once Sam went down the others realized they had to pick up the slack. Every one of them ran aggressively, it was inspiring. They ran courageously, not despite the weather, but because of it. They had anticipated and were prepared for this. Kara Beach amazed us placing third, Jessica Henry and Amy Harris became legends finishing fifth and eleventh. Grinnell took back the team conference title with a six-point edge over St. Norbert, and we did it with no returning All Conference runners. I have since retold this inspiring tale of challenge, courage, preparation for the unexpected, and of focusing on things within our "Circle of Influence" to numerous new student-athletes.

Such stories get retold because they contain powerful lessons. Recently I met Sam Babe on the street near U of T. Sam had been in the programme from a very young age and had been coached by Ross Ristuccia, whom I had coached three decades before at Monarch Park. When I asked what he was doing he said that he was completing law school and coaching in the Junior Development programme. Then he said, "We were talking about you just the other day. It was raining and cold and Jen told the athletes that was good because this was two days of training for us, the day we train and the day our competitors don't." He said they smiled at each other afterwards because they had heard that so many times from Ross, who had told them where he heard it, and now they were passing it on.

Alan Lindop has been a coach and team manager for numerous international teams representing Great Britain for many years. I met him in that capacity over 20 years ago and was always impressed with his attention to detail and his concern for the young people for whom he had responsibility.

Some years ago the Great Britain Decathlon and Heptathlon Under 20 and Under 23 teams were invited to compete with Russia and Germany in an International competition in Kiev. We had received no final written confirmation from Russia that the match was proceeding but we decided to go anyway.

Things started off badly for the team. Visas were issued only a few hours before departure from London's Heathrow airport. The twelve athletes arrived at the airport at 06.30 hours to be greeted by the announcement that British Airways had a cabin crew strike. This was terribly disappointing for the athletes, most of whom were making their international debuts in Russia. After a long delay and a change of aircraft, we were on our way. Upon arrival at Moscow airport we discovered that the vaulting poles had gone missing, which was not unusual except we were in Russia, which could make replacement difficult. After extensive searching they were located.

Our Russian guide was accompanied by the head of the German Delegation who was very upset. He advised us, much to the amazement of the athletes, that his team had withdrawn from the match. The hosts were not prepared to fly the delegations to Kiev, so we would have to travel by train. The Germans had arrived in Russia one day earlier and had ample time to travel whereas we arrived on the Friday afternoon, one day prior to the meeting. The Germans complained that the journey was too long and they were not going. Our guide confirmed that we could only travel by train and departure would be late at night, a long time after the team had left England.

Having a few hours to spare before we left Moscow station I arranged to give the athletes a short tour of Red Square, the Kremlin and surrounding areas, but even that did not go too well as the heavens opened and we were drenched. We arrived at Moscow station for our journey to Kiev to discover a train that appeared to be from the time of the Crimean War. The athletes stared open-mouthed at the relic and understood why the Germans had withdrawn. Not to be discouraged we boarded the train at 22.00 hrs, sixteen hours after leaving London, only to be advised that the trip would take thirteen hours.

We were all, by then, resigned to make the most of the situation. It did not get better. We arrived in Kiev at 11.00 hrs. on the morning of the competition. The Russians were pleased to see us, especially given the absence of the Germans, and they allowed us a couple of hours to freshen up before being taken down to the track to compete. We had warned the athletes that the food might be less than desirable so to a certain extent they were self sufficient in that regard. This was fortunate! Our hotel had very few comforts, and the water, which was cold, was not always running. However, the team spirit generated by all our trials getting to Kiev was of the highest standard. Due to all the hardships they had encountered, they felt they could not waste the opportunity. Despite the long travel and the lack of sleep, eleven of the twelve athletes gained personal best scores and one athlete broke the Scottish record which still stands today.

On the return journey our problems continued with luggage, poles and flights but our experience had taught them how to cope with the challenges. The events of the weekend could have been devastating and the team could have performed badly, but at every new setback and difficulty they chose to compete at their best. Each of them, as a person and an athlete, strengthened in character. They gained confidence, which not only helped them in their future in athletics, but also in life.

These young men and women were already people of good character and significant confidence or they would not have made the team. Coaches make certain that at every situation these qualities are reinforced or enhanced.

Gerald Steele lives, conducts his business, and coaches in Leaside, Ontario. He came to coaching late and has found his passion. Like John Haywood, Gerald has a deep concern for the personal well being of the boys with whom he works. He communicates regularly with the parents of the kids he coaches and makes his approach to coaching very clear. Here are excerpts from his season beginning pamphlet. As we would expect from a coach, it begins with a story.

"That wee fat boy will never make a footballer!" Today, Alex Ferguson, the perpetrator of the above statement, is the long-time, much revered Manager of Manchester United, one of the wealthiest and most successful soccer clubs in the world. Many years ago Ferguson, then an established player with Glasgow Rangers and Scotland, made that statement about a newcomer to professional soccer, Kenny Dalglish, after they had met in a reserve team match. Dalglish, then a teenager, was playing for Glasgow Celtic. He went on to enjoy a long and distinguished career with Celtic, Liverpool and Scotland. Recently, Kenny Dalglish was named one of the top 100 soccer players of all time in a poll conducted by FIFA!

The above anecdote clearly illustrates why it is important that we, who love and care about children and soccer, should avoid being judgmental about the potential of young children.

The wee ones must be given every chance to show their "stuff." We must be demanding of them but also be patient. We must expect high standards of them but must always be fulsome in our praise. We must try to be inclusive rather than exclusive. We must place enjoyment and the attainment of self-confidence as our major targets when teaching.

There are many important areas to work on when learning about soccer. In the coming months, I will be emphasizing the following six topics with our children: Enjoyment, Confidence, Self-discipline, Communication, Skills and Techniques, Speed.

Gerald Steele is a man who generously gives of his time to work with the children of his community and note the priority of what this coach will emphasize! Coaches support the development of character because they understand its significance in being happy and successful in the world. Successful people do what unsuccessful people don't do - they practice in the rain and cold, study when everyone else is partying, and make the time to be with a friend in need. It is not a matter of being difficult; it is a matter of getting the job done. The impact of a coach is not only long lasting, but it can be accessed again at a later time in life when it is needed once more and often in a very different way.

We heard Mike Dyon's story about what happened to his running when Hugh Cameron saw his potential as a marathon runner and Mike followed his passion in that direction. There is so much more to the story. There is also the story of what happens when one has the courage to pursue dreams, sees them in a larger context, commits to the process of discovering the limit's of one's ability, and takes responsibility for one's life.

Not long after that success at the Ottawa Marathon, Mike came to my office to talk. He wanted some advice about his future, which generally means someone with whom to talk candidly, someone who will not judge. There are times when all of us need someone who will allow us to hear ourselves clearly and who can ask the right questions. The dilemma Mike was facing was difficult: Attend Chiropractic College, where he had been accepted, for four challenging years that would preclude serious training or continue to train seriously full time to explore his ability as a marathoner.

I knew how important running and testing his limits were to Mike and I also knew the depth of his passion for excellence. Wrapped inside all of this was an Olympic dream. There was family financial support for continued education but none for this "youthful hobby" of running. Knowing this, I asked if he thought he could go to Chiropractic College in four years after he had explored his running. I knew the answer but he needed to hear himself say it. I then asked if he could still achieve the running dream after he graduated and became financially stable.

The answer was obvious and we talked about it. I then told Mike about Frank Shorter, a Yale graduate and decent runner who had chosen to go to the University of Florida for law school. When asked why he would even consider such a decision he explained it had to do with climate and running surfaces because he wanted to explore his potential as a marathoner. He wanted to make the Olympic team in four years. His friend pointed out that he wasn't even a top-flight college runner and asked why he dared think he might become an Olympian?

Frank Shorter's response was profound. He believed he had much more ability than he had shown in the limited time a Yale education made available for training. More than that, he had to do this so he could spend the rest of his life at peace with himself. He didn't want to live with a deadly case of "*the if-onlys.*" The story was definitely worth repeating because it had within it an inspirational message - Frank Shorter became Olympic gold medallist in Munich in 1972!

The key question then became, "Can you finance your running for a few years with some kind of part time work?" Mike's answer had more significance than anyone could ever have dreamed. "Yes, I think so, by selling training shoes to other runners." He competed in a number of road races in the U.S. and brought back Brooks shoes that he sold at local races. He believed with a little more effort he could get by. That was the path he chose.

Soon the trunk of his car couldn't carry enough shoes to meet the local demand and Mike had to borrow the family van for his trips to U.S. meets. His father saw what was happening and became the mentor that Mike needed. RMP Athletics was soon created to become the Canadian supplier of Brooks shoes. Robert Dyon, Mike's father had the business experience and brother Paul was the other partner.

His father, who with Mike's mother, had been the first best coach to give Mike the confidence he needed to be as successful in academics and athletics as he was, became again a significant coach to his son the business man. RMP Athletics has become a $100 million a year business!

I have seen many similar occurrences in different situations during my years working with people. W.H. Murray who led the first Scottish expedition to Everest wrote in 1951. "Until one is committed there is always hesitancy, the chance to draw back ... but the moment one definitely commits oneself, then Providence moves too."

Coaches support, in every way, the development of character, with its key partners in a successful life, confidence, courage and commitment, in all with whom they work. They model these essential qualities in all their relationships. The strongest statement we ever make is who we are.

Tim Scott is a former intercollegiate hockey player, a successful businessman who is married with children. He lives and coaches in North Bay, Ontario. Tim not only volunteers as a coach of kids in softball and hockey, he is also the Head Coach of the women's fastball team at Canadore College.

It was the beginning of my eighth season coaching the Canadore Panthers the Ontario Colleges Athletic Association. As with every new season, this one presented new opportunities and another chance to benefit from past seasons experiences.

Our team was mostly rookies and by our first tournament we had been together only three weeks. We were still getting to know one another and had yet to earn the mutual respect that would be the foundation to guide us the rest of the season. We have a team rule that once we start our pre-game warm-up the team must stay focused as a unit. No one is to wander about, talking to friends or family who may be arriving to support us. We socialize after the game. For two hours our minds must work together on the field. All coaches and players agree to this.

We had arrived at the ballpark and the players had organized the equipment in the dugout. It was pre-game time, our time together as we had all agreed. As the girls finished their stretches and were breaking up into station groups to continue preparing, one of the freshman players quietly approached me. "Coach, I know this doesn't follow protocol, but my dad just arrived and I haven't seen him in three months. Can I run over and give him a hug?"

Of course I said "yes," and I will never forget the special moment that followed. She quickly hugged her father. The look on her face, and the smile in her voice as she said "Thanks Coach" as she ran back to rejoin the team, will always be with me.

I am grateful for the opportunity sport presents me to make significant choices that shape and affirm the development of character and class in the young people with whom I work and in myself. Coaching allows me to witness and share a wide range of emotions with wonderful people.

Coaches understand and work with the concept of choice all the time. Tim addressed the issue from the coach's standpoint and in the next story we will see the effect of two very different choices being made by young men in sport.

Jim Cooke is a high school teacher and coach in Clinton, Ontario. Jim was Head Coach of the Men's Beach Volleyball Teams in the Sydney 2000 Olympics. He gave up the position in 2002 because he believed another coach could do a better job with two men he coached personally.

In more than fifteen years of coaching volleyball I have worked with individuals ranging from elementary school to Olympic athletes. Every skill level has its rewards and challenges and many of the rewards do not involve medals or prize money.

In 1999, I was coaching the senior boys' volleyball team at Central Huron Secondary School in Clinton, Ontario. I had worked with most of the players from grade nine up and I was looking forward to the season. After the try-outs I had all the players rank themselves and the other team members from one to twelve, in order of skill. I then held a meeting with each individual and discussed where they saw themselves on the list, what role I saw them playing on the team, and what they needed to improve in order to better themselves and the team.

Jason Lobb was one of the players that I had never coached before. He was a little shy and not a very strong player but he had an excellent attitude and always worked hard during the drills in the try-outs. He ranked himself twelfth on the team. I agreed with his ranking and told him that he would probably not play very much, if at all. I pointed out areas he needed to work on if there was to be any chance of him seeing the court. Jason was a very intelligent individual and I noticed how closely he paid attention to my instructions. It is not uncommon for players to decide to quit the team at this point. Fortunately for Jason, and our team, he chose to accept the challenge and continue with the team.

Halfway into the season, it was clear to me that one of the starting hitters was not being very effective. No matter how much I worked with this individual he had it in his mind to spike the ball as hard as he could every time. One out of six into the opponent's court was not helping the team. I gave my macho spiker some time on the bench to reflect on his choices and put Jason in as his replacement. Much to everyone's surprise, Jason passed the ball up to the setter any time it was served to him and hit every ball over the net into the opponent's court.

His hard work and dedication to improve his skills had paid off and had nurtured a confidence that he could be effective. He became our team's starting left-side hitter and we went on to win the Huron County Championship that year. At the Athletic Banquet he was also chosen as the Most Improved Player by his teammates.

Most of us are not destined for Olympic glory but we will all be faced with challenges and choices that define our character. It is gratifying to help individuals grasp the importance of commitment to both themselves and their teammates. Guiding players in developing focus, self-reflection and risk-taking skills makes coaching the rewarding experience it is, as all of these skills transfer into so many other areas of their lives, as they do in my own.

Hans O. Nilsson is General Manager and CEO of Bruce Municipal Telephone System, based in Owen Sound, Ontario. It is one of the most successful independent telephone systems in North America.

My parents were the foundation for me becoming a positive thinker and a motivator to the people I have worked with over the years. They told me I could accomplish anything I wanted if I put my mind to it. They were immigrants and their belief was that if you worked hard enough and had a positive attitude you would be rewarded with success. That is my approach to life and it is true.

I recall that in grade three we had spelling bees and I decided that I wanted to be perfect on all the tests the teacher gave us. With positive thinking and hard work I achieved this. Later, in sports, I maintained the same attitude. Along with motivating myself I motivated my fellow students and was always appointed captain of our teams. I believed that if we worked as a team we would succeed. We didn't win all of our games but we had a feeling of self-satisfaction with the process.

As I moved forward with my education and my career it became clear that a part of my life was to motivate and coach the people around me, especially my family. My wife and I raised two wonderful daughters who excelled in high school and college because I taught what I had learned - pay attention at all times in classes because this makes everything easier. It worked and today both have careers in which they excel.

I began my career with a major telephone company and quickly saw the need for professional development for all staff. I suggested to my supervisor that I write a syllabus for a two-week training course. It was so successful in our company that we offered it to three other telephone companies and I ended up with a full time job as an instructor. I loved it and received positive feedback, as did our company president.

Eventually I left the telephone company for a new challenge in sales. The first thing I learned was that I had to sell myself before I could sell someone my products. The key was to be truthful always. When asked a question for which I didn't know the answer, I made note of it and had an answer for the customer within an agreed upon time. It was critical to get back to the person within the time frame. By doing the little things I won over customers for an initial sale, and also for future business.

In one and a half years I became General Sales Manager. My number one objective was to meet or exceed the sales forecast that was given to me. By then I had eight sales people to motivate so they could do exactly the same. I also coached them to become leaders. During my first full year as GM of Sales we became "Region of the Year" for the World and one of our staff was named "Salesman of the Year." That person is still on my staff and has moved with me over the past twenty years. I continue to teach people to believe in themselves, stay motivated and to create goals that are achievable.

Since coming to my present job as CEO of an independent telephone company, I set my goals high and began motivating my direct reports and their staff to do the same. When I was interviewed for the job I made it clear that all major decisions would be team decisions and I would welcome input from all of my direct reports. That is the way I have been managing this company, which has grown from 35 employees in 1998 to 75 employees at the end of 2002.

We began to conduct "Town Hall" meetings with all the staff, which were held off site. I gave everyone an oak clock bearing the inscription, "Changing Time," counting down to the year 2000. The clocks are still visible as a reminder that we are in a changing world. We then formed a social club to organize events during the year. We work better together when we "play" together.

At a recent Town Hall meeting we involved everyone in EROC, which stands for "Effectively Reducing Our Costs." We formed five teams to come up with ways to reduce operating costs. Each will submit cost cutting ideas to a Committee. If an idea is used the team will get a cash reward based on the saving for the company. In all we do, we make every effort to keep all employees part of the team at all times. It is inspiring to see how motivated and committed people can be when they know their contribution is valued.

From supporting the development of the courage required to live positive values, to committing to a challenging process of personal discovery, to learning to do all the little things that over time enhance the way we feel about ourselves, coaches support the development of people of character. And always they do it as Hans Nilsson does by making them a part of a "team" something larger than themselves that benefits all of them - the family, school, community, country and eventually the world!

Seven Keys to Developing Character

1. Accept that character will make the difference in life.

2. Model and teach the qualities required to live well in the world.

3. Be patient. Understand learning and growth and development.

4. Accept your own and others "humanity" while expecting better.

5. Get commitment from those you coach to work on the personal challenges.

6. Support the courage to face what needs to be changed.

7. Do everything to support and enhance confidence.

Best ⁸ Practice

PERSPECTIVE

Best Coaches know that helping performers
gain perspective in their discipline and in their life
is essential for their success.

"Men are disturbed not by things,
but by the view which they take of them."
~ *Epictetus*

Every coach knows that helping performers gain perspective in their discipline and in their life is essential for their success. Peter Jensen, one of the finest sport psychologists and corporate trainers says, without hesitation, that the three key factors in successful performance are perspective, perspective and perspective. My experience is that when I lose perspective, I lose.

Coaching perspective is an ongoing process, day after day, week after week, and in elite high performance situations, year after year. Gaining perspective is an on-going process comprising many talks, frequent questions, daily reminders, and making meaning of a variety of situations. Rarely does a major event create an immediate "eureka!"

Mike Furlong, tells the story of his daughter Seona and how she lost and then regained perspective.

Since she was very young, our daughter dreamed of being an elite athlete. Fortunately, my wife and I had a strong background in athletics and coaching and were able to help her along the way. She was ambitious, aggressive, and determined. Her pursuit of a career in athletics led her from high school in Manitoba to a volleyball scholarship in Missouri. Neither we, nor several coaches who knew her had ever seen a young girl so determined to reach her goals.

Vince Lombardi, the famous coach of the Green Bay Packers once referred to a special trait he called "singleness of purpose." This is the ability to focus on specific tasks and to shut out all distractions. Seona had singleness of purpose in her career. As we all know, there are lows that accompany all the highs in sports, and we all stumble at times. Her first year in Missouri was somewhat overwhelming. She had to cope with a higher calibre of volleyball, a new school, a new culture and the difference between rural Canada and Missouri was more than expected.

Seona's academic performance plummeted and her volleyball performance was mediocre, partly because of a shoulder dislocation the previous year. She became seriously depressed. Fortunately, her mother had many years of nursing experience and an uncanny ability to provide counselling by phone, e-mail, and in person when we could be there. It was my job to provide the coaching and get her athletics back on the rails.

My coaching experience told me that when all else fails, return to the basics. In this case, the basics meant core values. After lengthy discussions, I encouraged her to identify her priorities. She was looking for some direction and in an attempt to address athletics, academics, and her personal life. I suggested that, in the simplest form, her priorities were: Be a good person, be a good student, be a good athlete, in that order. She needed to put her life into perspective. An athletic career is often short-lived, it can never be her sole priority.

Since that time she went on to captain her volleyball team as a senior, graduated from her master's degree programme with a 4.0 grade point average, coached college volleyball for three years before moving into the private sector where she is now a company vice president, and completing her MBA at thirty years of age.

A coach must be careful not to take too much credit for the success of his or her athletes. At best, it is speculation or subjective judgment that tells a coach what contribution they have made. I would like to provide you with a heart-warming anecdote that tells me that my coaching was valuable. During an interview for a college coaching job, Seona was asked by the panel, "If you could provide your athletes with one piece of advice, what would it be?" Without hesitation, she said, "My father always told me that my priorities were, "Be a good person, be a good student, be a good athlete, in that order." To which the panellist said, "I would like to meet your father."

We all love drama and are attracted to the sensational. For the young, life is always awesome or awful, beautiful or ugly. The media deals in extremes so it is natural that people tend to lose perspective. It took a long time to get decathletes I coached to think and speak differently about the tenth and final event, the 1500 metre run. Almost everyone refers to the decathlon as "gruelling" and that final run, after two days of competition, as "painful." I have frequently spoken with individual athletes about placing this in perspective. Until they thought differently and saw the situation differently, they could not act differently.

Pain is what you see on the newscasts, a child lying in a field mutilated by a land mine, a person badly burned after a harrowing escape from a house fire and a thousand other such examples. That is pain and it lasts for a long time. That minor "burning" in the chest and the intense feeling in the legs over the last two or three hundred metres is "uncomfortable" and in a few minutes is gone. "Gruelling" describes life in the gulag or the grinding poverty and oppression under cruel military regimes in too many parts of the world. The mental and emotional focus a decathlon demands are significant and after two days leave the athlete needing some relaxation. The physical effort is less than any two hard days of training, and the "uncomfortable" feelings last only a short time. The feelings of personal achievement and deep satisfaction are with the athlete forever.

Dr. Evan Mladenoff, a former sprinter and hurdler, is now a parent, a Chiropractor, and a wizard of Applied Kinesiology. He made an immense difference in my health and many athletes I coached. Evan tells the following story.

In January 1993, I was hired by the Kansas City Chiefs to help several players in the American Football Conference Championship. The Chiefs were playing the Buffalo Bills at Rich Stadium in the Buffalo area. Expectations were high. We had Joe Montana, Marcus Allen and a great defence one win away from the Super Bowl.

It did not go well for the Chiefs. Montana was knocked out of the game with a concussion early in the second half. The offence was handcuffed and our defence, the signature of the team's performance, couldn't stop Thurman Thomas, Jim Kelly and the Bills.

With less than two minutes to go the Chiefs had no chance of winning. The offence was on the field trying to salvage some pride. I was standing on the sidelines next to our All Pro linebacker Derrick Thomas. He was frustrated, upset, dazed, bewildered and downright furious all rolled up into one giant, emotionally scarring disappointment.

Nobody was talking to anybody on the sidelines. I turned and looked into Derrick's eyes and said, "Derrick, look around this stadium. Tell me, what do you see?"

After a slight pause, he replied, quietly, with absolutely no emotion, "A stadium full of fans, crazy and excited because their team is going to the Super Bowl."

I then asked Derrick, "Tell me, where else on the planet you would rather be than right here playing in the AFC Championship Game?" He made no answer and maintained his long face and blank stare onto the field. It was as if he hadn't even heard me.

I then said, "Derrick, I'd be willing to bet there are ten other teams watching on TV that would gladly change places for the opportunity to play for the right to go to the Super Bowl."

Derrick put his arm across my shoulders and gave me the best crushing hug I've ever had. He looked me in the eye and said, "Damn it Doc." He then looked at me and cracked a glimmer of his famous big smile for half a heart beat. There was no place else to be but on this football field on that day.

I remember reading when I was young that only those who are prepared to fail greatly can ever expect to succeed greatly. In any game in which a score is kept, winning and losing are equal possibilities. That is so obvious and yet so often not thought about, talked about, or put into perspective for young people. Evan Mladdenoff was not saying, "Don't be disappointed!" That is as silly as believing the possibility of losing does not exist. He was saying, be here in this moment and appreciate it fully, the energy of the stadium, the reality of this being the championship game and you being here, and, yes, you are disappointed, but experience all of it! This is a rare opportunity.

Coaches teach us that if we really need to dramatize something, dramatize positive actions and even minor achievements. Avoid "awfulizing." The price is too high in terms of happiness, life energy and long-term success. Negativity does not lead to useful achievement. If you have bought into a belief about anything similar to the "pain" concept, or about anger and silence when "losing," why not put it in perspective and change it now? Sport psychologists call this "re-framing" and it is a powerful tool. Try it.

In March 1992 we were in Winnipeg for the National University Indoor Track and Field Championships. In less than thirty minutes we were to board the bus to the field house. All the coaches and athletes were crowded into a small room and the feelings were becoming intense. As I was wrapping up this final team meeting I wanted every student/athlete to see this competition for what it really was, an opportunity to challenge themselves. I had already said a few words when I became aware that what I was saying came from more than thirty years of coaching, reflecting on and discussing competition.

"Remember, what you are going to do in the next three hours is the most important thing in your life!. and, it doesn't matter." I paused and let that much sink in. These were University of Toronto students, many in professional and graduate schools, all in demanding academic programmes. That statement had really got their attention. Every one of them had heard me say endless times that their academic work was their number one priority. I continued, "If what you are about to do in these next three hours is not the most important thing in your life, for these hours, then you have wasted endless time over the days and weeks and years you have been training for your event. But, we both know you haven't wasted all that time. Yet it does not matter even if one of you should, by some miracle of aligned stars and moons, set a world record. It would change nothing in the greater world that is of real consequence. Nothing.

The only thing that can be changed in the next hours by what you do, is you. Tonight the probability is high that a homeless person will freeze to death on the streets of this city, men will continue to beat their wives and children, and in far too many parts of the world humans will perpetrate inhumane acts on other humans. What you will do tonight is of extreme importance to you. It can change you, although in the grand scheme of the greater world it will change nothing. It does not matter. You, however, do matter. This is for and about you, as a person. It is an opportunity to find the joy in the challenge, to hold your focus, compete with courage and test your character. Do that and you have taken the first and only step you can to changing anything else."

Jim Thompson is the founder and director of Positive Coaching Alliance based at Stanford University where he was a member of the faculty of the graduate school of business prior to creating PCA whose website is: www.positivecoach.org. Jim tells this story in his book, *Shooting in the Dark: Tales of Coaching and Leadership.*

Years ago someone described to me how we waste most of our moments. He offered this example: When he is hungry, he rises from his chair and walks to the kitchen. He opens the door of the refrigerator and eyes the selections. He finally chooses something and takes it out. He then does whatever he needs to do to prepare the food, peels an orange, pours a glass of liquid, heats up some soup. Finally he puts teeth and lips and tongue to the sustenance.

Of all the moments described, he values only the final one in which he eats or drinks the food or liquid. The other moments are not valued for themselves, for the irreplaceable gifts that they are, but are hurried through to get to the prized moment of tasting the treat.

Now I love the pageantry and excitement of a basketball game as much as the next person. And the reality of an upcoming game against a worthy opponent gives an intensity to practices that is unlikely to occur in its absence. When the starting whistle blows and the ball is tossed in the air, the experience is as delectable as the first bite of a sweet orange.

I want to value the moment in which I get up out of the chair and the moment in which I walk to the kitchen and the moment in which I open the refrigerator door. I want to value the moments in practice as much as the moments in games. Each moment is a part of my life that, once passed, will never return. I suspect that the warm glow of memory may linger longer on those moments of practice than the more glittery ones of games.

Tom Watt is a lifetime physical educator and coach who has coached boys and men at the high school, university, NHL, and Olympic levels. He is a long-time friend of mine since university days when we were classmates at University of Toronto. In our first years of teaching for the Toronto Board of Education we met often to share ideas, swap information about teaching and coaching and to discuss our dreams. One dream that Tom and I often talked about was to be in the same school to create an ideal physical education and inter-school sport programme. We got that opportunity in 1964, and one evening that fall, after our games that day, I got a phone call from a rather quiet and shaken colleague. We talked about life and sport and what really mattered for only a few minutes, because that is all it took!

In the fall of 1964 I was coaching senior football in a brand new high school in Toronto that has been built to take the overflow from two very old and well established schools. In that first year no students in the upper grades were required to transfer, few accomplished athletes did. We had lost our first three games but had not been beaten badly. The fourth game was a 63 – 0 humiliation. I felt badly for the boys but I felt worse for myself. My young coaching ego was bruised.

My drive home took me across the Leaside Bridge high above a river and a freeway. Focused only on driving straight ahead and my own disappointment I was dimly aware of a car parked against the curb in the middle of the bridge. A man got out and stumbled to the immense concrete railing and began to climb up the bridge. I was brought immediately into the moment. I realized there was only one reason to be mounting that railing a couple of hundred feet above the valley floor.

I have no clear recollection of what I thought I was going to do or how I would do it, but I found myself stopping instantly and then I was talking to the man from some distance away. Eventually, I have no idea how long, I found I was standing close to him and he was then talking to me as well and crying. He agreed to step down to the bridge and as he did I was aware that there were now other people and the police had arrived. The man was taken to a nearby hospital and I drove home with a growing sense of the insignificance of a group of high school boys losing a game of football and my ridiculously out-of- perspective response to the loss.

I still have, in a file, a table napkin on which Tom had written a great truth about life and perspective. It was 1973 in the tuck shop in Hart House at the University of Toronto. Tom had been invited to coach and teach there a few years earlier. I was offered the same opportunity in 1971. Once again we were colleagues sharing our passion daily and still exploring perspective.

We were discussing the issue of the young men we coached becoming identified with their performances, and the problems that created for them. We briefly touched on how the problem even affected us as coaches. Sometimes it is a real challenge to get a youngster to understand that his worth as a person is not tied to his performance in sport or the classroom or anything else. During our discussion, Tom recalled something he had read recently on this issue, and wrote on a napkin, *"If you are what you do, when you don't, you're not."*

There are two sides to every situation, and we need very much to experience both to know, and appreciate the difference. You will recall the story earlier of Peter Warren's son Bill saying that he now knew how to lose well and could he be on a team next year that would allow him to learn how to win equally well. I smile every time I think of his request. We all need to learn how to win, to succeed, and to keep both in perspective.

Tom Bourne, from whom we heard before, is a parent and volunteer coach in South Florida. He comments on the simplistic thinking behind many attempts to place the loss a game in perspective.

We hear too often from people who want to put losing into perspective for kids that "it doesn't matter whether you win or lose, it is how you play the game," and it simply doesn't ring true. Part of the reason is, like so many famous quotes, it is wrongly interpreted and badly mangled. In his poem The Tumult and the Shouting, Grantland Rice comments on the character of great sportsmen writing, "When the one Great Scorer comes to mark against your name, He marks not that you won or lost, but how you played the game." Now that is a different notion and I agree with it.

As for the matter of winning and losing, well, if you are going to play the game then you play to win. I have yet to meet the coach or team who set out to lose a game! Nor have I met the person who enjoys losing. Why else would anyone engage in an activity in which score is kept?

Having said that, I believe there are shades of both winning and losing. Neither is as clear-cut as they might appear. At the beginning of every season I discuss both concepts with the players in the following manner.

The first question asked is, "Did you win or did they lose?" I suggest they think about it. In my experience it is an effective way to challenge them to address the issue of how he or she and the team performed. It is simple to say that if the final score was 5-4 in your favour you won - or did you? Hence the question did you win or did they lose?

I also tell them, "If you played your best and they played their best then you won today." I challenge them to think about this win or lose idea with more questions. I have found that questions get them thinking and talking and while there may not be any definite answers it keeps them evaluating the quality of their performances and places winning and losing into a healthier perspective.

Coaches find many ways to constantly remind performers that they are not their performance. We all need to remind ourselves daily: "I am not my performance. I am who I am and that is not changed by winning or losing a game, not by performing well or badly in the game regardless of the outcome. These are things I do. And, just as with the possessions I have, they do not change who I am."

Brad Morley, a former National Universities championship runner and now a parent and teacher of English in Owen Sound, Ontario, tells the following story.

My university coach taught me a valuable lesson in perspective and the definition of victory. Socially, we seem so tied to the idea of victory meaning coming first and that this is the best of all victories. It isn't and it should never be, no matter how wonderful finishing first in a track or field event can be. Victory is so much more about performing to your best ability on the day and in the conditions you are given. In this way a personal best, pb, for a tenth place finisher is more of a victory that matters than winning with a sub-par effort much slower than his pb. Accepting this simple truth relieved needless pressure in many race situations and allowed me to focus more on what I would be truly able to do in a race rather than on whether I should win the thing or on why I had, in my mind, already lost the thing.

It is October and we are just outside of Sudbury for the Provincial Cross Country Championships. The rain has been falling for several days. Even the long drive from Toronto has been almost entirely in a heavy rain. The course runs through a good deal of maple and cedar bush and part of it takes us across a beaver dam. When we arrive for a warm-up and course inspection spirits are low, water levels are high, and there is mud everywhere. Accepting the fact that we are going to be wet and cold no matter what we do short of driving the course in a heavy-duty military vehicle, we decide to try our luck at keeping our racing spikes dry while we trudge and slip through the slop on the 3k loop. Other runners from across the province move slowly and heavily through the rain, heads bowed, spirits sinking. I and my good friend John Sharp, who is contesting the senior race right after my attempt at the junior race, keeps in mind the real reason we are there: We love to run, racing is just a sideline. Winning doesn't matter, taking part well does.

"We can't change the weather," I tell John, "so let's not let the weather change us." We begin to jog, wet-footed but lighter of heart. John begins to sing "Singin' in the Rain" and I make the first move in what will amount to a long game of "I'll bet I can splash you in that puddle ahead before you can splash me." In this sort of game, winning does seem to matter. We are both soaked well before the course inspection and warm-up are over. We are covered in mud well above our knees and we are in great spirits while all around us people moan about the muck, the slop, and the constant rain.

I win the junior championships by close to forty seconds and John wins the senior men's by over a minute. We had a blast. Would I have had as much fun if I had come second? Who knows? I am convinced to this day that one reason I won was because I decided to not let the weather change me. Another reason I won was because winning wasn't the first priority, running and racing well were.

In my own coaching, I learned early to be sure to pass on to my athletes the idea that effort more than anything matters most when it is shaped by the belief that what one is capable of, is often a factor of how one feels about oneself and the situation one is in. It became a common chant for my high school boy's and girl's cross country teams: Whatever the weather is, that's the weather we want. It made a lot of late fall races much more enjoyable than they otherwise would have been, and I can trace it back to having learned in my first few weeks at U of T, that the greatest victory takes place within ourselves.

Gerry Desormeau is a retired sports journalist. He still remains an active member of the sporting scene in North Bay and was elected to the North Bay Sports Hall of Fame in 2002.

It's been said that you'll hear every excuse or reason why the team lost. After more than forty years as a sports reporter and twelve or so as a coach, I thought I had until the fall of 1996.

As an assistant coach with the Canadore Panthers, it's my job to not only work with the players but to keep statistics during the games. We were in Hamilton playing the Mohawk Mountaineers and the doubleheader meant a lot to our chances of making the playoffs. We lost the Friday night contest and Saturday, a beautiful, sunny October afternoon, we lost again. Moments after the final out I couldn't believe what I heard as I tallied up the final linescore.

"Is the game over? Did we win?"

I recognized the voice as one of our players and she wasn't joking. "Is the game over? Did we win?"

You can imagine what was going through my mind. I've never been fond of losing and to hear that made my temperature rise. Fortunately, my son Bob, who was at the game and who also heard the comment, suggested that I remain calm while the teams exchanged handshakes on the diamond. Of course, he later took great delight in kidding me. He kept reminding Roy Coxford, the team's trainer, to ask me if the game was over and had we won.

To this day, Tim, Fred and I still remember that moment. Now, it's hilarious. By the way, we missed the playoffs. Next time you think you've it heard all, think again. Somebody is sure to surprise you.

I know this hilarious laughter well. It is as much about my out of perspective reaction to a situation as it is to the "craziness" of the situation – in this case, "Did we win?"

Denis Sacks is Vice President of National Accounts at Pepsi Canada, a committed father, a generous volunteer to a number of organizations and a recreational runner with a background in highly competitive athletics.

It has been my experience that successful people have sport and life in perspective. They do not live through their children and if they coach sport, do not live through the young people they coach. I have known Denis for many years and he is a very competitive and a very balanced person.

For eight years I have coached my daughter's House League soccer team. In six of those years we did not win many games. In fact one season we did not win a single game until the final game of the season on Cup Weekend!

The girls never had a problem with this. Sometimes the parents and coaches did, but never the girls. This was House League and my over-riding goal was to make sure they had FUN! Somehow we were able to find a way for them to have fun and they kept coming back year-after-year requesting to play on this losing team.

By the way, in their eighth season they actually won the League & Cup Day ... and had fun doing it!

Kids always keep coming back to any activity when they are having fun. Imagine the difference in health and other social issues if every child had the opportunity to be engaged, every day, in activity that is "fun."

Debbie Muir is a corporate consultant living and working in Calgary, Alberta. She is the former National Coach for Synchronized Swimming and the Olympic coach for Canada to the Seoul Olympics in 1988.

When I was coaching Carolyn Waldo and Michelle Cameron for the Olympics we attended the Pre-Olympic competition in Seoul three months prior to the Games. We viewed this as an important meet for us because the outcome here would likely be the outcome at the Olympics. We took it seriously and trained and tapered accordingly.

The day before the meet Randy Starkman of the Toronto Star asked me about the importance of this meet.

I replied, "This meet is extremely important for us. Our goal is to win because we believe whoever wins here, will move on to become the Olympic Champions."

The next day Carolyn lost the solo event to her nearest rival, the 1984 Olympic Champion, Tracie Ruiz. Of course Randy couldn't resist asking me the question, "So yesterday you said winning this event was very important if you were going to win at the Olympics. Well, you lost. What do you think now? Will you even have a chance?"

If we were going to be successful I knew I had to change my perspective fast. My reply was, "I think it was very important that we lost here today. If we had won we would have gone along on the same path thinking everything was fine. We would have become complacent. Now we have a clearer idea of what the judges are and aren't looking for and we can go back and make some changes to our programme. It's almost a relief to have lost here because I would much rather lose here than at the Olympics."

When you change your perspective you gain new possibilities, and choices open up to you that you may not have had before. If we hadn't changed our perspective I don't think Carolyn would have won because winning wasn't one of the possibilities with our previous mindset.

Grant Connon is married with two children aged thirteen and seven. He has taught physical education for more than twenty years and has been involved in a variety of sports, mainly rugby and track and field. They live in Kerikeri, which is in the top of the North Island of New Zealand.

I have been involved in sport for many years and because I live in NZ my main sport to begin with was rugby. The first coach I remember vividly was my high school coach. I don't remember the specifics of the coaching sessions but what sticks in my mind is one time when I went to excuse myself from practice because I had a headache. My coach told me that exercise was good for headaches and to turn up. He was right and I use that same advice to my students today almost thirty years later. My coach's name was Graham Driver. A commitment to a team does put a headache into perspective.

I went to Dunedin University on the South Island where it is cold every winter. We would sit in the changing rooms until our coach, Duncan Laing, turned up. When it got close to training time and he wasn't there, I thought I might get home early to my nice warm house. But coach always turned up. I eventually understood that he had been doing that for years before I arrived and continues to do so after I graduated.

When I was 21 I left rugby and dedicated myself to the decathlon. Over the next five years, Max Steward and I spent a good deal of time together, during which I managed to win the national title twice and finished third once. Max and I lived thirty kilometres apart so we did a fair bit of traveling. Thinking back now, not once did I question what it cost Max to run around after me. I now see that his commitment was far greater than mine. Time has put that into perspective.

Time has given me another view of what all my coaches did and why. I have now been coaching for a number of years and it is amazing how rewarding it is when the young people achieve and I know that I have played some part in that. Before I questioned the fact that I did not think of what it must have cost my coach to do the things he did for me, but I realize now the joy I get from seeing my athletes perform and cost does not come into it at all.

After reaching the top in NZ by training part time, I wanted to train full time to see what I could do. I was fortunate to be able to go to Toronto and train at the U of T High Performance Centre under the expert eye of Andy Higgins and his extraordinary staff. I spent sixteen months training with great athletes and exceptional coaches. I had a wonderful time and I learned a lot about training for the decathlon.

Irene Wallace is head basketball coach at Camuson College in Victoria, British Columbia. Irene was a physical education teacher for many years before becoming the coach of the University of Saskatchewan Huskies Women's Basketball team from 1988 to 1994. After attending the University of Victoria for a Master's of Education in Coaching, Irene accepted her current position.

As coaches, we know that one of our biggest challenges is teaching athletes strategies for managing their mental game. If an athlete can develop the ability to focus on the here and now and is "competing in the moment," they will have less tendency to become distracted by events of yesterday or the worries of tomorrow. They will fully enjoy the experience of today. Athletes will remove fear of the next event or regret for the past because they can "see" they are living in a window of time that is their opportunity.

At the beginning of each season I ask team members to set up a glass bowl in a favourite viewing spot at home. They then go to the beach and select a stone for each day of our season, different coloured stones for practice days and competition days. It will be about 186 stones and they are to place them in their bowl. Every morning during the season the athletes take one stone out of their glass bowl and throw it away. They can "see" how quickly the stones and their days diminish one by one. This process helps them keep a more positive perspective and assists them with their decision-making around planning for exams, planning for social events and of course, planning for training commitments for basketball.

I have found that by watching the stones disappear, the athletes are able to focus more successfully on what is important and appreciate each day as it comes.

Jill Wooley neé Ross is a mother, an interior designer, and former two-time Olympian, who held the Canadian record for the heptathlon for eleven years. She still holds the North American indoor pentathlon record, which she established in 1982. Jill is married to Gord Wooley, who was an Olympian in bobsleigh.

Over the years, many people have asked me about my most memorable moments in my sport career. It is always a complicated answer, friendships, wonderful successes, all the life lessons sport has taught me, and certainly the significant coaches who have influenced my personal growth throughout my life.

The latter is a new revelation. It wasn't until I began coaching that I became aware of the impact a coach can have on a young person's life. Coaching is an intense, intimate and rewarding job that comes with immense responsibility. A great coach can guide, nurture and help an athlete become the best they can be. Coaching is synonymous with good and successful parenting, another job I cherish and value.

One of my most satisfying and memorable moments as a coach was when I was inducted into the Sports Hall of Fame at the University of Toronto. I looked into the audience finding faces of family and friends and right beside them were "my girls," my team from Branksome Hall, in full force smiling back at me. That they came and surprised me was significant, but in that moment I saw beautiful mature young women who had survived the high school experience still loving sport. What a great gift to me to have played a small part in that giving!

Andy Higgins is one of those special coaches. Thanks to him, I carry a lifetime of fond and warm memories. When coaching I often caught myself repeating an Andyism, just as, when I am parenting, I hear myself saying, "Oh my God I sounded just like mom!"

Glen Markle is a former professional football player who says he "was a pretty good all around athlete in high school who was fortunate to have played varsity football at university during the 1960s." He earned a PhD and began his own company The Ontario Skills Training Group www.ostg.ca, as a training consultant.

Our parents always provided their three boys with support and encouragement to participate in sports. At first they simply provided the requisite sports gear. There was always a new hockey stick under the Christmas tree. I can remember getting my first football helmet when I was in grade two or three and going out in the snow to test it out by diving into the drifts. My mother fashioned football pants by cutting off old jeans at the knees, sewing another layer of cloth padding in the front and then cinching below the knees with elastic. Wearing my new football helmet, my sort-of-new football pants, and my dad's old wool football sweater, I used to line up in the back yard head to head with Peter King where we would tear up the new lawn, tackling and scoring touchdowns. Peter was two years older and quite a bit taller and heavier than me, but I can't ever recall my parents expressing concern about the match up, although I'm sure they kept watch to make certain I was giving as much as I was getting. Nor did I hear any concerns for the lawn, which was getting a pretty good beating as well.

In the early 1950s we moved from Timmins to Toronto. In the new suburbs there were not a lot of organized sports activities. My parents volunteered their time to create opportunities for us and other kids in the neighbourhood to engage in sports. They frequently volunteered to drive us to games and practices. While this seems commonplace and expected today, I shall always remember my father getting home from work, having a quick bite, and then packing me off to an old freezing barn arena in Bolton, or Malton, or Aurora to play for my team.

I have come to realize that if our parents were not formally our first coaches, then they certainly provided solid values and pretty "good bones" for future coaches to work with in terms of skill development. We probably learned about sacrifice, dedication, overcoming obstacles, bumps, bruises, physical risks, and about setting and achieving goals from our parents. We learned the value of being provided with the opportunities and encouragement to just play. Joy is the freedom to just play.

Imagine if every parent, every teacher and every sport coach who worked with children understood and lived that as a first principle – "the freedom to just play."

Rob Town is an optometrist in Orillia, Ontario, a track and field athlete from the 1970s and early 1980s. He was a five time OFSSA champion and still holds the OFSSA midget discus record at 58.98m, the oldest record in the books. Rob was Canadian Decathlon Champion in 1981 and a member of the 1978 Commonwealth Games Team placing sixth in the decathlon. He is married to Andrea Wachter of 400m hurdles fame. They have four daughters ages seven to seventeen.

I have had many coaches and would say that the quality of instruction and commitment has been extraordinary. It began with my first swim coach who coached at 6 a.m. each weekday. He saw great possibilities despite substandard facilities. The way he choreographed interval training in a 50' X 16' YMCA pool for twenty kids, zig zagging lengths simultaneously is legendary among the swimmers of the day. I personally achieved three Ontario age group records. My brother Dave enjoyed an incredible career with multiple Conference and National University victories despite the humble beginnings.

What impresses me most about the quality coaching I received is the time that coaches were willing to devote to a motivated athlete. This is sometimes true to a fault. I appreciate Brent McFarlane for the time he gave to me and to the others in our group. He individualized our workouts for the non-group days. He would review and goal-set individually in his home, discussing the rationale for the training with a well conceived plan. He never missed our group training sessions. When the coach gives his time and expertise, you give back attention and effort.

Another significant coach was our pal Ian Macmillan, my high school and club coach for five years. He was intense and energized and never failed to make me think that the sky was the limit. We small town athletes need to know that the big city kids aren't necessarily better or stronger or work harder so he took a number of us and made us OFSSA champs.

Ian did the little things that made a big difference. He used predecessors as role models. I remember as an impressionable grade niner meeting Joe Watt, a great sports hero of the late 1960s. He held the records, won the medals, was the football star. I imagined him as eight feet tall by Ian's description. One day Ian brought him to a workout to offer inspiration to the new kid. He did seem as big as described and I don't remember him saying two words to me, but the presence of a sports hero, real or imagined, is important to a young athlete.

At the end of my high school career I held all of Joe's records, and I had broken his senior shot putt record by over two metres. I still see Joe at the Y as we both stay active. He doesn't remember the day, but I do. I also remember Bobby Orr shaking my hand and calling me "big guy" as an eight year old hockey player when our coach held a special practice at the Orr-Walton hockey camp. We have all been inspired by "heroes" and I make a point of going back to the track from time to time just in case I might be someone else's inspiration. I wonder sometimes if they have even heard of me. A good coach would make sure!

Jason Riley is a former member of the Hamilton Tiger-Cats, a high school teacher, a volunteer coach of several sports, and a strong supporter of amateur sport. I have excerpted an article Jason wrote for the *Hamilton Spectator* in response to a column about "a major decline in physical fitness on the part of Canadian girls." Jason quotes some of the public statistics that conclude with "only 11% are still active by age 16-17." He added, "The net result is a burden to our health care-services. This issue is obviously not only restricted to girls."

In this light, I want to share something special I experienced last weekend. I helped coach the Hamilton Hawks (#1) house league hockey team in the 9th Annual Hawkey Tournament, run by the Hamilton Girls' Hockey Association. It featured 130 teams in various age groups and divisions. Our team was in the Bantam House League pool of twelve teams from all over southern Ontario. This was a good challenge for the team after completing a successful season.

In the house league system all the girls are put through a clinic, and their talent is evaluated at the start of the season. Then the head coaches choose teams as evenly as possible based on their combined evaluations, hoping that all the teams will be competitive.

However, this process does not reveal the intangibles, like the coachability of the players, their desire, and team chemistry. Coaches often don't know what to expect with many different levels of ability, attitudes, and hockey experience coming together. Some of the kids were so shy they wouldn't say a word at the start of the season. As the season went on parents remarked about their kid's transformation as part of the team. We were pleased that our girls gelled quickly into a hard working team that showed a strong desire to win. They had a great deal of fun doing so, which in my mind is the main reason for sport, to have fun and improve fitness.

It was rewarding for the coaches to witness the girls' continual improvement as the season went on. They finished first in the overall league standings and won the city championship in an exciting final against Flamborough. This performance was outstanding for a team that started the season with few expectations. What was most gratifying was that many of the athletes' parents gave the coaches positive feedback about how the girls were enjoying the season, improving their skills, developing personal character, and forming new friendships.

Ultimately, the girls played inspired hockey and won the Hawkey tournament. They had the astonishing achievement of scoring thirty-two goals and having only one goal scored against them in five games. Even more impressive was that every skater on the team had a point, meaning either a goal or an assist. All the forward lines contributed to the offence and the defence was relentless in front of our goalie, who had four shutouts. There were no individual stars because the girls played so hard together as a team!

Jason deplores the lack of facilities for girls hockey in Hamilton and adds:

Perhaps knowing the great benefits that sports offer to our young people might help to spur the foot-dragging politicians in this city to finally build that new hockey arena that has been postponed again. The long-term gains far outweigh the short-term costs of building facilities that keep our kids active, reducing both the crime rate due to sheer boredom and health care costs due to unhealthy lifestyles. We need to provide broad funding for sufficient facilities, so that high user fees don't make sports elitist and exclusionary. We must make them available to everyone to benefit society as a whole.

What a truly wonderful perspective! Jason Riley sees sport in it's entirety, the need for a place for everyone at every age and ability level to be able to play. It is not only for high performance sport or children's sport. It is both and everything in between. Kids need excellence to be inspired by and to live up to as Rob Town told us. They also need opportunities in their communities to move towards that which has inspired them. Once again, Denis Sacks and Jason Riley remind me that successful people who are active in their lives have healthy perspectives – kids sport is about having fun!

Bruce Peckover lives in Toronto with his wife Ruth and three children. He has been a successful business man in the Insurance and Financial Services industry for almost three decades! Bruce shares his perspective on a successful life.

Life is a series of self-fulfilling prophecies. This is a perspective by which I lead my life. I have tried my best to pass this lesson on to my children and to people I have had the opportunity to influence in my working career. To state it another way, what you expect to happen, will happen. Choose carefully what you expect because both the best and the worst can befall you.

Do not confuse hopes and dreams with expectations. Buying a lottery ticket and telling yourself you expect to win is delusional. Setting a realistic goal and expecting to be able to accomplish it is healthy.

In the life insurance products industry, the epitome of success is to qualify for the Million Dollar Round Table. This is an international organization of the most successful insurance and financial service product practitioners. Less than three percent of insurance people attain membership in this organization in any year. I have qualified for membership twenty-four years in a row. I simply expect to attain the membership qualification level each year.

I didn't start out that way. I needed five years to develop the confidence, skills, knowledge, and contacts to attain this level of competence and productivity. I didn't do it the way the sales managers suggested. I didn't break down the volume of business needed for the year by the number of weeks available, and then into daily and hourly goals. I simply stated that I expected to become a member of MDRT and set about doing the best I could each day, safe in the knowledge I would attain my goal.

This is a far healthier way to approach life and the achievements of life's goals. Most of my peers who set these interim goals, failed to reach the final objective. I am convinced more of them could have reached the prize if they hadn't had so many little failures along the way. Each day they didn't reach their goals was a failure for that day. They then had to drag that failure along for the next day. The baggage of the past became too great a burden.

Setting expectations has worked wonders in raising the abilities and confidence levels of those around me. Many years ago, due to a change in work assignments among the sales assistance staff in the office, I had a lady reassigned to me with a reputation for shirking any extra effort. Her attitude had her walking under a dark cloud most of the time. Her work habits soon manifested themselves in the inability to find anything recent in my clients' files. Rather than hauling her on the carpet as others had, I asked a simple question. "How long after I put a piece of paper in the filing tray can I expect to find it in the appropriate client's file?" Possibly for the first time in her working life she was being given control of a situation. "One week," she replied. Now one week is far longer a time than is needed to move one piece of paper from resting horizontally in a filing tray to standing vertically in a filing cabinet four metres away but at the same time, instantaneous filing wasn't important. Dependability was what I wanted.

The exercise was a success. Within a short time, she suggested we move the time target to two days. This new "I can" attitude started to permeate other aspects of her job and her outlook on life. I am happy to report that she is now brokerage manager for a growing insurance operation to which she moved a few years later that was closer to her home.

When our children were younger there were very few rules in the home, but there were lots of expectations. Those expectations were mutually established. Failure to achieve the outcome weighed hard. And it weighed far harder on them than on us. Given the opportunity to set their own destiny the kids set far higher targets that we might have set for fear of pushing too hard. The expectations were theirs, so they worked harder to achieve them.

It is exactly the same with expectations in my business operation. When I first entered the insurance business, I had to get a car for all the night time and weekend appointments. I tired quickly of the endless work and the wasting of time and energy going from one part of the city to another. I set an expectation that eventually I would do all my business by TTC. It took three years until I traded my parking pass for a MetroPass. That was sixteen years ago. I now do almost all my business at my desk while my peers are still driving all over the city. My final expectation is to be able to walk to work. The lease on my current space is up in another four years and I'll be moving to Yonge and York Mills, a lovely twenty-minute walk from home, and overlooking the Don Valley golf course. Now, is breaking 100 an expectation or a hope?

I have jokingly said for many years that Flip Wilson of Laugh In days was a philosopher disguised as a stand up comic. His facile statement, "What you see is what you get," was totally misunderstood by most. I believe he was telling us that what we see, the perspective we hold, the view we take, determines exactly what we get. Perspective is everything and all these coaches and their stories make clear what Bruce Peckover has just told us: See clearly what you expect to achieve and work towards it. What a perspective on success!

Seven Keys to Creating Perspective

1. Separate the performer from the performance. "I am not my performance."

2. Know that "If you are what you do, when you don't you're not."

3. Focus on the process of the person learning, not on the outcome.

4. Understand you are not alone. You are part of the world.

5. Create opportunities for working with the less advantaged.

6. Explore your motivations – do not live vicariously!

7. Model that "joy is the freedom just to play."

Best **9** Practice

LIFETIME LEARNER

Best Coaches know that when
they cease to learn they cease to grow.

"Live as if you were to die tomorrow.
Learn as if you were to live forever."
~ *Mahatma Gandhi*

Coaches understand that all they can control is the way they respond to a situation. They can control how they feel, what they think, and what they do but they cannot control what anyone else does. They know, however, that it is possible to influence what others do, and that is the power and the wonder of coaching. The coach's ability to influence others is directly related to his or hers actions. Actions are determined by how and what we think, which are products of what we have learned. Coaches are insatiable learners.

Coaches learn from every possible situation because they know that the only way to be better at what they do is to know more and understand what they already know in different ways. Coaches constantly seek new information and more experienced people to help them understand that information. They know there is much to learn from people with different experiences and different disciplines, regardless of age or situation. The more they work with people the more they know that the human side of performance is where the greatest opportunities for improvement lie.

Coaches are observers of humanity and of themselves, students of the mental and emotional engines of performance. Coaches make the time to reflect on how this impacts on what they do. They are critical thinkers about new information, its relationship to what they already know and do, and to their particular situation. They reflect on and think critically about everything that happens in their lives. Coaches know that useful learning is not simply the acquisition of new information. It is how that information is processed and is then related to their particular situation.

Mike Badour thought a good deal about what happened in the following story. The events changed what he felt, thought and said in every situation afterwards.

As an executive with Canada Post, I was on a national tour and my final stop was Winnipeg. After a long day I was ready to go home. In the cab to the airport the driver asked me for whom I worked. I was reluctant to answer because I was concerned this might lead to a conversation about a letter we may have lost some time ago or the usual gripes about spending tax payers' money on meaningless things and so forth.

With reluctance, I told the cab driver that I worked for Canada Post. "Canada Post," he exclaimed, "man, say that with pride." He went on, "Canada Post allows me to keep in touch with my family across the world. I cannot afford such luxuries as Internet or even a computer, and the post office allows me to receive gifts and letters from the people I love. In fact, Canada Post is the backbone of this country. If the mail stopped, people could not receive cheques or money owed. It is the one crucial corporation that is needed to keep this country going. So when you say you work for Canada Post Corporation, say it like you're proud of it, it means so much to me." I thanked him for his comments and let myself be reminded that I do work for a Great Company. You never know where your coaching is going to come from.

Mike is correct. We never know where our coaching will come from or from whom we will receive the next useful lesson. We have to be open to coaching and learning at all times. The most successful people have benefited from coaching at every stage of development. Once anyone becomes aware of this they have the option to choose to open themselves to learning, change and growth. The wise choose to seek the best coaching they can find to support their development.

Many coaches are in a similar situation to that of a young coach in the National Coaching Institute programme who, when reflecting on feedback she received from a variety of people, was dismayed. She reported with real sadness and remorse in her voice, "I am becoming the coach I got into coaching not to be." At key stages in her own development she had "coaches" who were more concerned with the outcomes than the people and the process. There was a lot of yelling and negative feedback. Youngsters were singled out for "blame" and perceived misconduct or miscues were punished. Being sensitive and aware, she felt and reflected on the impact these messages were having on her and her teammates and considered ways to create a more positive outcome.

After beginning to coach with a real sense of the significance of working with the individuals on the team, she drifted into that which is easiest by focusing on technique and tactics and attaching to outcomes. As all successful coaches do, she took this feedback, thought about it and decided to act. It was time to learn the essential new skills and commit to a programme of personal change that was going to be monitored not only by herself but by all others involved, including the athletes. She had realized that knowing what she wanted to change was not enough. She needed to know how to change and she needed support for that process.

Coaches know that their own processes of learning and becoming more effective are identical to the people with whom they work. It is never smooth and linear. There are always "potholes" on the road to success; sometimes even major detours but there are never 'dead ends.' Coaches accept these as realities, adapt and move on.

Coaches understand that it is essential to be knowledgeable technically in whatever the discipline they work, from parenting to sports to leading a large organization. They understand they can never know enough and are always excited by new possibilities. Learning, growth and change is a given. Constant improvement is assumed.

They know that the real learning has to be about human beings and how to support their growth and development. It is not a student who attends school, nor an athlete who enters the arena, nor a salesman who goes to a sales meeting. It is a person performing a function. It is the person who performs that coaches need to learn about, and they do. Coaches know that learning begins with them, the person who coaches. The first changes necessary are always in ourselves if we hope to be able to influence change in others. This is critical for ultimate performance and for life-long success.

In a recent conversation with my friend Doug Clark, a former oarsman, national coach with Rowing Canada and for many years, a successful coach of personal performance in the corporate world, he spoke of this issue. Doug summed it up by saying, "Personal transformation must precede organizational trans-formation." That is exactly what the young coach in the NCI programme came to realize. She had to make personal changes to become the coach she wanted to be, to be able to create the success deserved by the young women on her team.

Richard Peddie, President of Maple Leaf Sports and Entertainment, in speaking about leadership to the coaches in the NCI programme in Toronto, talked about having to "re-invent" himself as a leader. Richard realized that if he wanted to develop other leaders in his organization he needed to do what Gandhi told us: "Be the change you want to see." He reads widely on the topic of leadership and has regular conversations with other leaders in the world of business. All coaches know that the moment they stop learning they begin to become less effective.

I have learned a good deal from all the youngsters, and men and women I have coached. One of the most memorable experiences happened when I was coaching at Monarch Park Secondary School.

I couldn't believe my eyes! This was John's year, and this championship 800m race, his to win. He ran poised right behind the aggressive front runner from our rival high school, ready to use his finishing speed when he came to the final straightaway. Approaching the last turn he remained on the curb in a position to be "boxed-in" should anyone come up to pass! Two runners did, and when they did not have enough speed to complete the pass there was John with nowhere to go when they came off that final turn.

I was both frustrated and disappointed because John was too smart and too experienced to have let this occur. Then it happened. The fast moving group hit the finishing straight and John came through on the inside and sprinted to a comfortable win. He had found enough space to use his superior fitness and speed. I congratulated him, and as we talked I commented that next week at the provincial championships he could not afford to lose focus like that.

I was shocked by his response. He said he knew exactly what he was doing and that the running room would be there, if and when he needed it. He did not want to run a lane wide on the corner just to protect his space with "these guys." He knew all the other athletes well and was confident of two beliefs - no one behind him was strong enough to beat him in the stretch and if they came up on his shoulder there would be room on the inside for him to pull ahead.

How could he be so certain of that? I asked.

"I've been a hot-walker at Woodbine Race Track for years and learned that from the jockeys. A tired horse, and they are all tired by the final stretch, cannot hold the rail coming off the corner and drifts wide. Always. It is exactly the same with runners,

especially at the high school level. The space had to be there and it was." John Hawkins had learned more applied physiology and biomechanics in a part-time job as a boy at the race track than I had at university.

It was not the first or last time I learned an important lesson in sport or life from a young person with whom I worked.

John Neufeld is a former national level high jumper and is now Manager of Coaching Development for SaskSport based in Saskatoon. He is a father of two young children.

This incident happened to me when I agreed to coach under-six co-ed indoor soccer. I am certified at Level 4 in Athletics and when soccer coaches were needed I felt that I had a responsibility to give something to the community. To do this I had to attend a short clinic on coaching skills that was excellent for exposing me to drills and teaching progressions. There was also a short session on the role of the coach, and safety issues, which prepared me even more for my tenure as the "coach." But I soon learned something was missing.

Armed with my new soccer knowledge I prepared my "plan" for the first practice. It included the usual warm up, mobility, drills, games, and cool-down. It was going to be a great kick-off to the season. I introduced myself to the seven starry-eyed participants and we were ready to go. I asked them to follow me as we started our warm up. After one lap of the small gym my future soccer stars were faltering, so we slowed to a walk for the second lap. At this point I heard one of the troops crying. At the same time that I got to the little girl to ask if she was OK, so did her Mom who scooped her up in her arms, mumbled that she hasn't been feeling that good, and carried her away, never to be seen again.

I was down to six, but they were eager. To keep them well hydrated I directed them to the drinking fountain. I waited in the middle of the gym. They wandered back and I noticed that Nicholas, my son, was the last to arrive with his friend, who said he thought Nicholas might have hit his head. I looked and saw a bump on Nicholas' forehead that grew in front of my eyes. It ended up about the size of a golf ball. He seemed all right but he was done with practice for the night.

Now we were five, a little thin, but we kept moving. I got the soccer balls and their eyes lit up. That's what they were really there for! With my assistant I demonstrated a simple pass, stop the ball, and pass back. I set up pairs but before one pass happened a little boy looked up at me and said emphatically "I don't pass to girls." Oh, boy, this wasn't exactly how I had planned the first practice! I explained that we were a team and it was important to pass to everyone on the team.

I survived my first practice and for the remainder of the year had a great time with these little boys and girls. The boy who said "I don't pass to girls" ended up being the leader on the team and he did pass to girls. The team scored some goals, they ran around a lot, they learned a bit about soccer, and most importantly they had a lot of fun, which was my #1 goal!

I enjoyed those twelve weeks as much as all my other coaching experiences. I learned so much from and with those kids. The biggest lesson was that they were children, and thus play and fun was the highest priority. They learned best when they were having the most fun. That, I learned, was the missing part in my training for "coaching" kids. I learned to be adaptable, to think on my feet, and that an intention was more important than a plan.

I referred to the idea of "age and stage of development" earlier as being significant to doing what is appropriate. I had a conversation recently with a coach who was asked to introduce his sport, Ultimate Frisbee, to a group of children at a large private club. Like many of us, his enthusiasm for promoting what he loved led him to agree before asking a key question: how young are these children? So he, like John Neufeld, had to change everything when he discovered the group was made up of more than twenty kids aged three to five! The point was that with children, whatever you do, it had better be fun! Unless of course, the intention is to drive them away from the activity. Later, as children develop, they become more complex and experience a broader range and deeper feelings such as pleasure and satisfaction. But fun is what kids seek first and it is what hooks them every time.

Coaches know that only if children are having fun will they remain to experience the pleasure and satisfaction that comes from mastering a skill and being a competent contributor to a team, whether that team is a family, a class-room, a sport team, a business, or the greater community in which we all live. The child in all of us still needs some fun along with its more mature aspects, pleasure and satisfaction.

I described earlier the difference between "knowing of" something and really knowing it. I believed for a long time that if my actions were not harmful in some way to anyone else then what anyone else thought of them did not matter. There are always those who are too quick and ready to judge others. I understood their opinions should never influence what I do or how I do it. I had that driven a little closer to "knowing" by one of Canada's finest distance runners at the stage when his international career was just beginning. Paul Williams was then a member of the cross-country and track and field teams at University of Toronto.

Low, heavy grey clouds assured us that the steady October rain that had been falling all night was not going to let up for our races that afternoon. It was our university conference cross country championships and we had not seen the new course.

Dressed in our rain gear we set out as a group to get a sense of what specific challenges the layout offered. Paul Williams, the dominant runner in Canadian universities at that time, and later a three time Olympian, was wearing a heavy pair of leather work boots! He was not about to get his racing flats soaked in mud any sooner than necessary. As the rest of us slipped and skidded down a steep narrow path that was essentially a mud sluice, Paul merrily placed each foot heel first into the mud getting a solid grip. He was in control all the way.

As the trail flattened out and I came up beside him, he jokingly said, "These Kodiaks are great, I think I'll race in them." I laughed with him and said that even with the heavy boots he would still win and "they" sure wouldn't like us for that. Paul's reply was wise beyond his youth. "They can't dislike us any more. We win too much."

Win with grace and generosity and celebrate every victory with the people who created it. They deserve to acknowledge accomplishment. Accept the reality, which Paul understood that not all who aspire to the success you achieve will admire and respect that success. Some will even resent it. That is life. Be successful anyway.

Konrad Lerch was for many years the Austrian National Coach for Decathlon and Pentathlon, and the personal coach of numerous high performance athletes in individual events. In 1975 he founded and is still the Meet Director for the de facto World Championship Decathlon and Heptathlon meet, held annually in Goetzis, Austria. He tells the following story.

I was coaching Klaus Bodenmuller who was a world-class competitor in the shot putt for many years. In 1990, Klaus was European Indoor Champion, and in 1991 was the Silver Medallist at the World Indoor Championships.

During this period we traveled frequently and one day after a stopover in Copenhagen we had only a few minutes left to connect for the flight to Helsinki. I tried to encourage Klaus to change his normal phlegmatic thrower's walk into a kind of running because it was the last flight to the capital of Finland where he was to compete that same evening.

Of course he did not change his speed, but he did say, "We won't be late because we have the time we need." He then added, "Besides, time is a relative matter, which passes faster and faster the more you hurry."

It is needless to tell we made the flight well in time.

Konrad had to learn from someone with a little more wisdom, this great truth of time. There is a difference in our lives when we accept the reality that moving quickly with a relaxed intent, when that is required, is far better than hurrying. I cannot recall how many times I heard my mother say, "Haste makes waste." Waste of life energy, waste of resources as we make needless mistakes, and strange as it seems, waste of time because we usually have to do it all over.

You will recall Greg MacNeill's story about telling his son that all he could ever do was his best. Greg demonstrated two key aspects of all life-time learners in that story, self-reflection and taking action. The latter he did twice. Taking the time to think about what has happened, what we have heard others or ourselves say or seen or experienced is critical to constant learning. Because coaches are reflective and Greg held "doing your best" as an important value, he simply had to think about what he had said to his son and apply it to himself. Then he acted on his new wisdom. Coaches put into practice what they learn. It seems significant that Greg began the discipline of Karate shortly after saying he was going to start "one of these days" and his son told him now was the time to do it. We can be certain that Greg reflected on that directive, and again, he took action.

I was discussing how and what we learn as coaches with Ozzie Sawicki who is a successful businessman and the national coach for disabled skiers. What he said was interesting: "The lessons I learned in coaching about working with people were responsible for my success in business." He pointed out that the organizational and technical material came easily to him as he shifted from being an athlete to coaching but he became aware that these were not what were going to create the ultimate success. He had to learn to understand the people with whom he worked, how they learned best, what motivated them and that all people need to be listened to and acknowledged as individuals. Ozzie said that this was all taken to an entirely new level of significance when he began to work with disabled athletes.

Coaches, like all successful people, have the ability that Einstein defined as "a great mind." They are able to hold two diametrically opposed ideas at the same time. They know what is essential to achieving success and they know they need to learn more. In the competitive arena, the opposed ideas are being able to accept that one is doing their best and believing that it is possible to do even better. Ozzie shares this learning with us.

After fifteen years of coaching, the specific moments that stand out in my memory involve victories, setbacks, and laughter and, most often, moments that are defined by individual strength of character.

I am often reminded of a cold, windy, artificially lit evening at the local ski hill on Calgary's perimetre in December 2000. Following a number of years working with able-bodied athletes in alpine skiing, I had taken on the new challenge of coaching the Canadian Disabled Alpine Ski Team. This was an exciting move because my initial coaching experience in 1989 involved working with athletes with a disability. I was now primed with what seemed like years of experience and a toolkit of impenetrable technical and tactical knowledge.

I was there to meet Lauren Woolstencroft, a young woman who was to be one of the athletes in my charge. Lauren is a double leg amputee and a single arm amputee who skis with prosthetics on both legs allowing her to ski as a "standing" athlete with respect to the three disability categories of standing, sitting or visually impaired. I knew that Lauren was talented and was one of the top women on the international World Cup circuit and I believed I could have an immediate impact on her continued improvement.

After introductions I skied with Lauren to assess her skiing technique. I could then provide feedback to coach her to the next level of technical prowess. Back at the top of the slope, we faced each other. Lauren, with both eyes fixed intently on me, waited for my words of coaching wisdom. I proceeded to provide a description of the mechanics of the three phases of the ski turn, continued to break it down into its various components, and completed my explanation by suggesting that a significant part of improving her turn would be to involve all the key body components with the ultimate focus on rolling her ankles to take advantage of the side-cut of the ski to assist in the initiation of the turn.

This, I believed, would be a defining moment in establishing my coaching relationship with Lauren. As I waited for a reply I saw the intense look turn to a somewhat cynical yet humourous one and I heard her say, "What if I don't have ankles?"

In that instant, my belief in the completeness of my knowledge simply vanished and I was left speechless, with a clear sense that I was looking at a new opportunity to learn.

We can be certain that Ozzie did learn and carry the lessons forward into the rest of his coaching and personal and business life. This story has a sequel and we will hear it in the next chapter.

Walter Adams is a retired educator who began as a physical educator in 1961, eventually became a principal and, when at Earl Haig Collegiate, was behind the development of a special programme for Elite Athletes. Walter ended his career as an administrator with the North York Board of Education.

In my first year of teaching and coaching, I was given the position of head coach of the football team at York Mills C.I. That year we made it to the championship game. The game was hard fought and close, and with only minutes left the score was 12 to 8 for Earl Haig. We had the ball on their five-yard line.

I was alternating quarterbacks for each play, which I called. On that critical last sequence I told quarterback #1 to call the fullback off-tackle play and we were stopped cold. I sent quarterback #2 in with a half-back dive play which got us to the goal line but not over. With the tension mounting, both on our bench and the team on the field, I told quarterback #1 to run the same play again, which in my mind meant the dive play. He ran the fullback off-tackle again which was once more stopped dead and we lost the ball on downs. Earl Haig ran out the clock to win the Championship.

I blamed quarterback #1 for not calling the dive play and it wasn't until that night after reviewing the game again and again, I realized that he did exactly what I told him and that the mistake was mine. My communication and perception were both incorrect.

It would have been great for all of us to win the championship, but the lesson learned has been invaluable for me as a teacher, coach, and eventually an administrator in the educational system. Far too often people in leadership positions do not communicate accurately or effectively and when staff perceives incorrect instructions they end up being blamed for the ensuing problems. That one lesson from a student's game in my first year of coaching taught me to be clear and check for the clarity of understanding with those I work with ever since. When we did have a problem related to a miscommunication, I made every effort to understand where we had erred.

Sheilagh Croxon is a mother who acts as a mentor to other coaches. She was a successful coach for many years before becoming the assistant coach on the 1996 Olympic team. In 1998 Sheilagh was appointed Head Coach for the Canadian synchronized swimming team to the Sydney Olympics. Their bronze medal was a testimony to her creativity and courage as a coach to take her sport to a new level.

In my earlier years of coaching I felt success was related to results such as medals, numbers on a page, titles, awards, and so forth. It was only recently that I experienced real success. By that, I mean the kind of wholehearted satisfaction one experiences when you make the conscious choice to acknowledge your greatest personal limitation. Let me explain.

The greatest challenge any coach, any leader will face in their career is getting athletes to believe in their abilities and to dare them to dream the big dream of being the best in the world. Fear of failure and self-doubt often limit us from being able to see what is possible. When I embarked on the journey of building the 2000 Olympic team, I quickly recognized that fear and doubt would be the team's greatest challenges. Not only did the team have no previous Olympic experience, for the first time in the history of our sport our international results were plummeting. These women and I were feeling the obvious pressure.

Although I was a coach with many years of experience and many talents, I had never learned to believe in my athletes or myself. Sure, at some level I knew that I was talented and skilled but when the going got tough my tendency was to become more self critical and more critical of those around me. Having a strong feeling that the 2000 Olympics would be my last opportunity working at this level, coupled with the knowledge that we had nothing to lose, I decided to embark on a personal journey toward increasing my self awareness and belief in myself while building the team's belief in itself. After all, if I couldn't stay on my own side under pressure how could I expect the same of my athletes?

In every team's journey there are critical moments or turning points where things can go either one way or another. There were several of these moments during our two years together. In 1998 I can remember a day when the athletes were having a session with one of our sport psychologists, Sandra Stark. The session was supposed to be about imagery and had been scheduled to last an hour. The session had gone overtime and I can remember waiting for the athletes on the pool deck wondering what was going on! Sandra emerged from the classroom and said " We didn't do any imagery. They wanted to talk, so we did and they want to talk to you now!"

At that moment I recalled some feedback I had received from Peter Jensen when working with the 1996 team. I can remember him sitting down with the head coach and me (I was the assistant at the time) and reviewing our test results. "Ladies", he said, "when God gave out ears, He gave you one, Sheilagh and He gave the other coach none! Believe it or not Sheilagh you are the listener in the group!" Now, feeling completely blindsided and overwhelmed, I listened to Sandra's advice that this would be a good thing to do if I was up for it and I entered the room. Every single athlete spoke about where they were at emotionally, saying they didn't think they could keep up the schedule for the next two years. I listened and acknowledged what they said. I did not judge and I was not defensive. They felt better after expressing themselves. Later many of the women wrote me notes about how important this was for them as individuals and for the team as a whole. It took me a week to recover! This situation was monumental in terms of building team trust and their trust and respect for me as their leader. I think if I had not been open to really "hear" them, things could have ended up differently. This particular experience affirmed my belief in the need to provide more opportunities for the athletes to express their emotions on a regular basis and for me to continue on my path of personal inquiry.

As a result of this journey, I have become a more open communicator. I welcome the opportunity to speak from the heart and actively encourage my athletes to do the same. I have learned the importance of addressing the little things, realizing that every fire is the same fire when it starts! By teaching what I needed to learn most, I was able to empower both myself and a phenomenal team of women to achieve the Olympic dream. I will always cherish the memory of the final team performance, the pride, the connectedness and, yes, the total conviction that they could be the best in the world.

Marion Lay is a former Olympic swimmer with a bronze medal from the Mexico City Olympics. She is the president of Think Sport Ltd., a Vancouver based sport management and consulting firm. Marion has devoted her life to making sport a better place for all and she has a passion for the advancement of women in sport and physical education. Marion has received many awards for her work in sport. She is the president of the 2010 LegaciesNow Society. Marion tells how an already successful woman learned a vital life lesson that moved her work to an entirely new level.

A turning point in my life came in 1985 when Rick Hansen asked me to handle operations for his epic 40,000 kilometre journey around the world, an achievement that most claimed was impossible. That experience taught me the truth of what has been attributed to Henry Ford: "If you think you can, or if you think you can't, you're right." I learned so much from that experience, not the least of which was discovering my unique gift of being able to help people like Rick achieve their dreams. I learned that for a dream to become reality, four steps must be taken.

The first is giving ourselves permission to dream. As Pamela Vaull Starr has written: "Reach high, for stars lie hidden in your soul. Dream deep, for every dream precedes the goal."

Next comes the realization that a dream can rarely be achieved without a team of special, committed people to help you, people who can translate the dream into reality. The anthropologist Margaret Mead said: "Never doubt that a small group of thoughtful, committed people can change the world. Indeed, it is the only thing that ever has." The Hansen experience showed me just how true that is.

Gathering the right team leads to the third step of taking the risk to succeed or to fail by sharing our dreams with the world and asking for support to achieve the dream. Yes, this is a risk, but if the dream stays inside us, it goes nowhere. When you weave the right team, with every person inspired to offer her or his own unique gifts, everything becomes possible. That, I learned, is my strength, weaving the team together to help achieve the dream, being a connector of people and blessed with the ability to sell a dream. Some call my gift being a dream weaver, others a team builder. The result is the same, being able to translate dreams into reality. When people ask for help I can set them on a course. I believe that asking for help is the greatest compliment you can give to another person.

Finally, it is important to realize that the outcome is beyond your control. You can only control the process and throughout the journey we learn that, in fact, the process is often more important than the end result. If you can accept that, then a dream and a small group of people can change the world.

"Only dreamers can teach us to soar." – Anne Marie Pierce
"Excellence can be achieved if you risk more than others think is safe, love more than others think is wise, dream more than others think is practical, and expect more than others think is possible." — Anon

Ted Schmidt has a lifelong but critical love affair with sports. He was a basketball coach at Mimico High School, and a baseball coach for Columbus Boys' Club. Ted is the editor of the *Catholic New Times*.

It wasn't supposed to be like this, the teacher burying the student, *but in life there are no guarantees. Al Smith, our Don Quixote, had come home to be buried in Mimico, the little town that had nourished him. To paraphrase T.S. Eliot, in his end was his beginning.*

The previous night at the wake in the town's only funeral home, Al's ex-wife Karen insisted I tell her two sons about their first break up, forty years ago. I was a first year teacher and the fiery Smitty had played on my basketball team. But this particular night at the school dance, he was in his cups having finished half a mickey of gin, to be exact, trying to assuage the pain of the first break up with the wonderful woman who would become his wife and mother of his three children.

Adam and James chuckled as I related the story, still so indelible in my mind, of walking their father around the football field as he poured out his frustration at the intricacies of the male-female dance. We were, as I told the story, one hundred yards away from the holy ground, which bound our friendship until the day he died.

That wasn't the first time I had walked him around the track. The other memorable time was when he missed a foul shot in the last second of play that same year. We lost the championship by a point and Smitty was inconsolable. We took another walk around the oval to talk about perspective, effort and learning about ourselves.

Al Smith was the quintessential hockey gypsy, chasing the elusive Canadian dream right across North America. His career reads like a bad travelogue: Starting in Toronto in 1965 he was off to Vancouver, San Francisco, Tulsa, Rochester, Baltimore, Pittsburgh, Detroit, New England, Boston, Buffalo, Hartford and finally Colorado in 1980-81. Close behind him was Karen, closing up apartments and meeting him in the next city.

Looking back Karen laughs at the hectic life and warm friendships formed during those years. Particularly memorable was the close friendship of the present Coach of the Toronto Maple Leafs, Pat Quinn and his wife Sandra. "The league had a rule," Karen says, "that you could have two players over 25, and Pat was the grey beard at 26. They were so warm and friendly to us 22 year olds."

Smitty was always conflicted and defensive about his lack of formal education. To make up for this deficit he became a voracious reader, eclectic in his taste. Even early in his hockey career he was driven to write. He simply could not hack the sales jobs after hockey, even though he excelled in each of them. The need to write had become a compulsion, his raison d'etre. Driving a cab gave Al the opportunity to concentrate, as well as fill his world with a steady stream of characters.

His life shifted between the cab to the word processor. He knocked off a couple of novels which he self-published. The results were the same for both: "limited sales and no readership," as he confessed to a friend. Then a gift horse smiled at him, a $30,000 cheque, courtesy of fellow player Carl Brewer's successful reclamation of money from the NHL pension fund.

With his new found stash, Smitty charged in, rented a downtown theatre, hired actors and staged his play Confessions to Anne Sexton. Nobody came. One night I showed up with six Mimico friends only to discover we were the only ones there. Over beers afterward he laughed at his failure as he always did. Another windmill down, more to come.

A month before he died, we were at lunch and he sighed. "I am just learning how to write." Later that night, blinking back the tears, I read the inscription he wrote at the front of his final novel, The Tragedy of Lake Tuscarora: "A mentor, unfortunately, is doomed to be a mentor."

At the funeral Mass of the Resurrection, so appropriate for one who had known so many, I marvelled at his indomitable and generous spirit. T.S. Eliot came to mind again. He seemed to have our beautiful dreamer in mind when he wrote: "We are only undefeated because we have gone on trying."

Like Al Smith, coaches go on learning so the "trying" becomes ever more effective. And like Al Smith, coaches know that the learning and the trying are easy or easier when we do what we love to do.

Adam Urbach teaches Elementary School in York Region, coaches juvenile boys' basketball with the Barrie Royals, and is Assistant Coach to Bob Bain with York University Men's Basketball.

Having drifted aimlessly for my first two years of university, undecided about where this high priced education was taking me, I finally was inspired to choose a direction. In my third year I was offered the opportunity, by coach Bob Bain, to be a part of a coaching team with the York Yeomen basketball team.

In the early discussions with Coach Bain it was stressed that such a commitment would mean sacrifice! I replied by saying, "I want to learn to do what you do!" His response shaped the next years of my life, "The decision is yours to make." I immediately made the decision to become a protégé of Coach Bain but had no idea at the time that it would take me to such heights.

Coach Bain saw that I had a gift, a hidden ability to coach this game well, and he looked past the fact that I had never played beyond high school level and that I was a mediocre player at best. He fostered my development through lessons and responsibilities unlike any I had been given to that time and he laid out the basis for my continuing to be a contributing member of his coaching team. Bob Bain inspired me to obtain a masters degree in coaching and recommended me as Director of a Summer Basketball Camp at Seneca College, a job I would not have known existed except through him. Through that job, I have found a new appreciation for life, love, and basketball. His lessons will never be forgotten, and I only hope that one day I can pass them on as selflessly and graciously as he did to me.

Bob Bain did for Adam what coaches do for others: He set him on a path of life-time learning with all opportunities that flow from it. He opened doors to real life lessons by first working with him in his programme and then encouraging him to enter the leadership role at Seneca College. Lifetime learners create other learners in the same way they teach all-important values; they model a way of being in the world.

Imagine how many lifetime learners who became coaches of others were created by Jim Deegan who, in 2003 celebrated his 47th season in the track programme at Mount St. Mary's College in Emmitsburg, Maryland. Jim is married with five children and seven grandchildren. He has coached numerous All-Americans and Olympians but as we read in the letter below, Jim impacted the lives of countless young men in even more significant ways. He gave them the opportunity and showed them how to become successful people.

The following letter came from Chris Hall, class of 1987. In a continuing learning programme, Chris was asked to write to someone who had made an impact in his life, and he writes, *"Coach, you were the first person who came to mind."*

When I decided I wanted to go to college, I found out quickly that my family couldn't afford Mount Saint Mary's. I was disappointed because I wanted to go to college and to play soccer. College is a gift. It is not something everyone gets to do. I remember going with you to the Dean of Admissions and talking with him while my mom waited in the hall. The Dean told me because my SAT scores were so low I would not be able to handle the demands of the college courses and I would probably not succeed. That made me feel horrible, but you said just as quick as he finished his sentence that you believed in me, and that you believed I could handle it, and you would make sure I succeeded. That made me feel great, coach, and because of you I was accepted to the Mount and I got to play soccer and flourish and grow as a man.

I know we banged heads sometimes over how we thought about the game, but you always came through for me when I needed help financially, and in your own way, when I needed it emotionally. I always gave 100%, on and off the field, for you, because I respected you and the Mount and my teammates.

Because of your help and support and your belief in me, I graduated from the Mount with a B average and a double major in economics and business and finance. I went on to success in business; I sold my three GNC franchises in May 1998 and made my first million at 33. I have now bought ten more franchises and I am opening them in Boston, North Carolina and South Carolina.

When I meet young men and women today, especially athletes, I always encourage them to believe in themselves and others. I know you don't realize it, but you have had a positive impact on many young men and women all your life. Thanks Coach, from myself and all the others with whom you shared your life and humour. We greatly appreciate it.

Coaches learn and continue to learn because they care deeply about the people with whom they work. Of course they always learn more about the practical areas in which they work, accounting to zoology and everything else imaginable. But they learn early that they need to learn the most is in the personal area, becoming more effective at working with people, inspiring excellence and joy in the process and enhancing confidence. Successful learners create other successful learners.

Seven Keys to Being a Lifetime Learner

1. Be curious about life, all of it.

2. Be fascinated by people, their differences, and how they grow and perform.

3. See every situation as a learning opportunity because it is.

4. Seek out new information constantly, exchange ideas with peers.

5. Think critically. Be self-evaluative and reflective. Make time to just think.

6. Find mentors and advisors and ask for feedback.

7. "Be the change you want to see." *Gandhi*

Best Practice 10

CELEBRATES LIFE

Best Coaches celebrate life by living fully engaged
with others in the challenge and struggles of becoming
better today than they were yesterday.

"My life belongs to the whole community, and as long as I live, it is
my privilege to do for it whatsoever I can. I want to be thoroughly used up
when I die, for the harder I work, the more I live. I rejoice in life for
its own sake. Life is no "brief candle" to me. It is a sort of splendid torch
which I have got hold of for the moment, and I want to make it burn
as brightly as possible before handing it on to future generations."
~ *George Bernard Shaw*

This book is filled with stories of lives that were changed and "turned around" by the intervention of coaches. The changing of lives, including their own lives is the strongest evidence that coaching is a celebration of life. Coaching is an affirmation that, at its best, life is filled with change, growth and becoming all we were meant to be. Living and supporting that process in all its forms is the most powerful celebration of being alive. The Lebanese poet Kahlil Gibran described the richness of life when he wrote that he wanted his life to be both a "tear and a smile." To be fully alive we need to experience it all. We cannot feel selectively.

Coaches change lives for the better because better is their focus. They see people as they can be and work towards that possibility, focusing not on the mistakes and problems but on what is done well and possible. The changes they foster have a lasting effect on people's lives. In turn, coaches lives are changed by the people they coach. They engage fully in life building relationships, and it is in their relationships that life is enhanced and celebrated. All this is possible because coaches are life-time learners. They reflect on their experience and think critically about all they see and hear. In particular they learn from the young people they coach who challenge everything that does not "feel right." Coaches treat seriously every question they are asked and provide thoughtful answers.

Bill Bradley, the All-American from Yale, a Rhodes Scholar, NBA Champion with the New York Knickerbockers, and a former U.S. Senator, wrote a powerful little book, *Values of the Game* in which he discusses the impact coaches have on others.

The really great coaches engage their players in a quest to be the best. In the right player-coach relationship, a quiet "well done" can go a long way. By talking candidly about the problems of adolescence or the vagaries of the parent-child relationship, some high school coaches extend their reach to life off the court. Their players may never become pros, but because they learned the values of the game they are better prepared for life. Many people in all walks of life will tell you that their lives were turned around by a coach who took an interest in their total well being.

How better to celebrate life than to work with young people in ways that improve them as whole people!

Stuart Neeley, who came to Canada from Scotland as a boy brought with him a love for the game of soccer and a belief that girls should not be involved in sport. Coaches and the culture of this country have not diminished his love for soccer but have taught him two major lessons: He has come to love Canada and he now supports girls involvement in sport. Stuart now works for the Canadian Soccer Association and coaches National Women's teams Under 21, U16, and U15! He got there by coaching his way up the system, starting with House League, and says that coaching girls and women in soccer has changed him. "They have taught me to be a better person and a better coach."

In a note I received from Stuart, he said that he "grew up in Canada and it has taught me well. I want to give everything I have to the kids and to coaching. They remind me daily to never forget the innocence of the game, that it is fun, that the whole range of emotions from fear to joy are there for us and that winning isn't everything. When victory is the goal, playing to win is everything until the game is over."

I asked him what the game means to him now and he noted that he continues to learn, and that is important. I could sense the contemplation in his writing as he concluded with, "But it is not about me, is it?"

Coaches consider as a first principle that the game is for the kids, for the young adults or for whoever is playing. It is about the experience of the players. Before I sat down to write this section, I checked the newspaper to see what was happening with our National basketball team coached by Jay Triano, a man whose character was moulded by his coach and mentor, the late Jack Donohue. Jay was quoted as saying, "I know how great it felt for me to go to an Olympics and how special I felt and how hard I had trained and everything. To help twelve players feel that same thing to me was the best."

Coaching is a celebration of life because it is about living life to the fullest and supporting others in doing the same. Coaching is about seeking and striving and engaging life fully. This is what Coach Triano had to say about the challenging preparation and committed focus of the team at the Sydney Olympics, "I think our players can walk away and say, 'We have no regrets'."

Hal Brown was a mentor of mine. He was the high school coach of Gord Stewart who was the first young man I convinced to become a decathlete. Recently, in an email exchange with Gord following Hal's death, Gord said:

"I don't know what life path I would have followed had I not crossed paths with Hal in Grade 9 at North Toronto C.I., then you in the years to follow! My early 'career' with Hal included amazing pole-vaulting with a 12 foot bamboo pole from Bamboo Interiors on Davenport Road. They cost $1.44 each (12 cents a foot!) plus countless dollars worth of friction tape between the 'knots'. Great days they were."

Great days, indeed. Sport for the pure joy of it. There is joy in acquiring new skills and greater fitness, then testing it all, and there is joy in healthy competition. Hal epitomized a relaxed attitude about the game and caring for the person and clarified these aspects of coaching for me. Hal made the joy of sport come alive for me in every interaction we had over the years. The athletes, such as Gord, who came to the East York Track Club to work with me in the summers, reinforced his message. He felt joy in the simple experience of the activity and he brought a relaxed commitment to excellence. I saw these qualities again and again in young men and women coached by Hal.

Celebration surrounds coaches who generate it themselves. They celebrate effort, learning, courage and all the other qualities that make life rich, including our human foibles and stresses. Until and unless one is in a high performance environment it is difficult to understand that a jujube or something equally meaningless, being an award celebrating a great effort in a training session. Do you really believe Harry Neale's millionaire hockey players were competing for the portable television set? Of course not. The television was a symbol of being judged the best in the challenge presented. Living fully, accepting the challenge to be the best one can be is a true celebration of life.

Coaches celebrate the achievements of others in a wide variety ways. Carolyn Broadhurst is a teacher and coach of Field Hockey and Track and Field at Colonel By Secondary School in Ottawa. She celebrates her own life and the lives of others by writing poetry. It is an expression of one of her talents and a way to acknowledge those who inspire her. She wrote to praise the commitment of Canadian Women's Olympic Hockey coach, Shannon Miller, to win the gold in 1998. When the team won the silver medal Carolyn wrote a beautiful poem that included these lines:

Do not despair
our silver standing-
golden desires
kindle
ambitious flames
in us
who watched you.

Hans Selye, the great Canadian scientist who defined stress and impacted the thinking of the world of medicine, said "Strive always for the highest attainable aim..." Life is a process, and while we strive for the highest aim there is no guarantee of achievement. When we are meeting life enhancing challenges and striving to overcome them we are fully alive. Only then can we have "no regrets." The "no regrets" is the second part of Selyes' tenet, "never put up resistance in vain." The ultimate life dulling experience is to live in the past, regretting what was or wasn't, and resisting reality. That was the basis of Mike Dyon's decision, go for it completely, explore his talent fully and then there will never be any "if-only's." Coaches encourage and support that in all with whom they work. Dreams are taken seriously.

Here is the second part of Ozzie Sawicki's story. It illustrates the human need to strive to be the absolute best we can be.

In March 2002, I was standing on the final steep section of the women's giant slalom leading into the finish area at Snowbasin, Utah, the alpine competition site of the Salt Lake City Paralympic winter games. For a reason that I will never know, I found myself reflecting on that cold, windy night in Calgary, and how many experiences Lauren and I had gone through since my "ankle rolling" advice.

Lauren was on course and skiing well. The crowd was cheering loudly watching Lauren's performance on the jumbo television monitor in the finish area, in part applauding her heroics earlier in the week. Lauren had recovered in only two days, from a dramatic high-speed fall in the initial downhill competition in which she injured her knee and went on to capture the gold medal in the Super G event. It was a truly fantastic achievement.

Now Lauren was closing in on the giant slalom finish. She crossed the line with a time that left her in third place, winning a bronze medal to go with her gold in the Super G. It was another moment to celebrate Canadian success and the audience cheered its support.

I skied down to the finish area where the athletes were being interviewed by the media and sought out Lauren and Karolina Wisniewska, who was Lauren's teammate. Karolina had secured the gold in the event. I received a fleeting glance from Lauren, a glance that took me back again to the first moment we met. I saw many things in her glance, but the most definitive was the same pure determination in her eyes that I had seen before. She approached me and apologized, with teary eyes for coming in third. The bronze, a podium performance, was simply not her goal.

Lauren's tenacity was unparalleled. Two days later in the final slalom event at the Paralympics, Lauren captured her second gold of the games. That defining look of determination transformed into a look of satisfaction, a look that I have become accustomed to seeing. The gold was her expectation. Nothing less would suffice. This is how Lauren lives her life both in sport and away from it.

I have had an impact on the lives of many athletes and all of them continue to impact on me. They remind me that we move ahead not as a coach making recommendations or an athlete following advice, but rather through a partnership. We create unified goals and share in and learn from both the failures and the successes allowing continued growth of each of us as individuals and as the team we are.

That first day in Calgary Lauren did not let the "ankle" incident interfere with her listening. We came to an agreement concerning what those partnership parametres would be so that there would be a better understanding of her expectations as an athlete and my ability to impact her growth.

An individual's quality of character often shines through in such diverse situations. My pride as a coach is to recognize my fingerprints on that character and just as importantly, to recognize the collective "soul" of the athletes' character imprinted on my own character. This is the "wisdom" of experience that we can pass on to each successive athlete with whom we have the opportunity to work.

I asked Ozzie what would define him in terms of challenges for change and growth. He answered: *What defines Ozzie? Do not see only that which is immediate to us, but look at life with the understanding that there is a landscape larger than the one we see. Dare to reach beyond what we already know.* Can there be a greater celebration of life than to work closely with another or others in the pursuit of being the best one can be?

John Byl is a professor of Physical Education at Redeemer University College in Ancaster, Ontario. He has been an educator at all levels in British Columbia and Ontario for over 32 years. John is president of the Canadian Intramural Recreation Association – Ontario and has published a number of books, which you can find at www.humankinetics.com.

When Terry was four he came home one day to find his mother in tears, speaking with a police officer. He ran, with fear in his heart, to his mother, and they held each other tightly. He was told that his father had died suddenly in a car accident. Terry cried then, and often, thereafter, when he thought about it. He missed his dad.

A number of years later he was a star basketball player, but he was plagued with injuries. We met when he came into our programme. Terry had been a determined person throughout his life. I applied rolls of tape and he played on as if he had no injuries. It took time to tape him before each practice and game but it was valuable time when I could be with him like his father might have been. We talked about everything from how to break out of a slump to dealing with relationships with girls. We enjoyed the four years we spent together on and around the court.

When I went to congratulate Terry at his graduation, we gave each other a long hug, and Terry let the tears flow freely. For four years we had a coach-player relationship but we realized when it was all over that it had become more. Through the hug I said: "You've become a son to me during this time," and through the tears he replied, "You've become a father to me during this time."

Norm Olenick is a retired educator who spent much of his career at Langara College in Vancouver, British Columbia. He is currently working at the University of British Columbia and teaches leadership and ethics for the National Coaching Institutes in Vancouver and Victoria. Imagine the "ripple effect" over a lifetime because a coach came into Norm's life when he needed it most. Imagine if every youngster had access to a coach.

Many people have had an influence on my development as a person and my thinking regarding leadership and coaching. The first was Merv Oveson of the Kivan Boys Club who presented the initial opportunity and challenge and then Jack Way, the club director, who continued, with Merv to "steer" me along.

Merv Oveson took me under his wing when I was on a path to become a juvenile delinquent. He saw something better in me and placed me in charge of a large group of young boys as their softball coach. My recollection is trying to justify his faith, trying to coach the boys to improve their skill and understanding of the sport, and trying to handle responsibilities of leading others for the first time. The influence of these two men, Merv and Jack, seemed to open many doors throughout the past several decades of my involvement in sport and recreation. They were not the only "influencers" but perhaps the most significant because Merv changed the direction I was headed and then Jack supported me in that direction.

Joel Donen is a member of the first graduating class of the National Coaching Institute in Ontario. He is president of Continuous Coaching Inc. He is passionate about working with organizations to foster accountability. He also coaches tennis. For more about Joel see www.continuouscoaching.com.

Is this your grandfather?" a middle aged tennis couple asked John and me after being on the court next to us during one of our training sessions.

In the last nine months, many people had asked about our training sessions, curious about this enthusiastic combination of a 17 and 71-year-old tennis player. "It is all about the love of the game," John Leicester would remind me over and over again on-court and off. He knew that an athlete who loved playing would be one of the few who pushed the limits of his performance, enjoying every minute. I was hooked.

This "old guy" who didn't sound old, related to everyone. He talked like a friend, drilled you like a sergeant, and joked with everyone. Best of all, he had stories. Stories of the local tennis legends he had coached, stories about mischief he got into in his teens, and stories about playing our game. We had so much fun that many people who saw us wanted to join in, including some parents who approached us to coach their children.

John backed up his statement about "love of the game" with a master's coaching style. He turned complicated, technical feedback from my previous coaches into simple concepts that made sense, felt right, and quickly improved my skills.

"Yes," we both answered the tennis couple. The idea of a grandfather and his grandson seemed easier to explain than the longer story of how a coach could so inspire a student, no matter the difference in age. Inspire was the right word. Whether it was maximizing my court time by getting extra fit so I could sprint to pick-up balls between drills, visualizing my strokes when I was in the car, or renting a video camera to analyze my strokes, I did whatever I could think of to improve my skills and unlock my best game for competition.

When the woman said it was great to see us training so hard, John replied, "Well, of course, we are preparing for a tournament." Her husband, curious, asked which tournament, and John said, "The Provincial Open. We are playing doubles."

"The Provincial Open, but you won't be able to play in the over 35s if you play together!" the husband stated as he realized our intent.

"No," I replied, "we are playing the open category."

We had a great tournament. After winning the first round easily, we gave the number one ranked team the best run of the tournament. We probably would have taken the second set if John hadn't twisted his knee while jumping for an overhead smash. It was great to see the top team's faces as we went after them full force, trying for the upset.

John's reputation for teaching "love of the game" spread. Soon, we started an academy in his name and were busy organizing provincial training camps, city wide community tennis programmes and a multi-sport fitness training centre.

Three months after John died of cancer at the age of 73 I had my interview for medical school. The interview went well but the committee was concerned that possibly I was more excited to be a tennis coach than a doctor. They were right. It excites me to challenge young people to train passionately for something they love doing. Over that first year the academy grew from four excited athletes to eighty, every one of them having learned, what I learned from John – "the love of the game."

John Leister, like all coaches brought his passion for "the game" every day and created an atmosphere of high-energy enjoyment. His passion was a simple, daily celebration of being alive!

David Kenwright is the Head Coach and Programme Director at the Abbotsford Twisters Gymnastics Club for the Girls Competitive Programme. He has coached for 25 years, and has placed gymnasts on national teams in two different countries. He "has had many successes and disappointments along the way." Inculcating joy among his athletes has always been important to him.

I have tried to teach my athletes that the greatest joy in life comes from desire and the drive to achieve. "If you can't earn it, it's not worth having" gets said everyday in training, even when the athletes don't like to hear it. We always laugh because I am consistent in my belief. Humour is the best medicine and the ability to laugh at oneself is the greatest gift.

One of the best things about reaching the top of your sport is that you get to be a part of the best in the world. Seeing the best gymnasts in training everyday, twice a day, for ten days before the Games begin is breath taking. One of the best gymnasts in the world, Svetlana Chorkina from Russia, trained in the same gym in Sydney as the Canadian team. Russia has always been the leader in our sport and to watch this team train was a coach's dream come true, because their gymnasts are the best and their artistic qualities are so refined.

The first day of team competition had been a bad day for the Russians and their head coach, Leonid Arkaev was having a coach's meeting in the gym. He was reaming out his coaching staff. Svetlana Chorkina's personal coach, Boris Pilkin, was in the meeting. He is in his late sixties and still produces top athletes. Svetlana, who was conditioning with the team near the meeting heard her coach getting into hot water. She walked over, pushed her way through, looked the head coach right in the eye, grabbed Boris Pilkin's hand and dragged him out of the meeting to "spot" her for some exercises.

This act of defiance took some courage especially since in Russia, one does not defy. Boris looked around in an amused, hopeless sort of way and winked at me as his champion was saving him. This moved me so much. It is always our actions and the choices we make, not what we say, that really speaks for the sort of person we are. I found out sometime later that Boris Pilkin had a heart attack in one of those meetings. Svetlana's love and wish to protect him says volumes. To me it said, "He is MY coach" just like the coach always says she is "my" athlete. I believe that the coach athlete relationship is sacred and must be revered. I do not know of any gymnast in this country who has her priorities as sorted out as this incredibly brave and caring individual. The bond between Svetlana and Boris was a huge part of their success as people as well as champions in sport. When Svetlana won the Olympic Gold medal on the uneven bars, her second Olympic title in that event, she said, "This medal is for the peoples of Russia and it is because of my coach that I stand here today."

My gymnast, Kate Richardson, was present while all this took place and we talked about the incident many times. One of the points I made to Kate was that I didn't think this gymnast and her coach would ever have any regrets.

In January 2002, Kate underwent back surgery and we were not sure if we would be able to continue her career. Kate found the courage and health to come back not only to her sport, but her life. She made the team for the Commonwealth Games and helped earn the team bronze medal. She also won the coveted all-around gold as well as a gold on the beam. She earned a full athletic scholarship to UCLA and left for her new college life in September. Before she went, she gave me her Commonwealth Games gold medal with a thank you card saying, " I will never, ever have any regrets." Such wisdom for an eighteen year old could not be any more real, honest or true. My work here is done.

In most of my conversations when the idea that coaches change lives is brought up, people have a "coaching story." I heard about Mr. Papich on a flight from Halifax to Toronto. The story below was written by Richard Luczyk, who graduated from Winston Churchill C.V.I. in Thunder Bay, Ontario in 1998. It was created for the school yearbook about "a remarkable coach, Walter Papich," upon the occasion of his retirement. The story says so much about the impact on others of those who give their time in a deeply caring and personal way.

It is often said that the greatest heroes go unnoticed. Every day these people give their time and energy to assist others in so many ways. However, in a world that grows increasingly selfish, such role models are often overlooked. Firemen, police officers, doctors, and teachers make the world a better place on a daily basis, with no fanfare. All too often they do not even receive a thank-you. Yet, for those whose lives these amazing people touch, their strength, caring words, or gentle touch will never be forgotten. For more than forty years, the community of Thunder Bay has been blessed by the presence of a remarkable person who has dedicated his life to enriching the lives of others. Thank you Mr. Papich, Sir."

Richard writes about all the sports Mr. Papich coached and the incredible successes the teams achieved. Then he writes,

However the numbers pale in comparison to the experiences and memories that Mr. Papich has left with his players.

On the field, Mr. Papich instils lessons about fair play, self-control, sportsmanship, and class. From his inspirational pre-game speeches to his one-on-one discussions with players, what Mr. Papich tells his athletes has as much bearing on life as it does the game. Year after year, he has ingrained in his players the watchwords of Trojan football that will remain with us and guide us for the rest of our lives: Intelligence. Integrity. Intensity. Dedication. Determination. Discipline. These words are lessons that each one of us has taken to heart and continues to apply to everything we do.

His ability to motivate students in a variety of ways is what makes him unique. He knows exactly when we as students need praise, or when we need a 'kick in the butt'. With a keen sense of humour he expertly measures out constructive criticism and wholehearted congratulations, inspiring thousands of young people to become leaders. Because of his guidance and example, we will never demand anything less than the best from ourselves.

The concluding sentence is a perfect summary of the significant impact this single individual had on the lives of so many young people. *"In every way, he has earned the nickname by which we so fondly refer to him... Sir."*

Only a man who treated others with deep respect can earn from them such respect. Coaches act that way, it is a large part of how and why they change lives.

And, the impact of these coaches has an immense ripple effect. Debra Gordon, now living in London, Ontario heard much about this "amazing teacher/coach Mr. Papich, Sir" from her daughter, who had never been coached by him but had him as a teacher. Debra talked so enthusiastically about him, I too was inspired enough to ask if I could get a copy of the yearbook article! None of us ever know where our impact ends and whom it touches.

Colin Hood is the Executive Director of OFSAA (Ontario Federation of Schools Athletic Associations), a former athlete and a passionate advocate for the value of sport and coaching for our youth.

Looking back on my life I can identify three key people outside my immediate family who really helped determine who I am and shaped my life to what it is today. Those were the coaches who helped me in my youth.

My school's cricket coach, Ray Knight, taught me more about the game than I can remember, but, above all, conveyed to me that cricket was only a game and that life was bigger than cricket. He taught me about respect for my opponents, the importance of enjoyment in participating, and the values associated with teamwork and fair play. My physical education teacher, John Learmouth, instilled in me the love of physical activity, and the desire for a career in sport. He showed me that nothing could be achieved without hard work and dedication and further, that in order to succeed in life, and in sport I would have to develop a whole series of skills around time management, goal and priority setting, as well as skill development. My college teacher and coach, Jim Biddle, showed me that I could get immense enjoyment out of teaching and coaching others and that, while my own skill development was important, I could play an even more vital role in helping develop others to their full potential in life and sport activities.

I suspect that at the time I was not very conscious of their efforts to make me a better player or athlete, and I was probably not fully aware of what I know today, which is their commitment to help me as an individual in the journey of life.

Jeff Adams, Canada's great paralympic athlete summed it up perfectly when he said, "Coaches sometimes have an opportunity to help an athlete become a great athlete. Coaches always have an opportunity to help all athletes become better people."

Harry Sawchuk is currently a partner in H&H Associates – Consultants in Lifestyle and Personal Growth Programmes. Harry spent 32 years as a physical educator at Governor Simcoe S.S. in St. Catherines, Ontario. During all those years he contributed to professional and community organizations, wrote texts and journal articles, and presented at dozens of workshops and conferences across Canada and internationally. Harry's work has been recognized with several professional and community awards.

About forty years ago there was this little scrawny, bony-kneed kid with the proverbial coke bottle glasses from the east side of a little town called Port Colborne. On his first day of high school, during his first PT class, he sat nervously and in awe amongst all the big guys while a tall, fit, good looking "Mr. MacDonald" explained what the class could expect in PT.

Then came the time for Mr. MacDonald to pick "squad leaders." He looked across the group and pointed a finger at the little scrawny kid and said, "You will be squad leader number one." I was that kid.

I was so thrilled and proud to be a "squad leader" that I silently vowed that I would NEVER let this man down. I would be the best squad leader ever! I wanted to be just like him!

It was that very day that I decided that I was going to become a physical education teacher, so that I could have the opportunity to help some unknown little kid.

Mr. Don MacDonald left Port Colborne shortly thereafter to become the principal at Pauline Johnson Collegiate in Brantford Ontario. I often wonder if he ever realized just what an impact he had on my life!

Hugh Spooner is a first generation Canadian, born in Toronto and a graduate of Newtonbrook High School. He acknowledges his many blessings in life from exceptional coaching when he needed it to become an Olympian in 1976 and earn an athletic scholarship that he turned into a fine education. Hugh states emphatically "my greatest blessing from athletics is my wife of almost nineteen years, Antoinette (Toni) Bryan Spooner, and our son."

In 1975, at the age of seventeen, I was one of the finest junior sprinters in the nation. Because of my potential I was encouraged by Gerard Mach and Fred Foot to commit to training for the 1976 Olympics. I remember thinking I didn't have a chance of making the Canadian team for the 1976 Olympics, but at least it would be a positive experience to train with older, more developed sprinters laying the foundation for my future. In October 1975, I committed to training at least four to five days a week for the Olympic Trials in June 1976. I had nine months to mentally and physically commit to the process with no guarantees of anything but the experience of trying.

As most athletes soon learn there are usually setbacks in athletics, most often in the form of injury. Mine came in January 1976, after a strong two-week training camp in Gainesville, Florida. I was training at the "old pig palace" at the Exhibition grounds in Toronto. The conditions were not good. There was a less than perfect 200 metre banked track, with a less than adequate ventilation system. We usually cracked open doors to allow the cold air outside to provide some semblance of fresh air inside. In the middle of this training session, I tore my left hamstring, not an unusual injury for a sprinter. The next day as I went off to school on crutches, I believed my training towards the Olympics was over, but I was wrong.

My first night away from the track after my injury I received a call from Gerard Mach instructing me to meet him to resume my training. My first reaction, albeit a silent one, was that Gerard was nuts and didn't fully understand that I couldn't walk properly much less run. Nevertheless, on a Friday evening after school, I made the hour plus journey, through a snow storm, down to the track to meet Gerard. My decision to meet Gerard that evening was a turning point in facing a setback head on. It helped propel me on a course of great and unimagined life experiences .

Gerard created a workout that allowed me to continue to condition my body and assist the healing process of my hamstring without any danger of further injury to the muscle. The additional upside for me was this new programme required more discipline and commitment, which not only built up my body, but it helped to focus and strengthen my mind. My very first competition was in April 1976, at the Dogwood Relays in Tennessee, where I ran a relaxed 100m. My training and rehab had begun to pay dividends and I believed that I would be ready for the Olympic Trials.

I was selected to attend a month long training camp in May 1976, at Longbeach California. *The camp essentially provides fine tuning for training and competition. The focus was on speed and technique, with select competitions to get us ready for the all-important Olympic qualifying meets in June.*

My commitment and hard work paid off. I performed well in a series of meets throughout late May, June and early July 1976. I raced well in California and in the first

Olympic qualifying meet in June in Quebec City I was sixth in the final. In the second qualifying meet in Montreal I ran a personal best 100m, and placed fourth behind Marv Nash, Hugh Frazer and Bob Martin. I continued to run well in a meet at Crystal Palace in London, England, and back at the Pre-Olympic meet in Olympic stadium in Montreal.

Then came the second setback. In early July I injured the back of my right knee. I couldn't sprint at all; the pain was just too great. Gerard organized a special session with the doctors at the Olympic village and I received my first and only cortisone shot. Two days later I was ready to go fast again. After the second qualifying meet I was named to the Canadian Olympic Sprint team. Although I didn't run fast enough to qualify for the open 100 metres, I was the fourth fastest Canadian going into the games and had made our relay team.

From the entire process, albeit a brief nine month duration from the time of my personal commitment, I learned a tremendous lesson about not giving up and being tough minded through setbacks. With determination, great coaching and mentoring and proper preparation and planning, I was able to make the best of an earned opportunity and represent my country on the marvellous international stage of the Olympics.

All that said, my greatest rewards from athletics have come not just from actually competing in the Games and gaining recognition from my peers and community, specifically North York at the time. My greatest rewards have come from the extensive travel, a strong university experience and the friendships established with so many good people along the way.

Denis Sacks, whose story appeared earlier, believes that his friend Tommy Bacher really does celebrate life – every day!

Dr Tommy Bacher is a very busy general practitioner in the Toronto area. He volunteers on many charitable boards and is currently Executive VP of the Canadian Maccabi Association. Tommy has a full schedule! He is also a runner and a voluntary leader, organiser and coach of a group of diverse forty and fifty year olds who call themselves the Rocky Road Runners.

In spite of Tommy's jammed schedule he somehow finds time to organise and inspire this group, including organising two teams of seventeen runners who compete annually in a road relay, between Jasper and Banff and more recently along the Cabot Trail. Team registration, flights, van rentals, uniforms, food, hotel rooms, race tactics, logistics - you name it, he does it. He trains and motivates and, if necessary, coaches others. Oh yes, not to forget motivational poems and his annual song the night before the relay which includes a verse for every one of the 34 runners plus traveling supporters!

The team comprises joggers and former Olympic runners. All are motivated by Tommy and all marvel at his ability to be a great and caring doctor, volunteer, parent and organiser. He also plays competitive softball and somehow finds time to play golf!

That is celebration to life!

Yes, it is that celebration that coaches are committed to – a joyous, powerfully affirming "yes" to all that makes us fully alive!

Tom Nease is retired from a successful life in business. We first became acquainted when Mr. Nease was President of Adidas Canada and I was coaching high school track and working with Fred Foot at East York Track Club. Mr. Nease's generous support made a huge difference for a large number of struggling young athletes. His generous nature led to his association with many charities and not-for-profit boards. Like so many parents, Tom brought his children to skate at the local arena. It was there that he met Percy Gee, known by all as "Mr. Gee."

Fifty years ago Woodbridge, Ontario, was a tiny village northeast of Toronto with an interesting history. Like so small many Canadian villages and towns it had its own indoor arena with quality artificial ice. It had been built almost entirely by volunteers, people who gave generously, engaged in money raising schemes and provided the muscle power and construction skills required. The local Legion was also a contributor. The arena served Woodbridge and the surrounding area.

Games are played, the score is kept and only one team wins. This is generally determined by the degree of proficiency developed in the players and the natural talent nurtured by practice, practice, and more practice! For a hockey player something else must take place first, the youngster must learn to skate on those narrow pieces of steel laced to the feet.

Enter Mr. Percy Gee who for years took the youngest of the N.H.L. dreamers under his wing at the Woodbridge arena. With sure hands and soothing words Mr. Gee guided his young charges in a series of well thought out manoeuvres and motions so that, quicker than any would have thought possible, they became gliders and skaters. It was not an easy task for any youngster and I am certain many thought of giving up. Few did because the ever patient and dedicated Mr. Gee soothed their feelings and made them think they were the next Bobby Hull. He exuded such an expectation of success and created an atmosphere of accomplishment that it was even felt by the mothers in the stands who were longing for the day when their kids could lace up their own skates.

For decades Mr. Gee spun his magic with hundreds and hundreds of youngsters who grew up to be accomplished skaters. Many would not have lasted that first season had it not been for this remarkable man. Mr. Gee could have moved up the coaching ranks, but he never did. His personal satisfaction lay in watching youngsters develop the essential skills that are so important to all that follows. He took pride in showing that real learning was possible, that practice makes a difference, and that only by being patient with one's progress was anything worthwhile ever achieved. Mr. Gee knew these life skills absorbed early would last a lifetime.

I had four boys who came under Mr. Gee's spell. None of them ever thought of calling him anything other than Mr. Gee even after they all grew up. I never called him anything else either, nor did any of the other parents, which was the most sincere expression of gratitude and respect.

The great ice dancer and Olympic medallist, Paul Martini, to this day still says, "Thanks, Mr. Gee."

The wonder of the work that coaches do with children is they create foundations upon which lives grow and take many directions. All the participants are gratifying to know about but the real thrill comes when a person arrives at the top of what they do and the coach knows he or she contributed a small part in the beginning. I can only imagine the images that ran through the mind of Mr. Gee when that little boy who wobbled onto the ice one day stood atop his first major podium.

John Reeves is a former holder of Canadian Masters' records at all distances from the half mile to the ten miles, and age group winner in several marathons. As a member of East York Track Club and later the University of Toronto Track Club, he was coached by Fred Foot. Now in his mid-seventies, he still trains regularly and occasionally races. John was inspired to begin running in 1963-64 when he produced an award-winning documentary on Bruce Kidd, the teenage sensation of distance running, when the world still believed this was the domain of much older and much more experienced runners.

Fred coached our group workouts Mondays through Fridays in the late afternoon and early evenings. Weekends, we were on our own. During the late fall and winter, we worked out in Hart House where the track was reserved for Varsity runners from 5-7 p.m., when it was not crowded with joggers as it was at other times. In spring and summer we worked out on the track at East York stadium and when university resumed we returned to Varsity Stadium.

I have many treasured memories of those sessions, of my fellow athletes, and of Fred's coaching. One session in particular stands out in my mind. The Varsity Stadium sessions used to occur at the end of daylight saving time in late October. This was before good lighting had been installed which could allow us to continue well into November, weather permitting. In 1967, the last Friday in October happened to be a rainy day. When I arrived at the stadium, I discovered that everyone else had decided to skip the workout or go indoors because of the weather. The only other person there was Fred Foot, conscientious as ever, braving the weather in a raincoat. At that moment it would have been easy for Fred to say, "Okay, if you're the only one here, why don't we just call it a day?" Most coaches would have. Not Fred, though.

I urged him to go on home and get in out of the wet but he wouldn't hear of it. If I'd taken the trouble to show up, he said, he'd give me a workout. What did I have in mind? The best compromise, it seemed to me, was a time-trial. Interval training was precluded by the conditions, and a two-mile run would be over quickly so Fred wouldn't

*have to hang around too long in the foul weather. He agreed. We discussed the tempo
and he said he would give me my lap times.*

*My training had gone well that fall, leading up to a number of Canadian Masters'
Records the following summer. There was no question of running a really fast time on a
soggy cinder track with no competition. However, looking for excuses is not the way to
approach a run, psychologically. We settled for a tempo that would be quite demanding
even in good weather. Encouraged by Fred's faith in me I set out as best I could, and
was spurred on at the end of every lap by hearing Fred announcing my splits and calling
out that I was right on schedule. Plugging away, I managed to finish the eight laps in
what was then a Personal Best.*

*But that little achievement, later bettered, is not why I remember that particular
day with fondness. What stays with me is Fred's generosity and loyalty as a coach.
There I was, an undistinguished forty-year-old, in no way comparable to the young elite
runners who were the backbone of his squad, and yet he was willing to give me the same
time and attention he gave to them.*

*That, in fact, was what made him a great coach. He never trained his runners
dogmatically, as though there was some magic athletic formula that should be applied to
everyone. To him, each athlete was an individual, with his or her discernable needs and
abilities. The only demand he made of us was that we try our best, whatever that best
might be. If anyone could appreciate that, I could: for I was only a journeyman runner of
small significance among the young stars on the team. Nonetheless, from the day I joined
the club, Fred paid just as much attention to the development of my potential as he paid
to nurturing far superior talents, some of them Olympic calibre.*

Every athlete should be so lucky in his coach!

Yes, every young person should be so lucky. Fred Foot's coaching was a
celebration of life. He was still coaching only weeks before he died – well into his 80s;
still sharing his passion, still making a difference.

Doug Clement is a former Olympic athlete, physician, coach, and Professor of
Sports Medicine at the University of British Columbia, Faculty of Medicine. Honoured
with the Order of Canada, an inductee in the Canadian Olympic Hall of Fame and
recipient of numerous awards, Doug is a co-founder, with wife Diane, of the Richmond
Kajaks track and field club. He is also a founding member of the Achilles International
Track and Field Society, The Vancouver Sun Run, and the Harry Jerome International
Track Classic.

*There have been situations in which I have been driven to a take a stand in my
relationship with athletes, and it has become confrontational. Often this is a repetition of
a particular behaviour by the athlete, on or off the playing field, which in my view, was
not in the best interest of the athlete in the long run. There were times when this
confrontation became a wedge in the relationship and led to the athlete terminating their*

involvement. This is never what I wanted it to come to, it was always difficult, and I am certain it created emotional upset in both of us. These confrontations always left me feeling uncertain as to the outcome of the situation on the long-term development and maturation of the athlete. It was never pleasant, but always necessary.

A few years ago I had a cerebella infarct, or stroke and was in intensive care for several weeks. The initial prognosis was uncertain. This short-term critical situation precipitated a torrent of communication and support from family and friends. Amongst the letters and cards were a substantial number from athletes with whom I had limited contact for many years. Some letters came from athletes who parted following confrontational situations. The common thread in these letters was "Thank you for taking a stand, as this was a pivotal point in my life."

Best Coaches always take stands for that which is best, in the long term, life, living and the daily celebration of it. Here at the end is the beginning, the end of this book and the beginning for each of us, of the next moments and days of our lives. As the medicine wheel suggests we have come full circle and to celebrate the gift of life we can only go forward – with more experience and greater wisdom. I am so grateful to all the coaches who took the time to come to this place and share their stories with us. I have been given information, insights, and inspiration. I hope you have as well. It is also my hope that you use these stories and your own stories to support yourself and those around you. There is no greater way of celebrating life than to engage fully in the life of your community and give of your time and energy to make a positive difference.

Yes!

Seven Keys to Making Coaching
a Celebration of Life

1. Choose to do what you love and share that passion with others.

2. Find joy in simple things - celebrate the innocence of the game.

3. Bring humour to every situation, especially by laughing at yourself.

4. Celebrate the joy of effort, of learning, of facing challenges and all that makes life rich.

5. Celebrate the exceptional and the extraordinary.

6. Create traditions that acknowledge and celebrate our achievements.

7. Honour the need to experience, to learn and to change

The gift of

Best Coaches, Best Practices

to your friends and family

Send a copy of **BEST COACHES, BEST PRACTICES** to the people you care about. Help them to be the best they can be!

For an autographed copy or copies of
BEST COACHES, BEST PRACTICES complete the order form and include a cheque for $25.00 plus 7% GST for Canadian residents, US$20.00 for outside of Canada. Add $4.00 for shipping and handling on each book ordered.

Name_____

Address_____

_____

Telephone#_____

Internet address_____

# of copies_____

Amount enclosed_____

Send your orders to:

Higgins House
P.O. Box 84668
2336 Bloor Street West,
Toronto, Ontario M6S 4Z7

Email: best_coaches2004@yahoo.ca

**HIGGINS
HOUSE**